LATIN AMERICA THROUGH SOVIET EYES

Soviet and East European Studies

Series list continues on p. 250

LATIN AMERICA THROUGH SOVIET EYES

The evolution of Soviet perceptions
during the Brezhnev era 1964–1982

ILYA PRIZEL

The right of the
University of Cambridge
to print and sell
all manner of books
was granted by
Henry VIII in 1534.
The University has printed
and published continuously
since 1584.

CAMBRIDGE UNIVERSITY PRESS

Cambridge
New York   Port Chester
Melbourne   Sydney

Published by the Press Syndicate of the University of Cambridge
The Pitt Building, Trumpington Street, Cambridge CB2 1RP
40 West 20th Street, New York, NY 10011, USA
10 Stamford Road, Oakleigh, Melbourne 3166, Australia

First published 1990

Printed in Great Britain by Redwood Press Limited, Trowbridge, Wiltshire

British Library cataloguing in publication data

Prizel, Ilya.
Latin America through Soviet eyes: the evolution of Soviet
perceptions during the Brezhnev era 1964–1982.
– (Soviet and East European studies; 72)
1. Latin America. Policies of Soviet Union, history
I. Title II. Series
980

Library of Congress cataloguing in publication data

Prizel, Ilya.
Latin America through Soviet eyes: the evolution of Soviet
perceptions during the Brezhnev era, 1964–82/Ilya Prizel.
　　　p.　　　cm. – (Soviet and East European studies: 72)
Bibliography.
Includes index.
ISBN 0–521–37303–4
1. Latin America – Foreign public opinion, Russian – History –
20th century. 2. Public opinion – Soviet Union – History –
20th century. 3. Latin Americanists – Soviet Union – Attitudes.
4. Scholars – Soviet Union – Attitudes. 5. Journalists – Soviet
Union – Attitudes. 6. Politicians – Soviet Union – Attitudes.
7. Latin America – Relations – Soviet Union. 8. Soviet Union –
Relations – Latin America. I. Title. II. Series.
F1416.S65P75 1990
980.03'072047– dc20　89–33198　CIP

ISBN 0 521 37303 4

For Kate Rothko

Contents

Preface

This study evaluates the evolution of Soviet perceptions of, and attitudes toward, Latin America during the Brezhnev period (1964–1982). The Brezhnev era is especially significant because it was during this period that the USSR rose from being a regional world power to a global power able to exert its influence throughout the world. I look at three major components of Soviet perceptions: the changing Soviet perception of Latin America's domestic politics; the new role of Latin America in the international arena and the ability of the United States to influence regional events; and emerging Soviet–Latin American relations.

The purposes of this study are to clarify the data base the Soviets use to formulate their policy toward Latin America and to see whether greater interaction has resulted in a more sophisticated and subtle Soviet approach. I examine and discuss how the various changes that took place in Latin America, the United States, and the Soviet Union altered Moscow's perceptions of Latin America's internal and external structure and, thus, of the region's international posture. In addition, I look at how these altered perceptions influenced the USSR's policy toward the hemisphere, and I explore whether, by the end of the Brezhnev era, Soviet political and academic communities were emerging with a new model and prognosis for the future political course of Latin America. Since Soviet–Cuban relations have an entirely different character from those between the Soviet Union and the rest of Latin America, discussion of Cuba is excluded except where the Soviet–Cuban link directly affected the Soviet Union's relationship with the rest of the hemisphere.

One central hypothesis is that, because there are very few Soviet specialists on Latin America, the role of these scholars in policy formulation is significant and that changing Soviet perceptions, as reflected in the Soviet scholarly and journalistic communities, have a profound impact on official thinking in the USSR and on its policy formulation. Another important hypothesis is that, as the Soviet data base on Latin America increased, the USSR abandoned its rigid stereotyped perceptions of Latin America and realized that the Latin American states and societies contain within them a very wide range of interests and opinions, some of which are actually sympathetic to the USSR. In addition to the social diversity within each country, some Latin American states, because of their relatively high levels of development, more closely resembles the South European states, while others certainly remain a part of the Third World. Given the Soviets' new awareness of these realities, it stands to reason that the policies of the USSR toward Latin America would become more flexible and imaginative.

Research supports the notion that, indeed, there was a fundamental reevaluation of Latin America in Soviet eyes that led to a series of new Soviet initiatives toward the region. This increase in Soviet sensitivity toward Latin America also led to a wide array of different schools of thought regarding Latin America, ranging from people who were very optimistic about future developments in the region to those who retained an essentially Stalinist perspective. However, for a variety of reasons Latin America has remained the area of lowest priority for the USSR.

Initial research included reading the available Western literature on Soviet–Latin American relations. The key sources of data, however, were Soviet academic journals, such as *Latinskaia Amerika, SShA, Mirovaia Ekonomika i Mezhdunarodnye Otnosheniia, Voprosy Istorii, Nauka i Religia,* and *Voprosy Filosofii.* The information in the scholarly journals was greatly enhanced by the numerous books published by the Latin American Institute of the USSR Academy of Sciences. In addition, communist party journals, such as *Kommunist, Rabochii Klass i Sovremennyi Mir, Kommunist Vooruzhionnykh Sil,* and *World Marxist Review,* provided insight into the views of the communist parties of both the Soviet Union and Latin America. Soviet newspapers, such as *Pravda, Izvestiia,* and *Krasnaia Zvezda,* along with Cuba's *Granma,* also proved to be valuable reflections of Soviet perceptions.

So far as my sources are concerned, it is important to note that in the USSR there are very few serious analysts of Latin American affairs – fewer than fifty individuals. Given this and the small data base on which the Soviets form their perceptions and policies toward Latin America, many academics and journalists play a far more significant role in policy formulation toward this part of the world than their peers who study Western Europe, the Middle East, or Asia. Although it is certainly true that statements by members of the Politburo or the Central Committee of the CPSU are more authoritative than statements by academics and journalists, in the case of Latin America, academics and journalists do play a disproportionate role in Moscow's policy formulation. It should be noted, for example, that it was the journalist, Alekeseyev, who served as the key link between Castro and the Kremlin before becoming the ambassador to Havana in 1962. Therefore, when I deal with "Soviet" perceptions of Latin America, I include prominent academics and journalists associated with major publications as well as political figures.

Acknowledgments

Many people have helped in the writing of this book. I am especially indebted to Bruce Parrott, Riordan Roett, Piero Gleijeses, and Thomas Perry Thornton, all of The Johns Hopkins University, as well as Karen Dawisha of the University of Maryland, who read various drafts of the manuscript and provided me with wise and constructive comments and criticisms.

Stephen Sestanovich of the Center for Strategic and International Studies read the epilogue to the book and provided some very useful comments which helped to bring the book into greater focus. Mark N. Katz read the manuscript and was generous in his insights as well as intellectual support.

This research project would not have been possible without the patience and help of the staffs of the Library of Congress in Washington, and The Johns Hopkins School of Advanced International Studies library. I would like to thank Nancy McCoy and Margaret Jull Costa for excellent editorial work.

Special thanks go to Michael Holdsworth at Cambridge University Press, who remained supportive throughout the long process of producing this manuscript.

Finally I would like to thank my wife Kate, and my children, Peter and Natalie, for their ongoing interest and support for the project.

Introduction

Lenin was not interested in the socialist movement in Mexico. He realized it was bound to be rudimentary. But he was interested in the people of Mexico, in their relationship to the United States, in whether there was strong opposition to the United States.

Manuel Gómez (Charlie Philips)
upon return from the Second Comintern, 1920

Latin America is a collection of US satellites.   Stalin, 1946

The Monroe Doctrine is dead.   Nikita Khrushchev, 1960

The Soviet attitude toward Latin America is analogous to that of the United States. It is a colonial attitude; the Soviets have respect for American power and contempt for Latin American weakness.

Herbert Dinerstein, 1968

Two decades ago there was only Cuba in Latin America, today there are Nicaragua, Grenada and a serious battle going on in El Salvador.

Marshal Ogarkov, 1983

The traditional Soviet perception of Latin America was totally determined by two key factors. First, because of the great distance between Russia and Latin America and the paucity of historical contacts, a salient feature of the Soviet perception of the continent was Moscow's inordinate ignorance concerning Latin America and its inability to comprehend fully the political dynamics of the continent. Second was the Soviet perception of the region, from Lenin on, set almost entirely in the context of Latin America's relationship with the United States.

Although the Comintern did establish its presence in Latin America as early as 1920 and supported several communist-led uprisings on the continent during the 1920s and the 1930s, Latin America was perceived by Moscow as the "strategic rear" of the United States. Despite these

1

occasional intrusions into Latin America by the Comintern, Soviet policy toward Latin America, until the 1960s, was defined almost entirely in terms of Latin America's relations with the United States.

In Asia and Africa Soviet analysts saw a rapid diminution in the European colonial presence and a social structure that would encourage the emergence of elites inclined to follow a "noncapitalist path of development." In Latin America, however, the Soviets saw the continued expansion of an ever more powerful and assertive United States and the continued domination of the region by a dependent bourgeoisie. This perception of US political hegemony over Latin America was reinforced by the fact that all Latin American states signed a military pact with the United States, the 1947 Treaty of Rio, that all (except Argentina, Mexico, and Uruguay) broke diplomatic ties with the USSR during the cold war, and that almost all watched the ousting of the democratically elected Arbenz regime in 1954 without a murmur of protest. In terms of Latin America's domestic structure the Soviets perceived the region as one dominated by a well-entrenched oligarchy and a large *comprador* class, backed by a conservative church and reactionary armies all heavily dependent on the United States.

Given the distance from the USSR, the absence of a history of Russo-Latin American ties, the perceived US dominance in the region, and the region's reactionary social structure, it is hardly surprising that most of Moscow's attention during the 1950s was devoted to the Afro-Asian bloc. Until the 1960s much of the Soviet leadership perceived Latin America as being "out of reach" for the USSR. Hence, Moscow's interest in the region was minimal.

During the 1960s and 1970s several major changes took place in the international arena that caused profound changes in Soviet perceptions of Latin America. The survival of the Castro regime (only 90 miles off the US coast), despite Cuba's nationalization of billions of dollars of US assets and despite US hostility, convinced Moscow that the United States' ability to dominate events in Latin America was severely constrained. The war in Vietnam, which fragmented the US political consensus and reduced the United States' sense of political confidence and global assertiveness, also altered Moscow's perception of the United States' ability to dominate events south of its borders.

Within Latin America the emergence of several relatively developed states with a global economic presence, such as Argentina, Brazil, and Mexico, convinced many Soviet analysts that the era of US economic hegemony in Latin America might be coming to an end. The changes in political attitudes within various Latin American political institutions, such as the armed forces, the church, various political parties, and trade unions, also played a role in shattering Moscow's stereotyped image of Latin America.

By the early 1970s most of Latin America had ceased to identify itself with "Western Christian civilization" and began increasingly to perceive itself as a part of the "Third World." This new self-perception of Latin America, which transformed the region from a pliant backer of most US diplomatic positions in international forums to a major exponent of Third World aspirations, again altered the traditional image of Latin America held in the USSR. Finally, the attainment of nuclear parity with the United States, the construction of a "blue water" navy, and abandonment of an autarkic economic model enabled the USSR to establish, for the first time, a modest presence in Latin America.

Part I

Soviet perceptions of Latin America's global role

Introduction

Although most of Latin America attained formal independence in the early nineteenth century, and in fact most of the region's states predate many European states, Latin America played only a peripheral role in the world arena. The center of the arena was Europe, geographically distant from Latin America. When British policy severely limited European influence in the Americas (and enabled President Monroe to develop the so-called Monroe Doctrine), Latin America's global political role became further marginalized.[1] After the end of World War II, as Britain, Germany, and France withdrew from the Latin American scene, the area fell almost entirely into the US sphere of influence.

Given the preponderant US domination of both Latin America and the OAS, it is hardly surprising that the USSR retained a contemptuous attitude toward the hemisphere. For years the prevailing Soviet perception had been that Latin America, although nominally politically independent, in reality was little more than an adjunct to various colonial powers. Stalin and Molotov often described the region's states as "US satellites" or "pseudo-colonies of the US."[2]

This attitude continued well into the Brezhnev era, unmodified until the late 1960s. Latin America was not included in changing Soviet perceptions of the Third World after Stalin's death, when Soviet analysts conceded that newly independent states governed by the bourgeoisie were not necessarily stooges of imperialism. Khrushchev recognized that such states as Egypt and India were indeed capable of severing their ties with their imperialist patrons. However, the Soviets believed that, unlike the case in Europe, the United States had actually consolidated its grip on the hemisphere.

By the late 1960s, US influence in the region was clearly beginning to decline, and the USSR began to recognize that elements within key Latin American social institutions – such as the church, the armies, and the middle class – had started to deviate from their historical positions

7

of staunchly supporting the region's existing political order. This section traces evolving Soviet perceptions of three key aspects of Latin America's changing role in the international system: Latin America's efforts to enhance regional integration, its role within the capitalist division of labor and its ties to capitalist centers other than the United States, and its role within the Third World and the Non-Aligned Movement. Discussion then turns to Soviet perceptions of US–Latin American relations during the Brezhnev era and the impact the Soviets considered these relations to have on possibilities for regional transformation. Finally, the section presents Soviet conclusions regarding Latin America's new assertiveness and its potential for conducting an independent foreign policy. Changes in Latin America's global role *vis-à-vis* the USSR will be addressed in Part IV.

1 Soviet perceptions of US–Latin American relations

Pre-*détente* (1964–69)

Given that the cornerstone of Soviet foreign policy was to avoid direct confrontation with the United States, especially in an area as remote and marginal to the USSR as Latin America, the Brezhnev era began at a rather inauspicious moment for Soviet interests in the region. Gone was the euphoric perception of the early 1960s that the Latin American continent was ripe for a shift from the capitalist path of development. It had been less than two years since the Cuban missile crisis, and the Johnson administration had quickly made clear that it was ready to defend US interests in the region by all the means at its disposal. Yet Soviet policymakers were being pressured by China and Cuba, which relentlessly browbeat Moscow over its failure to fulfill its internationalist duty by supporting "wars of national liberation" throughout Latin America.

Thus, during the pre-*détente* era Soviet policy followed two somewhat contradictory tracks. On the one hand, Moscow attempted to preserve its fragile *détente* with China (1964–65) and, more important, its influence in the radicalized Third World, by supporting wars of national liberation in Latin America, albeit most modestly and discreetly.[1] On the other hand, Moscow carefully studied Washington's policy toward and position in Latin America so as not to overstep the limits of US tolerance of Soviet activity in the United States' backyard.

Early on in the Johnson administration Soviet analysts had concluded that the United States was willing to resort to the doctrine of the "big stick" in Latin America with an assertiveness unmatched by any US administration since Franklin Roosevelt had declared his "good neighbor" policy toward Latin America in 1933. President Johnson from the start had been perceived by the Soviet establishment as representative of the most reactionary and anticommunist elements

9

within the Democratic party. He would further impress Moscow with his hard-line approach by ordering the bombing of North Vietnam in February 1965 (ostensibly in retaliation for a Vietcong raid on the US airfield at Pleiku).[2]

The generally aggressive tone of the Johnson policy, the buildup of US conventional forces (including the "counterinsurgency" component), and the appointment of Thomas Mann as assistant secretary of state for Latin America confirmed Moscow's belief that President Kennedy's "soft" policy in Latin America had been abandoned. Several prominent Soviet scholars equated the US shift from the mild reforms envisaged in Kennedy's Alliance for Progress, and toward reliance on military force, with a return to Washington's traditional alliance with Latin America's oligarchy and military establishments.

Soviet analysts, in fact, had viewed the Alliance for Progress as doomed from the start, given the weakness of Latin America's middle class, the only natural ally of the effort. Anna Matlina observed that for such "controlled revolutions" to be effective, social restructuring must occur on a vast scale and include substantial agrarian reform. Matlina felt that the United States could not force such a reform, since the oligarchy of Latin America's countryside was a key ally of US multinationals. Pointing out that even the most liberal US supporters of the Alliance for Progress had never suggested a change in the alliance between the multi-national corporations (MNCs) and Latin America's most reactionary elements, the author stated: "The middle class proved to be unable to carry out the mission assigned to it by US liberals, since in times of tension the bourgeoisie leaned toward the oligarchy and their army."[3]

Under the Mann Doctrine, which established the basis for the United States' Latin America policy in 1963–65, several events firmly convinced the Soviets that the Alliance for Progress days were over. The first occurrence was in 1964, when the Johnson administration applauded the military coup in Brazil and offered the new regime massive economic aid – literally within hours of the army ousting the reformist Goulart, who, two weeks earlier, had announced major agrarian reforms. Although the Soviets were not surprised that the United States was instrumental in the coup (and, indeed, hard evidence points to US cooperation with the military conspirators), they were surprised that, despite Goulart's apparent ability to draw enormous crowds of supporters and despite active peasant unrest in Brazil's countryside, the army had been able to smash all opposition with virtually no resistance.

Of greater significance was the 1965 US intervention in the Dominican Republic. Not only did the United States demonstrate – in the face of increasing difficulties in the Vietnam War – that it was willing to defend its Latin American interests, it also forced the OAS – despite strong opposition to the US intervention by such democratic members as Mexico and Chile – to legitimize the move in a manner reminiscent of the 1950s, if not the 1920s. In response, *Kommunist* warned that "if there was anyone in the United States or its allied countries who entertained the illusion that the Johnson administration was willing to act in a realistic fashion in the international arena, that illusion was crushed by the intervention in the Dominican Republic."[4]

The new assertiveness of the Johnson administration also aroused concern in Moscow that Johnson might renege on Kennedy's pledge not to invade Cuba. Commenting on Congress resolution of 20 September 1965, which stated that the United States would defend its interests in the hemisphere by all available means, *Kommunist* observed: "The resolution . . . allows the Pentagon to deal with Latin America in an uncontrolled manner, without any limitation on the means to be applied . . . against *any* Latin American country"[5] (emphasis added). It is noteworthy that neither *Kommunist* nor *Pravda* excluded Cuba from the list of threatened countries nor offered any promises of Soviet aid if the US threat materialized.[6]

Whereas the Soviets had considered the Mann Doctrine a return to the United States' traditional alliance with the region's oligarchy, the Johnson Doctrine that emerged after September 1965 was viewed as a return to a "gunboat diplomacy" unknown since Woodrow Wilson's "protective imperialism." Thus, by late 1965, the Soviet press reduced its emphasis on the power of US corporate investments in Latin America and highlighted US willingness to intervene alone or in concert with Latin American paladins. According to *Pravda*, in its condemnation of the September 1965 resolution, the Johnson Doctrine, with its emphasis on "ideological frontiers" that disregarded national boundaries, was "a new blow to the national sovereignty of the countries of Latin America, the worst form of gangsterism in the Latin American policy of the present administration."[7]

By late 1965 the USSR was reverting to a more traditional "geographic fatalism" and, taking its cue from US policy, was attempting to improve its ties with almost every regime in Latin America. As discussed elsewhere in greater detail, Moscow extended large lines of credit to Brazil and Chile, regardless of the ruling regimes' political complexion, and by 1968 had revived its diplomatic missions in almost all Latin American states. Yet simultaneously, responding to pressures from China and Cuba, the USSR lent support – if often only verbally – to guerrilla warfare in the hemisphere.

An incident surrounding the 1966 tricontinental conference in Havana highlighted the difficulties of walking such a narrow line between competing interests. Sharaf Rashidov, the Soviet delegate at the conference and a Brezhnev crony, provoked an almost universal outcry from Latin America when he stated that the Soviet Union would continue its support for wars of national liberation in Latin America, especially in the cases of Colombia, Guatemala, Nicaragua, and Venezuela.[8] Within days the Soviet mission at the UN circulated a *note verbale* disassociating the Soviet government from such statements, which it emphasized had been made by social organizations and were not representative of the government's position.[9]

In reality the USSR was accepting the fact that the United States remained the dominant force in the hemisphere, and it was attempting to derive the maximum benefit from the existing Latin American situation. Thus, while Moscow extended economic ties with the region, the Soviet press continued, for example, to castigate the Brazilian military leaders as "gorillas" and "Washington's puppets." Part of that reality, the Soviets recognized, was an increase in US influence in Latin America because of growing US investment in the region. As one article implied, increased economic penetration might enable the United States to control events in Latin America by means of covert economic pressure rather than direct military intervention.[10]

Soviet analysts offered various explanations for the robust rebound in US investment by 1964. Some attributed it to inter-imperialist competition and the division of the world by the capitalists into spheres of influence, with the United States responding to increased European investments in other parts of the world, especially Africa.[11] Most, however, linked the increased inflow of US capital to confidence inspired by the Alliance for Progress and the aggressive policies of the Mann and Johnson doctrines. Almost all agreed that growing US investment would result in greater US interests in the region and, therefore, in greater US assertiveness.

Soviet analysts were also deeply disturbed that Latin America's state monopolies – which they viewed as critical to the attainment of economic independence – were falling under US control. An article in *Pravda* characterized Chrysler Corporation's takeover of Brazil's state-owned Fábrica Nacional de Motores as "a calculated blow to the concept of state-owned enterprises in all of Latin America and not just

Brazil." The article went on to state that to "liquidate" Latin American state-owned corporations, US monopolies "would not be adverse to using any means ranging from blackmail to military intervention."[12]

Given the Soviet Union's traditionally negative view of the prospects for change in Latin America, the speed with which Soviet perceptions changed during the last days of the Johnson administration and early days of Nixon's rule is remarkable. The weakening of the United States as a result of the war in Southeast Asia, the disintegration of US political consensus, and the challenge to what Schlesinger called the "imperial presidency," along with an increase in nationalist agitation in Latin America, all took a toll on the administration's ability to impose its will. The decline of US global power since 1965 had become evident as international events unfolded. In Latin America, the US retreat manifested itself primarily in the diplomatic arena, especially within the OAS.

Historically, most Soviet as well as Western observers had viewed the OAS as the American equivalent of the British colonial office. Until the mid-1960s the Soviets had standardly referred to the OAS as a "tool of US imperialism,"[13] and history had indeed justified such a perception. The organization, created by the United States, had primarily been used to implement and legitimize US hegemony over, and interventions in, the hemisphere.

The US victory in arranging for OAS participation in the occupation of Santo Domingo is generally accepted as the "last hurrah" for US domination. The Soviet commentator Vitalii Levin noted that although it would be "an exaggeration" to say that the OAS was "no longer under Washington's control," increasing opposition to US policies, both from within and without the OAS, had deepened with the US intervention in the Dominican Republic.[14] *Pravda* observed that the OAS was being torn apart by contradictory visions of the organization's purpose: the US aim being to retain dominance over Latin America, and the emerging interest of Latin American states being to use the OAS as a forum in which to assert their political and economic independence.[15] Although most Soviet observers were still concerned about accelerating US economic penetration of the region and had no illusions about a parallel increase in US influence, a growing number concluded that the OAS was slipping away as an instrument of US policy in the region.

Thus, by the end of the Johnson era Soviet perceptions were beginning to come full circle – from precluding the possibility of any change occurring in US–Latin American relations, to considering that US control over events in Latin America was entering a phase of decline. Reassessments of the prospects for change caused the Soviets to re-evaluate their view of many events that were taking place in the region; for example, the US call for a Latin American "common market."

The typical Soviet view held this to be a ploy to increase US investment in Latin America and, by dealing with supranational organizations of the market, to deflect the growing anti-US nationalism.[16] Anticipating that this "market" would become a source of friction between the United States and Latin America, however, M. Gerechev was one of the first to suggest that US economic hegemony might be challenged in a way similar to the political challenge that had arisen in the OAS: "In order to calm down anti-American feeling in Latin America and . . . retain the interests of US imperialism in the area, Washington resorted to regional integration . . . However, broad layers of the Latin American bourgeoisie see in a regional market a means of defending themselves from US competition."[17] Nevertheless, Gerechev believed that the region's bourgeoisie was too dependent on the United States to oppose US interests.

Some Soviet analysts, however, were convinced that Latin America's economic integration would not only fail to help the United States reinforce its dominance over the region but actually aid the Latin Americans in forming a united front in their confrontation with the United States. The emergence of nationalist leftist regimes in Bolivia (1966) and especially in Peru (1968) fostered the belief that the changes occurring in Latin America were sufficiently fundamental to alter the region's relationship with the United States permanently. By 1968 the Soviet press was lauding some of Latin America's military regimes as progressive forces, and by 1969 the Andean Pact was depicted as an anti-imperialist bloc[18] (in sharp contrast with the charges leveled by the Soviets against previous efforts to facilitate regional integration).

By 1967–68 the only stumbling block to improved ties between the USSR and Latin America was Castro's constant drive to ignite revolutions in other parts of Latin America and his endless attacks on Soviet ties with "oligarchic" Latin America. China no longer posed a serious challenge to Soviet domination of the communist world, having been compelled to withdraw from the international arena and concentrate on domestic problems resulting from the Cultural Revolution. In addition, in 1966 the Sino-Cuban friendship had totally disintegrated.

By mid-1967 recriminations between the USSR and Cuba had reached a climax, and Kosygin traveled to Havana to demand that

Cuba tone down its anti-Soviet rhetoric during the upcoming OLAS (Organización Latinoamericana de Solidaridad) meeting. Not only did Castro fail to heed Kosygin's request, but he pushed through a resolution condemning the USSR for instigating the withdrawal of the Venezuelan communist party from armed struggle.[19] Moscow, no longer fearing that a Mao–Castro axis might undercut its authority within the communist and nonaligned movements, responded to this and other blatantly anti-Soviet actions by attacking Castro's dogma.

Criticism of Castro appeared in the pages of *Pravda* and *Kommunist*. An article in the latter made an undisguised attack on both Castro and Guevara. It criticized certain "left-wing elements" in Latin America that "have vigorously popularized the ideal of a revolutionary who invariably considers partial demands as illusory and ineffective" and who "dedicate[s] himself only to organizing open armed actions." The article continued, "Although propagandists for these revolutionaries sometimes, to give the appearance of being Marxists, speak of the role of the masses, their arrogant disregard for any form of struggle except armed struggle is all too clear."[20]

By mid-1968 Castro was facing grim problems. The USSR had slowed its oil deliveries to Cuba in late 1967, causing serious fuel and food shortages and forcing Castro to impose severe rationing. The sugar crop, which provided 80 percent of Cuba's exports, dropped to 5.1 million tons – barely enough to meet the 5 million tons promised to Moscow.[21] Castro's hopes of creating a chain of socialist states throughout Latin America that would collectively oppose the United States and, thus, lessen Cuba's dependence on Soviet military protection had not materialized; Guevara's efforts to start a "foco"-style uprising in Bolivia had failed, and Guevara had been killed; and the Castroite uprising in Venezuela had collapsed.

In August 1968 Castro submitted to Soviet demands regarding socialist foreign policy. Historians generally agree that Castro's support for the Soviet invasion of Czechoslovakia was the turning point in Cuba's foreign orientation from a defiant maverick to one of the most loyal allies of the USSR within the socialist bloc.[22] After August 1968 Cuban foreign and domestic policy became more and more like Moscow's, and few if any criticisms were made by either Castro or the Cuban press about Moscow's efforts to improve its ties with the rest of Latin America.

Other reasons can be cited as well for the change in Soviet policy toward Latin America and for Soviet overtures even to right-wing regimes. Herbert Dinerstein believed that the Soviets had become less willing to commit their increasingly limited resources to support potentially "progressive" regimes, because by 1967 they had witnessed the downfall of several close allies in Asia, Africa, and the Middle East.[23] Another explanation for Moscow's willingness to expand diplomatic ties with even the most pro-US regimes in the hemisphere may lie in the redirection of Soviet priorities after the 23rd congress of the CPSU. During that congress it was declared that the Soviet state could fulfill its internationalist duty by building *its own* socialism.[24] It is also understandable that Moscow was eager to derive as much economic benefit as possible from its dealings with Latin America rather than undertake any new burdens: in 1966–68 the USSR was making a supreme effort to attain nuclear parity with the United States and was supplying North Vietnam with military and economic aid at great cost while rebuilding the shattered Syrian and Egyptian armies.

Improved Soviet–Latin American ties may be further explained by the marked improvement in US–Soviet relations after 1966. US bombing raids against North Vietnam were reduced, and bilateral trade between the superpowers was expanded. Furthermore, in 1967 Kosygin offered to attempt to find a diplomatic solution to the war in Vietnam.[25] The United States improved its relations with the Warsaw Pact countries of Poland, Romania, and Hungary at the same time as Franco–Soviet relations significantly improved and a slow but noticeable improvement was occurring in Soviet–West German ties. In 1968 the superpowers signed the nonproliferation treaty, and Johnson planned to visit Moscow.

It was only natural that a by-product of the new atmosphere would be better ties between each superpower and the other superpower's allies. Thus, while the United States was able to improve and strengthen its ties in Eastern Europe, the USSR was able to strengthen its ties in Latin America. Soviet perceptions took into account both the diminished ability of the United States to impose its will on the Latin American states and the increased freedom that these states would have in their dealings with the USSR in light of the warming in US–Soviet relations. Furthermore, given the corrosive effects of the Vietnam War on the American body politic, the US administration was perceived to be less likely to pressure Latin America over its ties with the socialist community. Thus, the USSR was ready to act on its new perceptions of possibilities for state-to-state relations with Latin America even before the onset of *détente*.

Early *détente* (1969–74)

During the first phase of *détente* both superpowers were sufficiently interested in the potential fruits of *détente* to show a greater degree of flexibility in the conduct of their foreign policy. From the US viewpoint, the draining war in Indochina and the subsequent weakening of the US economy (and the unprecedented pressure on the dollar in world money markets) made it desirable to avoid a costly new round of the arms race by arriving at some sort of arms control agreement with the USSR. From the perspective of the USSR, which in 1969 attained a crude nuclear parity with the United States, greater access to Western credits and technology was a priority, given the regime's inability to sustain extensive economic growth. Further, growing hostility between Moscow and Peking made the Soviets anxious to avoid hostile situations on both its Eastern and Western frontiers.

The election of Richard Nixon in 1968 and the initiation of *détente* prompted a Soviet reevaluation of the United States' capacity to influence events in Latin America. Most Soviet analysts had recently agreed that US–Latin American relations were undergoing a process of adjustment whereby US influence was rapidly declining. Yet Nixon, given his political identification with large corporate interests and the right wing in the US political spectrum, did not appear likely to forgo US influence and control over the region without protecting the interests of the US business and military elites. Thus, Soviet analysts debated the following questions: Did the emergent new order in Latin America indeed represent a diminution in the United States' ability to influence events in the region, or did it merely reflect a change in the format rather than the substance of US domination? Was the United States, because of *détente*, likely to become more tolerant of progressive regimes in the region and, if so, to what extent?

Two schools of thought emerged. Those in the optimist school largely based their evaluations on political events in Latin America and held that the United States' ability to influence Latin America was progressively declining and would soon be no greater than the European powers' ability to influence their former colonies. Those in the pessimist school stressed economic trends as markers in their assessment of the regime. They warned that the challenge to the United States was mainly rhetorical and that the US economic presence in Latin America was expanding in a manner that would make it harder than ever to dislodge. Although both schools interpreted the same key events as a vindication of their different views, there was one point of agreement: that if the United States felt its vital interests were seriously threatened, it would ultimately resort to force.

The optimist school

The "optimists" responded to what they perceived as a broad-based challenge to US influence that included such traditional support-ers of the United States as the church, the armed forces, and the bourgeoisie. Matlina was convinced that there was no longer room for centrist political solutions within the region, as demonstrated by the failure of the Alliance for Progress. She believed that the drift to the left was bound to continue, since the United States could no longer impose a rightist model, as it had done in Brazil.[26] Maidonik, the doyen of Soviet scholars of Latin America's internal politics, agreed.[27]

V. G. Bushuyev stated that the unity of all major social groups against the United States had put Washington on the defensive: "In reality the North American politicians are being compelled to drop some of their crude methods of coercion in Latin America. The anti-American mood of the Latin American people is so intense that direct intervention by the United States in the affairs of Latin American states may well cause an explosion."[28] Rubén Souza, the first secretary of the Panamanian communist party, was even more sanguine about the prospects for cross-class opposition to US influence and observed that even the conservative regimes had been compelled to adopt an anti-US posture.[29]

In their common belief that opposition to the United States was universal among all segments of Latin American society, the optimists gave particular emphasis to the armed forces. Given that the Latin American military was traditionally a vital pillar of US hegemony, and given the importance of the military in regional politics, the impli-cations of an emerging progressive wing within the armed forces were substantial, according to V. G. Bushuyev.[30] In fact, almost all the Latin American armies were moving away from dependence on the United States.

This movement had begun in the late 1960s, when Argentina initiated its "Plan Europa," whereby it shifted to Europe as its major supplier of arms. The Argentine precedent was soon followed by Brazil, Peru, and even the Central American republics.[31] Several opti-mists accorded such efforts the additional significance of representing a move away from the role that the United States assigned to Latin America's military. Antonov and Karpov noted that Latin American states were simultaneously reducing allocations to counterinsurgency weapons urged upon them by the United States.[32]

The pervasive Soviet view was expressed by Shul'govskii: "The armed forces are becoming an ever more important factor in the political lives of the Latin American states; and it is the positions of the armed forces that will determine the long-term development of Latin America."[33] Even those who discounted the strength of the progressive element within the armed forces appreciated the move away from dependence on the United States. Shul'govskii, however, was generally optimistic about the future, stating that "it is clear that the policy of the United States and of the Latin American ruling classes of using the armed forces to suppress anti-imperialist movements has proved ineffective."[34]

The emergence of a leftist military regime in Bolivia (1966), the Torrijos coup in Panama (1968), and, most important, the leftist military coup in Peru (1968) appeared to vindicate the optimist view. Analysts noted that by the late 1960s the Latin American countries, even if divided by different political systems, maintained a united front when dealing with Washington – thereby reducing US leverage in dealing with an errant regime. The effectiveness of this solidarity, they argued, was especially apparent in the weakened US position in the OAS and UN and in the United States' unwillingness or inability to oppose regional efforts to achieve greater economic independence.

In the case of the OAS there was almost unanimous agreement among Soviet students of Latin America that the United States now represented a minority of one developed capitalist country – in a sea of more than two dozen developing countries challenging it with serious demands. The crumbling of the OAS blockade of Cuba soon demonstrated the erosion of US control over the organization. In 1971 the majority of the OAS membership voted to lift the trade embargo. The United States, with the aid of several right-wing regimes, such as Guatemala, Nicaragua, and Paraguay, was able to prevent a majority vote that would have lifted the embargo, but the extent of US efforts to retain the embargo convinced both Soviet and Western analysts that a radical transformation had occurred within the OAS. Washington's weakness had peaked in 1970, when the OAS membership, led by Chile and Peru, blocked a US proposal to pass a declaration condemning international terrorism. Such a resolution, it was alleged, was attempted US interference in Latin America's domestic affairs.

At the UN the United States could no longer count on Latin America's voting *en bloc* in support of US positions, something which in the past had been decisive in passing such controversial resolutions as those concerning the partition of Palestine, the dispatch of UN troops to Korea, and the question of PRC membership. By the early 1970s the Latin American vote was far more likely to side with the nonaligned bloc. According to A. P. Baryshev, "The change of Latin America's position at the United Nations reflects the major socio-economic changes that have taken place within Latin America, and the growth of Latin America's struggle for full independence."[35] Baryshev also noted that Latin America was challenging the United States not only on contentious inter-American issues, such as the Panama Canal and North–South relations, but even on global issues that did not affect its immediate interests.[36]

In the economic sphere – the historical basis for US hegemony in the region – the United States was also unable to force Latin America to part ways with its nonaligned brethren. The optimists emphasized Venezuela's leading role in the creation of OPEC, which by the late 1960s, they asserted, was viewed by the United States as a threat to the entire capitalist world order. Yet not only did Washington fail to deter Venezuela from taking a hard line within OPEC, but it also proved powerless to prevent tiny Ecuador from joining, despite US threats of economic reprisals.[37]

In addition, efforts by Latin American states, even by right-wing military regimes, had succeeded in reducing the US share of the region's external trade to below 50 percent. The reemergence of "inter-imperialist" rivalry, to use Soviet parlance, was weakening US influence over Latin American economies. European and Japanese penetration of Latin America in fact took many forms and included the replacement of the United States as the region's main weapons purveyor.

Members of the optimist school, many of whom believed the United States to be dependent on Latin America's mineral wealth, attributed great significance to the rash of nationalizations of extractive resources that occurred in the late 1960s and early 1970s. Peru, in 1968, was among the first to nationalize the properties of such US giants as Exxon and the Grace Corporation. Under the Hickenlooper amendment, the US government was required to cut off all credits to any government that nationalized US-owned assets without prompt and adequate compensation. Yet Washington did not invoke the amendment, nor did it take any direct punitive action against Peru. In fact, despite prolonged negotiations and Peru's payment of only a fraction of the funds demanded by the United States, the Nixon administration continued to deal with Peru in a manner unheard of only five years earlier. V. G. Bushuyev proclaimed that the common denominator in events in South America was "the general crisis of capitalism and its inability to reassert the initiative needed to regain its lost position."[38]

Between 1969 and 1973 almost the entire extractive industry, 85 percent of which had been owned by the United States, was nationalized. In almost all cases the US reaction was mild if not passive, with Washington taking a flexible position and attempting to arrive at a speedy agreement on compensation claims. G. F. Vishnia believed that Washington was willing to enter a constructive dialogue with Latin America because of the realization that the region no longer existed in isolation. Since Latin America was integrated with other parts of the developing world as well as within its own hemisphere, direct intervention in any one Latin American state would cause other conflicts.[39]

Some analysts, especially Bushuyev, were encouraged by the regional integration efforts of the Andean Pact, which, as noted, had won Moscow's approval despite earlier suspicions regarding such efforts. The optimists were convinced that the change in Latin America's political and economic orientation was deep and fundamental. V. G. Bushuyev noted that the unprecedented, unified position of Andean Pact members in regulating US capital would alter the opportunities for US multinationals not only within Latin America but also throughout the developing world.[40] Turkatenko called the 1969 joint Andean declaration, which imposed region-wide controls on US capital, a watershed that would force a permanent readjustment in the role of US capital in Latin America.[41]

Finally, the optimists took the opposite view of those who linked the slow and prolonged decline in Latin America's terms of trade with the United States to declining Latin American leverage *vis-à-vis* the United States. Instead, they maintained, the United States was becoming more dependent on Latin America. They pointed to the fact that Latin America's economic position was improving at a time when the United States was rapidly losing its ability to control the economic posture of the capitalist world. Some argued that, in light of the US defeat in Vietnam, the United States' ability to compete successfully in the markets of Asia and Africa was becoming gravely limited. Thus, they believed that the United States was now forced to rely almost exclusively on Latin America as a source of minerals vital to US industry and as a buyer for US goods that could not find a market elsewhere.[42]

The pessimist school

Almost every event that encouraged the optimists only intensified the gloom of the "pessimists" regarding the prospects of Latin America's independence from the United States. The pessimists acknowledged that the region had achieved some minor lessening of its dependence on the United States, but they asserted that US dominance was continuing to deepen and strengthen only in a less obtrusive form. In the political sense, they were referring to what came to be known as the Nixon Doctrine.

In July 1969 President Nixon stated that although the United States would continue to support its allies in Asia with economic aid and military material, it would no longer deploy its own troops on Asian soil. The United States would rely on local subpowers to uphold regional order. Although Nixon claimed that the doctrine applied only to Asia,[43] Soviet and Western commentators soon predicted that the policy would be implemented in other parts of the developing world. In fact, the Nixon administration began to concentrate US military and economic aid in a handful of strategically positioned recipients in the developing world (for example, Brazil, Iran, Israel, and Pakistan). Empirical evidence suggests that the United States did indeed rely on regional powers to uphold world order.[44]

Soviet analysts identified Brazil and El Salvador as the countries assigned the role of regional power. Several Soviet observers believed that the Nixon Doctrine was adapted to Latin America with the special feature of "ideological frontiers," intended to convey a sense of responsibility for defending the world from the international threat of communism. Most analysts felt that the doctrine of ideological frontiers both served the US interest in repressing progressive forces in Latin America and fulfilled Brazil's ambition to dominate South America.[45]

Thus, Moscow perceived the demise of Torres' leftist regime in Bolivia as a clever application of the Nixon Doctrine, by which the United States managed to oust a regime it found objectionable without getting directly involved.[46] To the pessimists, Nixon's "low profile" approach to Latin America, coupled with the applications of the Nixon Doctrine (as the Soviets understood it), appeared a new and frighteningly effective means of retaining US influence at a very modest cost to the United States.

Pessimists also doubted that a cross-class convergence of anti-US feelings would pressure Latin American regimes into adopting an anti-US policy on substantive issues. Instead, they linked regional industrialization to the creation of a large bourgeoisie and a "labor elite" that was employed by the multinationals and that identified with the United States. Moreover, they argued that the *petit bourgeois* origins of Latin America's officer corps limited how far the armed forces would go in supporting a restructuring of their societies. The Nixon administration's reintroduction of US-made arms into the region reinforced the view that the bond between the United States and the Latin American military was more enduring than it may have appeared. In addition, the pessimists believed that Nixon's shift from a hemispheric to a bilateral approach in Latin America was eroding the newfound regional unity *vis-à-vis* the United States.

In terms of US economic presence, the pessimists foresaw a deepening US penetration of Latin America's economy and, therefore, greater Latin American dependence on the United States. Zoia Romanova asserted that a new pattern of dependence was emerging that was far more dangerous and subtle than its predecessors. By using joint stock companies, US multinationals were able to hide behind locally owned or even state-owned enterprises and thus avoid public pressures to control or nationalize foreign capital. Since the jointly owned US–Latin American companies were totally dependent on the North American partner for technology, research and development, and capital and distribution systems, the multinationals were able to acquire effective control of a joint enterprise with as little as 3 percent of the stock.[47] Thus, the United States was now able to control the most dynamic sector of Latin America's economy – the manufacturing industries – with a relatively small capital investment.

Furthermore, the Nixon administration's shift away from direct US aid to the use of such international agencies as the Inter-American Development Bank – while the United States retained control of the purse strings – was perceived by some pessimists as yet another means for the United States to make its *de facto* dominance less obtrusive. S. Onskii claimed that in this way Washington obtained a veto power over the investment policies of the region's bourgeoisie and retained control over the Latin American economies without directly confronting public opinion in the region.[48] Some analysts even claimed that there was a direct correlation between the degree of US penetration into Latin America and the level of loans advanced to specific countries through these international agencies.[49] The fact that the shift removed foreign aid granted by the United States from congressional supervision was also not lost on the pessimists.

Whereas the optimists saw a growing American dependence on Latin America's mineral wealth, the pessimists saw a decline in the region's economic leverage *vis-à-vis* the United States. The pessimists noted that Latin America's terms of trade were declining, along with its share of US trade and foreign investment. They also stressed that, since Latin America's share of global trade had fallen every year since the end of the Korean War, the continent's vulnerability to US pressure was increasing.

Colonel V. N. Selivanov concluded that the expansion of state power in Latin America during the previous twenty years had greatly benefited the US multinationals. He felt that, given the dependent nature of the bourgeois regimes of Latin America, any expansion in the power of such regimes would only aid the region's penetration by US capital.[50] It is significant that Selivanov and other pessimists took this position, since the standard Soviet line was that the first step toward abolishing imperialism in a developing country was to enhance the power of the state.

Even greater pessimism was voiced by Soviet analysts associated with the Soviet political establishment. Vasilii Kuzentsov, a close associate of the CPSU's Central Committee secretary Boris Ponomarev, observed: "The economy continues to carry an imprint of colonialism and remains the a-territorial extension of the United States' economic complex beyond its frontiers ... the basis of US neo-colonialism in Latin America continues to be the export of capital, which continues to grow."[51] Klochkovskii of the CPSU Central Committee concluded that common markets had enhanced the US economic presence, despite the efforts of regional economic groupings to defend themselves from economic penetration by US concerns.[52] He also noted that, aside from Latin America's social structure, which inhibited the region's ability to resist US exploitation, the shifting terms of trade against Latin America and the decline of the region's share of US and EEC trade seriously hampered Latin America's drive toward greater independence.[53]

Late *détente* (1974–79)

At no time did either the USSR or the United States claim that *détente* would end superpower competition for influence in the developing world. In fact, after 1974–75, the USSR came to believe that the risk of a direct confrontation with the United States was relatively low, given the US aversion to direct involvement in the developing world following Vietnam and the serious limitation on executive power imposed by the War Powers Act. With regard to Latin America, although most Soviet observers agreed that the United States was now more constrained (and while these observers increasingly analyzed regional events in terms of Latin America's own political reality), the debate persisted about whether Latin America was becoming more or less dependent on the United States. The growing US political and military weakness encouraged the optimists, who foresaw an accelerated move away from the capitalist model of development. The pessimists held firm to their belief that Latin America's economic dependence on the United States was growing and deepening.

Perceptions of the changing correlation of forces

The 1973 Arab–Israeli war is often cited as the watershed of *détente*, since it appeared to reverse the traditional relationship between the West and the developing world. The 400 percent increase in the price of oil profoundly shook the economies of most Western countries, which found themselves competing for loans, investments, and deposits from Middle East oil producers. Those in the optimist school believed that the United States' new dependence on the Third World would weaken the US position and influence in Latin America. Similarly, they were heartened by rapidly increasing Latin American identification with the Third World.

Yet the pessimists maintained that despite the change in the global economic order, there was no immediate alternative to the Latin American economies' dependence on the United States. They argued, for instance, that although the few Latin American states that exported oil had benefited from recent events, most of the region would now have to compete with the developed capitalist countries to import capital and so would suffer. Furthermore, the recession that had been caused throughout the capitalist world by the oil crisis meant a shrinking US export market for Latin American goods.

Disputing the notion of declining Latin American dependence on the United States, Viktor Vol'skii, head of the Latin American Institute, made the following points: (1) Latin America's industrialization represented merely a new division of labor rather than a changed regional position within the capitalist system; (2) the economic gap between Latin America and the developing countries was growing; (3) in 1961–76, although Latin America's gross domestic product had grown by 230 percent, US investment had increased by 400 percent; (4) by 1976 multinationals controlled 59 percent of Latin America's exports, compared with only 40 percent in 1966; (5) Latin America's legislation limiting foreign ownership in some enterprises had proved ineffective; and (6) Latin America was more dependent on foreign capital than either Asia or Africa.[54]

Klochkovskii, reaffirming his earlier statements that shrinking markets for Latin American goods enhanced the multinationals' power and the region's dependence on the United States, observed:

> Despite measures directed at limiting the area of activity of foreign capital (including nationalizing foreign firms in extractive industries and infrastructure) the position of foreign monopolies was not only weakened but actually expanded ... and unlike the past when the activity of most multinationals was directed at the export of minerals, current activity, which consists of industrial output, is directed at the domestic market, further integrating it into the fabric of the local economy.[55]

The key method of control by the capitalist world in the postwar era was generally acknowledged by Soviet analysts to be technological know-how. Thus, as early as 1970 Romanova had attributed the growth of US economic muscle in Latin America primarily to the region's growing technological dependence on the United States rather than to the increased volume of US capital investment.[56] Numerous Soviet analysts claimed that even in Asia and Africa, where the presence of foreign corporate interests was much smaller than in Latin America, dependence on Western technology was preventing fully independent economic development in both relative and absolute terms. According to Karen Brutents of the CPSU, "Neocolonialism's strategy remains essentially the same: the only alteration is the scientific technological revolution."[57]

The debate also continued as to the implications of Latin America's nationalization of mineral resources. Optimists credited OPEC's success in altering the terms of trade for petroleum with at least some shifting of the North–South balance of power toward Latin America.[58] If anything, the pessimists viewed the oil price hike as a negative development for the region, since the developing states were themselves large importers of raw materials and would be less able than the developed countries to absorb any increase in the prices of mineral imports. Furthermore, the pessimist school argued that, given the fact that the United States remained by far the largest trading partner of Latin America, any decline in Latin America's share of the US market automatically meant a decline in the region's share of global trade.[59]

Serious differences between the two Soviet schools of thought also persisted with regard to the potential for cross-class coalitions to oppose the United States. The pessimists discounted the optimist belief that the changing social origins of the Latin American officer corps were eroding the US orientation of the military. Moreover, Klochkovskii and V. Shermet'ev declared that the decline of US influence in the region had reached its limit in the absence of a radical transformation in Latin America: "Experience has shown that in order to put an end to imperialist dependence and exploitation one must turn the struggle against the entire capitalist system which is exploitative."[60]

Similarly, the pessimists remained unconvinced that the United States had lost its capacity to intervene directly in Latin America. For example, V. N. Selivanov argued that the region had become even more prone to intervention because Latin America's economic and strategic importance had greatly increased since the US defeat in Southeast Asia and reversals in Africa and the Middle East. He cited the fact that the United States was building a vast network of military transport facilities throughout the hemisphere so as to retain its ability to intervene in the region, and he described the United States as being willing and able to resort to the "most extreme of measures" to maintain its sphere of influence in Latin America.[61]

The belief that the United States retained the ability and will to shape events in Latin America was not confined to academics but extended to members of the party hierarchy. In an address on 29 January 1974 Brezhnev observed:

> Experience teaches us that wherever the positions of imperialism and its servants are in danger, the bourgeoisie forgets completely its propaganda talk of "democracy" and a "free world" and does not stop at any violence, any cruelty. This is clearly shown by the recent events – the bloody fascist coup in Chile and the onslaught of reaction in some other Latin American states.[62]

Perceptions of the impact of détente

Since *détente* was the official state policy proclaimed by every Soviet official from Brezhnev on down, there was no direct criticism of *rapprochement* with the United States. The optimists, in fact, embraced the official line that a global relaxation of tension would restrain the United States from exerting its power against the developing countries that displeased it. The pessimists maintained that although *détente* may have made direct intervention a measure of last resort for the United States, the new instruments of policy – regional subpowers and new economic levers – allowed the United States to continue its domination of the continent.

The optimists Glinkin, Lunin, and Martynov praised *détente*'s ability to alter the US posture in the region, saying that "under the impact of *détente* favorable possibilities have opened up in this region for the development of liberation movements and for the acceleration in the restructuring of inter-American relations."[63] Not only did they believe that the United States had been forced to show greater flexibility in its Latin America policy, but they also claimed that *détente* had forced Washington to accept a radical change in the ideological orientation of the region:

> The process of liberation can only be achieved on the basis of peace and it is for this reason that the people of Latin America were striving for peace, *détente* and arms limitation. It is precisely because of the relaxation of tension in the first half of the 1970s that it had been possible to achieve the abolition of the anti-Cuban sanctions which had been thrust upon Latin American countries at the beginning of the 1960s by Washington. In the words of the Brazilian sociologist, Octavio Ianni, this was tantamount to the recognition of socialism as a political reality in international relations.[64]

If the United States' toleration of Allende's election did not fully confirm this view, it at least seemed to indicate that Washington's power was diminished.

Several analysts in the optimist school noted an ideological shift toward pluralism, which enabled numerous Latin American states to oppose the United States jointly, regardless of their different political systems, and which they asserted denied the United States the advantage of bilateral relations. Furthermore, the optimists interpreted the acceptance of regional "centers of power" by US political analysts as US acceptance of a devolution of power that would result in the permanent decline of US influence.[65]

Pessimists, however, held to their belief that growing US reliance on regional powers was merely a shrewd tactical move on behalf of US hegemony. They denied that *détente* had inspired a new flexibility in Washington, explaining that US policy instead reflected the specific role that Latin America played in the US political scheme. For instance, Y. Yelutin, writing in 1970, had commented that the United States was experimenting with new policies in Latin America – which had always been a good proving ground for US foreign policy – because of the reverses suffered in Asia.[66] (Using a similar emphasis, N. V. Mostovets stated that it was because of the US political climate, and not *détente*, that the United States was increasingly constrained from using military force.)[67]

Yet Vishnia, while observing that reversals in Asia and Africa had indeed deepened US dependence on Latin America, argued that it was *détente* that had allowed the region to pursue more independent foreign policy and that had altered the quality of inter-American relations.[68] Sergeev and Tkatchenko said that *détente* had created a climate in which even communists could participate in governments – despite Latin America's growing penetration by US capital and increasing technological dependence on the United States.[69] Selivanov, unique in his belief that *détente* in itself could block direct US military intervention, stated, "The spread of the principles of peaceful coexistence blocks any direct military intervention by imperialist powers against states that embark on an anti-imperialist independent policy, and allows the revolutionary progressive forces to embark upon the social and economic reorganization which is in the interests of the majority of the population."[70]

The thesis that *détente* constrained the US ability to use force against Latin America was by no means limited to Soviet academics and journalists. For example, the Declaration of Havana, signed by all the pro-Moscow communist parties of Latin America, stated openly that *détente* denied the United States the possibility of using force against developing countries as it had been able to do during the cold war.[71] It should also be noted that there is a similar divergence of opinion about whether *détente* induced the Soviet Union to follow a more moderate policy toward Latin America and US interests in the region.

Although Moscow did increase its activism in Latin America and became more assertive than during the early 1970s, the absence of opportunities for influence in the region and doubts among many Soviet analysts as to whether the United States and Latin America were capable of giving up their interdependence led Moscow to maintain a relatively low profile. The Ford administration's efforts to improve US–Latin American relations through such means as a biannual meeting on the ministerial level between the United States and Brazil, the declaration of a "new dialogue" with Latin America, the rewriting of the OAS charter, and the promise to relinquish US control of the Panama Canal, were all viewed by Moscow as nothing more than an attempt to deflect Latin America's resentment of increased US economic penetration of the region.

Thus, in the view of Soviet observers, the Nixon–Ford era ended on a paradoxical note. As the United States' political influence in Latin America was rapidly vanishing, US penetration of all spheres of the region's economy continued to expand, creating an ever deepening dependence on the United States.

The Carter administration and the twilight of détente

In terms of US–Latin American relations, the Soviet reaction to President Carter's election was one of utter confusion. Initially the administration perceived Latin America as a North–South, rather than an East–West, issue. It thus attempted to improve relations with the "South" by making several meaningful political concessions, including: agreement with Panama regarding the future of the canal, guaranteed denuclearization of Latin America, and abandonment of the claim of "special relations" with Latin America that led to a shift toward almost total reliance on bilateral relations. Further, US military aid and identification with right-wing military regimes was greatly curtailed. Suddenly "human rights" paced center stage.

The issue that divided the Soviet academic and political community was whether Carter's adjustment of policy represented a new level of tolerance for change on Washington's part and, if so, what that level was. Invariably, the debate centered around the question of whether the US position *vis-à-vis* Latin America was improving or eroding. Despite numerous blows to US–Latin American relations during the Carter years, the Soviet political community reached no consensus as to the future of the United States' economic role and US power in the region. Optimists focused, for instance, on the increased Japanese and European penetration of Latin America; pessimists pointed to Latin America's growing debts, greater technological dependence on the United States, and shrinking share of global trade.

Nothing in Carter's "enigmatic" policy toward Latin America confused Soviet observers more than his emphasis on human rights. The most common reaction was that this was a cynical attempt to deflect anti-US feelings that were prevalent in Latin America, especially after the revelations of US covert action against the Allende regime.[72] While some analysts attributed the human rights emphasis to the growing US isolation within the OAS, others, such as M. Vasiliev, claimed that it was a US ploy to allow Washington to interfere in the domestic affairs of other Latin American states.[73] Some posited that the United States was attempting to compensate for the weakening of its economic bonds to the region by seeking an ideological identification that stressed the "Western tradition," "human rights," and so on.[74]

Carter's human rights policy and its effects on Latin America drew similarly divergent views from the various communist parties of the region. For instance, Costa Rica's Manuel Mora Vallverde asserted that the human rights campaign was designed to blunt anti-US feelings and to isolate Cuba. Dominico Ramoz Bejaprano of Honduras called the policy nothing more than a clever sham intended to defame the world socialist system. Yet Rubén Darío Souza of the Panamanian communist party, in considering Carter's human rights policy and the Panama Canal accord, believed that a genuinely progressive wind was blowing in Washington. The strongest champion of the policy was Jorge Shafik Handal of the Salvadoran communist party, who noted that the hallmark of US imperialism was its adaptiveness: Since the United States had discovered that it could not control the rightist regimes it had installed, and since it no longer had the capacity to follow the traditional hard line, the Carter administration had shifted to human rights as a means of creating friendly, stable regimes while isolating revolutionaries.[75]

The middle period of the Carter administration (1977–79) was perceived by Soviet analysts as the ebb of US influence in Latin America. Carter's effort to be on the right side of change had yielded few visible results by mid-1978, and his human rights policy was under attack by such diverse Latin American regimes as those of Mexico and Brazil. Furthermore, by 1979 it was clear that the United States under Carter had come to face a global political and economic retreat.

What intrigued most Soviet analysts was the question of how the Carter administration would deal with the crisis in Central America. The region's regimes – mostly creatures of US economic, political, and military presence – were simultaneously being challenged by guerrilla warfare and losing the support of the emerging middle class, vital to the regimes' survival. By 1978 the Central American crisis had become the most serious challenge to US hegemony in the region since Castro entered Havana on New Year's Day in 1959. Unlike South America, Central America was unquestionably perceived as a vital part of the US strategic rear, yet Soviet analysts were equally aware that the Carter administration was operating under a set of constraints not faced by any other US administration since World War II.

The most significant constraints were as follows: Since the unhappy experience in Vietnam, the US public and US military and civilian bureaucracies were fearful of becoming involved in another guerrilla war. The change in the political atmosphere in Latin America ensured that, unlike in the cases of Guatemala (1954) and the Dominican Republic (1965), the OAS would not provide the United States with a diplomatic fig leaf legitimizing direct US intervention. The decline in East–West tensions, along with the emergence of greater solidarity in the Third World, also ensured that a US intervention in Central America would create a ground swell of anti-US feeling not only in the developing world but even in large segments of West European public opinion. Furthermore, Carter's earlier emphasis on human rights and his reliance on the liberal wing of the Democratic party, which was committed to nonintervention and support for democratic forces in Latin America, made a shift in favor of the existing Central American regimes awkward if not impossible.

Even given their interest in the United States' apparent dilemma in Central America, much of the Soviet academic community remained skeptical about the outcome of that struggle and did not anticipate a Sandinista victory in Nicaragua. Moscow did not take a clear position regarding the uprising in Nicaragua;[76] however, it may be assumed that Shafik Handal articulated the position of the Soviet elite in an article that was published by *Kommunist* at a time when Central American issues were of major concern to Soviet policymakers. Handal, the first secretary of the Salvadoran communist party (PCES), warned that military struggle against a repressive regime was a dangerous proposition, which experience had shown could bear tragic results. Never directly referring to events in Nicaragua, Handal concluded by stating that the PCES would remain true to the resolution of its sixth congress, which called for a united front against the dictatorship formed in coalition with the Christian Democrats and other progressive forces.[77] S. A. Sergeev was more obvious, noting that because of the modern weapons of Somoza's army, "the possibilities of conducting a successful guerrilla war against it are very limited . . . Thus illustrating that the 'peaceful road' remains a valid form of struggle."[78]

Nevertheless, it is significant that eight months before the Sandinista victory in Nicaragua, some in the Soviet press were talking of this ultimate outcome as a foregone conclusion. Obviously, the belief that the United States could impose its will on Central America was losing currency. The theory that the Carter administration had lost control over its Latin American policy was echoed in a *Kommunist* article that concluded that Carter's trip to Brazil and Venezuela demonstrated that the US had run out of ideas for dealing with Latin America.[79]

The FSLN victory in Nicaragua forced both a change in US policy toward the region and a radical change in Soviet perceptions of the region's revolutionary potential. US policy shifted back to its emphasis on East–West competition and downplayed the human rights strategy. The US administration significantly increased its regional military presence, establishing a new naval command responsible for the Caribbean. It ordered several highly publicized "assaults" on the base in Guantánamo, Cuba, using "live" ammunition. It also agreed to supply El Salvador's army with "nonlethal" military equipment, despite that country's persistent human rights abuses.

Soviet observers oscillated between fear that direct US intervention in Nicaragua was possible, if not imminent, and a general sense of elation that led some to claim that Central America was entering a new stage of "anticapitalist development" that Washington could not control. For example, *Pravda* cautioned the Sandinistas to remember that US tolerance of their regime was far from assured: "The fear that Nicaragua will become a 'second Cuba' or that Somoza's overthrow will cause a chain reaction in such states as Guatemala, Honduras, or El Salvador could prompt direct intervention in Nicaragua."[80] Yet *Pravda*'s anxiety soon gave way to almost unanimous euphoria. By mid-1979 the Carter administration, which from its first days had been characterized by vacillation, was beset by a series of foreign and domestic crises. As US public attention became almost totally absorbed in the theatrics of the Camp David process, the fall of the Shah of Iran, and the subsequent "hostage crisis," the administration's ability to act assertively in Central America weakened. The Soviet perception of US vacillation with regard to Latin America was probably reinforced when Carter called the Soviet "combat brigade" in Cuba "totally unacceptable," only to contradict himself within the next few days.

In conclusion, by the period of late *détente* the United States had no political clout left with which to dissuade the USSR from expanding its diplomatic, economic, and cultural presence in almost all the countries of Latin America. Soviet economic activity in the region was limited primarily by the fact that the Soviet and Latin economies could not be easily integrated for expanded trade. Throughout the period the USSR and the Latin American communist parties had remained aloof from guerrilla movements for reasons which included: *détente*; the fear of a direct confrontation with the United States in an area of marginal importance to the USSR; the pessimism of many Soviet analysts regarding the possibility for change in Latin America (especially after the demise of the Allende and Velasco regimes); and Soviet preoccupation with the more promising situations in Angola, Ethiopia,

Mozambique, and Iran. It may be argued that, in the case of Latin America, *détente* ended in July 1979 when the Sandinista guerrillas marched into Managua. Moscow became convinced that there was now little reason to fear US intervention against a progressive regime in Latin America, and during the last three years of the Brezhnev era pursued an increasingly bold policy toward Latin America – in the face of an increasingly assertive US response.

Post-*détente* (1979–82)

Response to the Sandinista victory in Nicaragua

The victory of the Sandinistas, along with the emergence of a Marxist regime in Grenada and increased guerrilla warfare in Guatemala and El Salvador, convinced many Soviet observers that Latin America was indeed ready for a major transformation along a "non-capitalist path of development." The new orthodoxy shared by academic and political circles in the USSR held that the United States had totally lost control over events in Central America. In fact, the strong support that the Sandinista regime received from most of Latin America and Western Europe seriously constrained President Carter's ability to challenge the new Nicaraguan leaders. As Politburo member Andrei Kirilenko proclaimed in November 1979, "Soviet people rejoice that in recent years the people of Angola, Ethiopia, Nicaragua, and Grenada have broken the chains of imperialist domination."[81]

Thus, the last few months of the Carter administration were filled with high hopes on the part of Soviet observers, somewhat reminiscent of their upbeat spirit in the early 1960s. Georgi Arbatov, a member of the CPSU's Central Committee and director of the US and Canada Institute, asserted that the United States would be no more able to control events in Central America than it was in Iran and that the region confronted the United States with a series of "delayed-fuse land mines."[82] His deputy, V. Zhurkin, stated that the USSR "will not accept the Monroe Doctrine in Central America."[83]

The invasion of Afghanistan in late 1979 and the withdrawal of the SALT II treaty from Senate consideration removed the last remnants of *détente* as a factor inhibiting Soviet policy toward the United States and its global interests. Moscow, apparently having no fear of a direct US intervention in Central America, hastened to embrace the FSLN regime. In March 1980 the CPSU signed a party-to-party agreement of mutual help with the FSLN, along with a series of agreements covering economic, technical, and cultural issues. The USSR also signed a secret military protocol with Grenada, which allowed the USSR to use Grenada as a landing base for its reconnaissance flights.[84]

As the Soviets evinced greater hopes for near-term revolutions in Latin America, similar views appeared in the writings of the pro-Soviet communist parties in the region. Shafik Handal now enthusiastically supported the idea of armed struggle, stating that in objective terms revolution was "an attainable reality"[85] and concluding that the Salvadoran communist party would win by military means.[86] Similarly, the Chilean communist party now endorsed active struggle and a tactical alliance with the ultra-leftist MIR (Movimiento de Izquierda Revolucionaria).[87]

The apparent impotence of the Carter administration convinced numerous Soviet analysts that the United States would now have to accept a historic reorientation of its backyard. Valerii Skliar, for example, argued that Washington would now have to "change its strategy and tactics" and would thus seek to side with change in Latin America.[88] V. N. Dmitriev noted that Washington had accepted the FSLN victory and was offering $75 million in aid to Nicaragua's private sector so as to retain some semblance of influence and as a bribe with which to influence the FSLN's foreign policy.[89] Despite Washington's attempts to create "reformist" regimes to stabilize Central America, many Soviet observers felt that such efforts were doomed to failure.

It should be noted, however, that there were some Soviet observers who did not discount the possibility of a US reaction to the Central American crisis and who apparently feared that such a reaction might (1) place the USSR in the uneasy position of not helping "progressive" regimes challenged by the United States and (2) lead to a clash with the region's bourgeoisie that might destroy the existing communist parties in Central America. For example, Boris Ponomarev warned that the United States had never abandoned the "hegemonic pretensions" endemic to its system and that the recent bout of political transformations in the developing world had induced the Carter administration to spend vast amounts of money on the rapid deployment force.[90] He seemed to caution against too much direct Soviet involvement, especially in Nicaragua, since this might provoke a US response. Furthermore, he rejected the "revisionist" position that had emerged regarding Guevara's "foco" theory, stating that "in no country [can] the transformation to socialism be induced and established by a group of revolutionaries."[91]

M. Vasiliev observed that President Carter's indecisiveness had sparked a debate over US policy in Latin America and an even sharper reaction against Carter's policies within the United States.[92] Vasiliev warned that the 1979 congressional amendment banning US aid to anyone who opposed the Monroe Doctrine was an indication of the emerging mood in the United States.[93] E. V. Mitiaeva also warned that just because the United States did not prevent the victory of the FSLN, one should not assume that it would remain indifferent to events in Central America:

> The ruling circles in Washington are determined to use any available means to prevent a "second Nicaragua." Numerous leaders in Washington feel that the Carter administration, when it finally got involved in Nicaragua, did "too little and too late" thus failing to prevent the FSLN from attaining power; therefore in El Salvador the US must act differently ... Since the victory of the Sandinistas in the summer of 1979, the US has been engaged in frantic efforts to prevent a similar sequence of events in any other Central American country.[94]

Such views, however, were in the minority. The perception that the United States was a rapidly declining force in Latin America prevailed and was further reinforced when Brazil and Argentina not only refused to join the grain embargo against the USSR but agreed to fill the void with their own shipments of grain. Paradoxically, during the twilight of Carter's administration, Latin America's position as the historical "strategic rear" of the United States had become the "strategic rear" of the Soviet Union, at least in terms of grain supplies.

The Reagan years

The election of Ronald Reagan to the presidency in 1980 represented the sharpest political break in US history since Roosevelt's election in 1932. Reagan's harsh anti-Soviet rhetoric drew two reactions from Soviet observers. One group felt that once in office Reagan would drift back toward the mainstream of US politics. A second group believed that Ronald Reagan represented a qualitative change in the US attitude, a shift to the right of the traditional political mainstream in the country.[95]

With regard to Latin America, Moscow clearly became very concerned that the Reagan administration might indeed resort to the "big stick." The fear of the new and assertive Reagan administration prompted Moscow to "create fact," or achieve various *faits accomplis*, during Carter's final weeks in office. The basic logic of this Soviet policy appeared to be that although the Reagan administration might attempt to reassert itself in Latin America, it was more likely to concentrate on preventing "new Nicaraguas" rather than on becoming involved in long guerrilla struggles against existing regimes – a process bound to strain the US political consensus.

Thus, by stepping up weapons deliveries to various Latin American regimes, Moscow attempted to convince the new administration that, despite the assertiveness of its rhetoric, it should not expect easy victories. In 1981 the USSR sent more weapons to Cuba than during any other year except 1962.[96] To demonstrate Moscow's commitment to Cuba's defense, Brezhnev, for the first time, listed Cuba as a member of the "socialist community."[97] The USSR had initiated substantial arms transfers to Nicaragua as early as the spring of 1980, and by 1981 Nicaragua possessed 25 т55 tanks, more than 100 armored vehicles, 800 East German military trucks, and enough light weapons for its new army of more than 40,000 men.[98] While helping Nicaragua build by far the largest military establishment in Central America, the USSR also sent 70 military advisers. Furthermore, in a secret agreement, Moscow agreed to supply the tiny island of Grenada with 10 million rubles worth of weapons.[99]

Yet perhaps the strongest indication that the USSR attempted to "create fact" before the Reagan administration took power was the "final offensive" launched by the Farabundo Martí Liberation Front (FMLN) in El Salvador in January 1981. The offensive is logically explicable only as an attempt by the newly formed FMLN to take power before a hard-line administration took control in Washington, since it acted with little or no groundwork laid and without a coherent plan of action (unlike the FSLN). Although there is no direct proof that Moscow ordered the final offensive in El Salvador, or that it determined the date, it is unlikely that the offensive would have taken place over Soviet opposition.

The defeat of the final offensive in El Salvador, and the increased US aid to that country's regime, convinced Moscow that, although there was no reason for it to accommodate the United States in the region, the Reagan administration intended to back up its rhetoric with some degree of action. E. V. Mitiaeva noted that Latin America's economic importance to the United States had increased sharply at the same time that US potency in the region had declined and that this assured an unstable relationship. Further, the Reagan administration had not only abandoned the policy of human rights but actually linked it with international terrorism, thus freeing Washington to work with even the most right-wing regimes in the region.[100]

Glinkin, Martynov, and Iakovlev conceded that the shift to the right in the mood of both the United States and Latin America had occurred even before Reagan took office. They referred to the 1979 La Paz meeting of the OAS and its final communiqué, which failed to link ideological pluralism to *détente*.[101] The authors concluded: "Speeches by the Vice President and the Secretary of State leave no doubt that the US is willing to follow an interventionist course in its dealings with its southern neighbors."[102] Nevertheless, they observed that Nicaragua was in a position to survive the new pressure and must negotiate a settlement to reschedule its debts, improve its ties with Western Europe, and gain the support of the Social Democrats in Europe and Latin America. It is interesting that they assigned no role to the USSR in the FSLN's survival, commenting instead that "the Nicaraguan revolution is ready to defend itself."[103]

Reagan's ability to appease right-wing Republicans and yet not drag the rest of the country into a paralyzing debate, combined with the defeat of the final offensive in El Salvador, convinced a growing number of Soviet analysts that the United States might indeed deny the revolutionary possibilities that so many Soviet observers had predicted after the FSLN's victory. M. A. Oborotova pointed out that Reagan had more maneuverability than Carter had possessed, because he was more interested in a Latin American regime's survivability than its nature and had dropped all pretense of reformism. She also noted that Reagan's pressure tactics on Latin America had worked to the extent that Venezuela and Costa Rica had cooled toward Nicaragua and had started to support the junta in El Salvador. On a less pessimistic note, the author stated that although Latin America might be increasingly divided on Nicaragua, the region remained united in its opposition to any US intervention. Nevertheless, she concluded her article with a warning that, despite the hazards, the Reagan administration would not accept a political solution in El Salvador.[104]

Glinkin and Iakovlev published an even gloomier article asserting that the Reagan administration considered Latin America to be as important to the United States as Western Europe and Japan. They observed, "A deep imprint on the imperialist strategy in Latin America and the Caribbean basin is that in this region there is an extraordinary concentration of so-called 'vital' US interests." The authors also rejected the notion that revolutionary change was inevitable in Latin America – one of the most dynamic regions in the capitalist world, which would be able to create for itself a new niche within the capitalist system.[105]

Anxiety that Washington might assert itself in the Caribbean basin resulted in Moscow's decision to downgrade its own presence. Thus, the Salvadoran communist party, which had received so much attention from the Soviet press only a few months earlier, was the only communist party not even mentioned at the 26th congress of the CPSU.[106] Although the CPSU did sign a party-to-party agreement with the New Jewel Movement of Grenada, this fact was never revealed, unlike the public agreement signed with the FSLN in March 1980. It would be wrong, however, to assume that Reagan's assertiveness drove Moscow back to a modified version of its traditional geographic fatalism. Moscow no longer accepted that Latin America was in the United States' exclusive sphere of influence, but it still accepted the possibility that the Reagan administration would halt the emergence of new revolutionary regimes.

From the Soviet perspective, at the end of the Brezhnev era there were still encouraging signs in Latin America. Despite a major effort by the Reagan administration to eradicate the FMLN, the guerrillas still retained control of more than 25 percent of the country and had managed to force a military deadlock. Nicaragua, in the face of severe US pressure, had managed to survive, and the FSLN had consolidated its power under adverse conditions. The regimes of Guatemala, Honduras, and Colombia were engaged in apparently endless struggles with guerrillas, and Brazil's military regime, long-time pillar of US influence in South America, reeled under an economic crisis and sought to retreat from power (while retaining its institutional integrity).

Thus, although the Soviet press no longer predicted near-term revolutionary transformation in Central America, traditional references to the entire Western hemisphere as an extension of the United States were similarly absent. In late 1982 the Soviet press described Latin America as a volcano where "a prolonged struggle toward national liberation" would ultimately result in social transformation and the end of the colonial US presence. And Moscow was almost certain to continue with its activist policy in Latin America, despite modifications imposed on it by the possibility of direct US intervention in the region and despite the Soviet leadership's reluctance to undertake new economic and military commitments.

2 Latin America's role in the capitalist division of labor

Until 1930 Latin America's place within the capitalist division of labor had remained essentially unchanged since the middle of the nineteenth century, when most of the Latin American republics had developed highly specialized monocultural economies, generally designed to serve a specific market either in Europe or North America. Thus, Argentina and the other states along the Río de la Plata had specialized in meeting Britain's needs for primary products, in exchange for British capital and industrial goods; Brazil, Central America, Mexico, and Peru had developed similar relationships with the United States. Dependence on foreign markets produced an infrastructure that was totally export-oriented and that often completely ignored necessary development of the continent's interior.

As noted earlier, the Great Depression and the collapse of demand in the industrial world for Latin America's primary products permanently destroyed the previous world economic configuration. Unable to sell its primary commodities in Europe and the United States, Latin America could not purchase industrial products and so in general embarked on a policy of "import substitution." By the late 1930s almost all of the region's countries had greatly expanded their light industries, and the major states had started to lay the basis for their own chemical, iron, and steel industries. Local industrialization was further stimulated by the inability of Europe and the United States to provide the region with industrial goods, by the outbreak of World War II and the Korean War, and by Europe's continuing failure to supply Latin America with the industrial products it needed.

Thus, although one result of World War II was the demise of Europe's economic presence in Latin America and the massive expansion of the US presence there, the traditional center–periphery relationship was not reestablished. By the time Brezhnev rose to power, the predominant economic position attained by the United States as a result of World War II had started to erode and the level of industrial development in several Latin American countries surpassed that of parts of Europe. To this would be added the greater participation of non-US corporations in Latin America's economy. Whereas during the 1950s and early 1960s US MNCs had accounted for the overwhelming share of foreign capital in Latin America, by the mid-1960s German, Japanese, British, French, Canadian, and even Israeli companies had made significant inroads into all spheres of the region's economic activity, including mining, industrial production, agriculture, banking, and the service industries.

In addition, Latin American leaders displayed greater diplomatic assertiveness during the Brezhnev years. By the 1970s they had become some of the most visible diplomatic travelers, with Mexico's presidents Echeverría and López Portillo visiting most major capitalist centers of Europe and the Orient and Brazil's President Geisel visiting London and Paris, soon to be followed by the presidents of Venezuela and Costa Rica. Not only were these leaders often able to exploit the different attitudes and interests of capitalist countries, but, because of divergences between Europe, Japan, and the United States, they were able on several occasions to conduct foreign and economic policies in defiance of Washington.

For example, during the early 1960s, Britain, Canada, and Spain refused to support the US-led economic embargo against Cuba and actually expanded trade and credits to that country. Similarly, during the late 1960s and early 1970s, Britain, France, Italy, and West Germany agreed to supply Latin America with weapons refused by the United States in an attempt to dampen the arms race in the region. In 1970, at the height of the clashes between the United States and Peru over the nationalization of US capital, Japanese mining concerns agreed to assume some of the previously US-held mineral rights, on economic terms that the United States resisted. In 1977 West Germany, despite strong protests from the Carter administration, agreed to supply Brazil with several nuclear reactors and a complete reprocessing cycle. During the late 1970s and early 1980s, Canada and Europe refused to support the United States in its economic warfare against Nicaragua.

Given the industrial growth of Latin America, the greater participation of non-US corporations in its economy, and the region's greater diplomatic assertiveness, Soviet analysts started to debate the following question: Was Latin America economically still a mere appendage of the United States, or was it becoming a significant new bloc (albeit still the weakest) among the various capitalist blocs? In other words, had Latin America's growing industrialization lessened the region's economic dependence or altered its position within the capitalist division of labor? The prevailing Soviet attitude during the Brezhnev era was that it had not.

Zoia Romanova, unswayed by Latin America's growing industrial capacity, was one of the strongest proponents of the theory that Latin America's global role was shrinking and thus increasing economic dependence on the United States. Romanova noted that Latin America's terms of trade had been sliding for more than two decades. In other words, the price of Latin America's exports was actually falling, at a time when the price of its imports was steadily rising – a conjunction that pushed Latin America into increasing debt. The author also observed that the institution of the common agricultural policy by the EEC and of preferential import policies for Europe's former colonies severely restricted Latin America's once extensive trade opportunities with Europe. Again, these realities implied a marked increase in regional dependence on the United States.[1]

An even more pessimistic assessment was articulated by A. N. Glinkin and P. Iakovlev, who asserted that most Soviet analysts seemed overimpressed with Latin America's industrialization and that, in fact, the region's share of output in the capitalist world remained the same in 1976 as it had been in 1938 – only 3.7 percent.[2] Thus, the authors continued, Latin America's global position had deteriorated, both because of the European bias toward its former colonies and because of the region's diminished importance for the United States. Whereas in 1950 Latin America had accounted for 50 percent of US overseas investment, by 1973 the share had fallen to a mere 18 percent, accounting for less than 8 percent of US corporate profits.[3] The authors further contended that the Brazilian economic miracle, which manifested itself in the rapid economic growth of the early 1970s, had collapsed, leaving the country deeply indebted and failing to reverse the decline in Latin America's share of global trade from 6.2 percent in 1960 to 3.9 percent in 1973.[4]

Greater economic development, according to Lev Klochkovskii and Shermet'ev, did not create a greater economic role for Latin America. The authors pointed out that although the region might have reached the "mid-level" of capitalist development, similar to Spain and Ireland, Latin America's technological base and its trade position were unimproved. This was because almost all of its economic development during the preceding twenty years had been directed by foreign corporations and aimed mainly at the region's internal markets.[5] In a later article, Glinkin contended that despite the improved terms of trade resulting from the "mineral crisis" of the 1970s, and despite the growth of Latin America's trade with Japan and the EEC at the expense of trade with the United States, the level of Latin America's dependence on the United States had not really changed.[6]

It was Viktor Vol'skii, director of the Latin American Institute, who most strongly attacked the thesis that Latin America's industrialization enhanced regional independence from the United States. Vol'skii denied that industrial growth had, in any way, altered the region's position in the capitalist global economic system; the emergence of some industries, such as steel, simply reflected an updated division of labor.[7] Regarding Latin America's efforts to diversify its economic activity away from the United States, Vol'skii noted that between 1966 and 1976 the percentage of goods made by local affiliates of US corporations had risen from 40 to 59 percent of the region's exports.[8] Vol'skii also ridiculed those who compared Latin America's level of development with that of southern Europe. His comparison described southern Europe's current trade account deficit as manageable, whereas Latin America in 1976 had spent 43 percent of its exports in servicing its debt – up from 18 percent in 1950.[9] The author concluded that Latin America was now more dependent on foreign capital (both in absolute figures and on a per capita basis) than either Asia or Africa[10] and that any discussion of a new role for Latin America within the capitalist world was not merited.

Although some countries in fact reached the mid-level position of economic development during the Brezhnev era, most Soviet analysts remained convinced that Latin America had failed to attain sufficient economic weight to exploit "inter-imperialist rivalries." Although some parts of the Third World (such as the Arab world) had managed to become sufficiently important to the United States, Europe, and Japan to trigger rivalries among the capitalist powers, Latin America increasingly suffered from the reverse problem of decreasing importance to both Western Europe and the United States, and only marginal importance to Japan.

Viktor Lukin touched upon Latin America's declining importance to Europe when he cited a drop of from 6 percent to 2.8 percent in Latin America's share of Europe's external trade between 1960 and 1975. He felt that this deterioration was bound to continue, since under the provisions of the Lomé Convention the EEC had committed itself to cut imports of Latin American commodities by 50 percent to accommodate the needs of Europe's former colonies. All this was despite Latin America's view of the EEC as a counterweight to the United States and despite the region's improved position within the capitalist world, which had resulted from the increased price of primary commodities during the mid- and late-1970s and the fall of the Shah of Iran.[11]

Lukin further asserted that the only growth in European–Latin American economic intercourse was an increase in European capital investments in Latin America, aimed at Latin America's domestic market.[12] He noted that even West Germany, with its large investments in Latin America, close ties with Brazil, and an absence of colonial responsibilities toward Africa, had never seriously deviated from EEC policies in order to be helpful to Latin America. This was despite West Germany's self-proclaimed role of "defender" of Latin America, within the councils of the EEC, and of "mediator" between "North" and "South."[13] The essay concluded that, of the three major capitalist world centers, Japan alone remained an area where the prognosis for expanded Latin American trade remained good, and through which some displacement of US hegemony might occur.[14]

Similarly, Iu. Paniev asserted that the growing inter-capitalist struggle between US and European monopolies over Latin America yielded only marginal benefits for Latin America. For example, US monopolies tended to acquire existing plants; the Europeans tended to build new plants and introduce new technology, but the output of these investments was aimed at Latin America's domestic markets. Paniev further noted that a paradoxical situation was developing in Euro–Latin American relations. Although Latin America was becoming increasingly important to the EEC's corporations (such as Volkswagen, Olivetti, and Philips), it was becoming increasingly marginal to the EEC economies as a whole.[15] According to Paniev, the obligations undertaken by Europe at the Lomé Convention, combined with preferential agreements with the semi-developed states of the Mediterranean, the Association of South East Asian Nations (ASEAN), and India and massive subsidies to Europe's own farmers, blocked almost all trade opportunities open to Latin America.[16] He predicted that this situation, which almost eliminated Latin America as a trading partner for the EEC, would worsen when Spain and Portugal joined the EEC. This was because Spain would no longer import Latin American meat and wheat and because Spanish footwear would be able to replace Latin American leather goods on Europe's markets.[17] Finally, Paniev observed that, despite Europe's declared sympathy for Latin America, the EEC through its policies was perpetuating a global system in which Africa remained within its sphere of influence while Latin America stayed within that of the United States.[18]

If the Soviets perceived Latin America as a continent of diminishing importance to both Western Europe and North America, the situation was somewhat different in the case of Japan. Japan, with no mineral base of its own and with fewer enduring colonial ties, consistently attempted to diversify its sources of primary commodities as well as its export markets. Although Japan had few economic interests in Latin America before World War II, the collapse of the Japanese empire in Asia, along with the massive inflow of Japanese immigrants to much of Latin America (particularly to Brazil), created the necessary conditions for expanded trade between Japan and Latin America. Increased Japanese penetration of Latin America started to draw Soviet attention in the early 1970s, when Japan's investments in the hemisphere surpassed those of West Germany, thus making Japan the second-largest foreign investor in Latin America.[19]

The growth of Japanese trade and investment in Latin America, however, did not convincingly signal to the Soviets an alternative to Latin America's increasingly dependent predicament. Soviet analysts noted that although Japan's trade with Latin America was rapidly expanding, the nature of that trade was returning Latin America to an economic position analogous to the one it had occupied before the 1930s. Furthermore, most of Japan's investments in Latin America were concentrated in extractive industries, which did little to advance Latin America's level of development.[20] V. O. Kistanov pointed out that although Japan's investments in Latin America might indeed challenge some US multinationals in their traditional strongholds, the net effect of the Japanese penetration was nevertheless the consolidation of Latin America's traditional role within the capitalist division of labor.[21]

Only toward the end of the Brezhnev era did some Soviet analysts begin to perceive Latin America's industrialization process as a possible vehicle for pushing the region toward a new position within the capitalist division of labor. Evgenii Primakov asserted that those countries of the developing world that managed to attract large amounts of foreign investment did indeed develop an industrial base and the capacity to generate internal capital, which, according to most Soviet analysts, was the first step toward economic independence.[22] Thus, such countries as Brazil, Venezuela, and, to a lesser degree, Mexico and Argentina, were on their way toward greater economic independence. This implied a new role within the capitalist division of labor.

Klochkovskii, although he did not anticipate an immediate change in the correlation of forces between the economies of Latin America and the developed capitalist world, believed that Latin America's role within the capitalist world had indeed changed and that the region was on the road to greater economic independence. He noted that Brazil, for example, had attained all the prerequisites of an industrial power, with an output of steel exceeding that of Britain; Latin America as a whole had become a key export platform of industrial goods (such as automobiles) to the rest of the world, including both the developing countries and centers of capitalism, such as the United States.[23] Although Klochkovskii remained very critical of the activities of the multinationals in Latin America, he noted: "On the whole, one must concede that the establishment of the 'new economic order' during the 1970s has become one of the leading factors in the industrial progress attained by the region in the restructuring of Latin America's export profile, and a change in the region's position within the international economic order."[24]

Yet even those Soviet scholars who believed that Latin America's industrialization, albeit financed by foreign concerns, would ultimately lead to structural changes in the region's economies and greater independence, did not believe that the change would take place in the immediate future. Primakov, despite his belief that the Third World might be able to exploit for its own economic benefit the growing competition being waged over it by the capitalist countries, did not link the emergence of economic multipolarity to a devolution of American political hegemony:

> The growth of the economic potential (of Western Europe and Japan) was not accompanied by the loss of the dominant position of the United States in the military-political region which permits it to preserve its position of hegemony in the capitalist subsystem of international relations and impose its approaches on questions of principle on other capitalist states.[25]

Thus, although many aspects of Moscow's perception of Latin America changed during Brezhnev's tenure, most Soviet analysts did not alter their traditional belief that Latin America was a dependent continent with no immediate prospects of emancipation.

3   Latin America's role in the Third World

Latin American attitudes

Before 1961 Latin America often expressed ambivalence toward the Third World. Its unwillingness to consider itself part of the Third World was, in fact, similar to the viewpoint of the Soviets, who usually referred to the Third World as the Afro-Asian bloc. That many Latin American elite felt little communality with the emerging states in Asia and Africa was due largely to the region's long experience of independence and traditional self-perception as being a part of "Christian Western civilization."

Only in 1961 did Latin America begin to participate in the Non-Aligned Movement (NAM), which had first convened in 1955.[1] Several explanations may be given for why Latin America started to identify more with the Third World. First, Castro's regime, with its activist policy among nonaligned nations, convinced many in Latin America that the NAM might be a new forum in which Latin America could air its grievances against the United States. Added to this was Latin America's need for greater cooperation with the new Asian and African states, whose inclusion in the UN reduced the numeric weight of Latin America within that organization.

Other developments, of course, aided Latin America in shifting its policy toward the Third World. For example, the success of OPEC led Latin American states to join eagerly with other developing countries in price cartels for primary commodities in an attempt to offset the region's declining share of global trade. These cartels dealt in various commodities, such as copper and bauxite. Brazil found it preferable to begin stressing its African heritage, over traditional self-identification with Christian Western civilization, when the 400 percent increase in the price of oil in 1973 left the country with a massive current account deficit. This forced Brazil to make an all-out effort to expand exports

47

to the oil-exporting states of the Middle East and Africa and led Brazil to abandon its traditional support for Portugal's efforts to retain its empire in Africa. Similarly, both Brazil and Argentina made strenuous efforts to cultivate their ties with the Arab world and developed significant trade contacts with Iraq, Libya, and Saudi Arabia.

Latin America's evolving attitude toward the Third World also related to its changing perceptions of world tensions, away from East–West issues and toward North–South conflicts. In addition to Brazil, other Latin American countries (particularly Argentina, Guyana, Mexico, Peru, and Venezuela) took leading positions both with the "Group of 77," UNCTAD (United Nations Conference on Trade and Development), and other North–South forums that demanded a new international economic order.[2] The growing assertiveness of Latin American demands for changes in North–South relations was also reflected in a changing diplomatic posture, which began with Brazil's refusal in 1961 to support fully the US sanctions against Cuba. Next, most of Latin America broke with the United States and voted in favor of admitting the People's Republic of China to the UN and ousting Taiwan. Similarly, Brazil, Guyana, and Mexico broke with the West and voted in favor of the UN resolution equating Zionism with racism. In 1975, when the United States attempted to rally Latin American support against the Cuban intervention in the civil war in Angola, these efforts fell on deaf ears.

Thus, the 1960s witnessed a dramatic shift in Latin American attitudes toward the Third World and its position within that world. No longer was Latin America aloof and patronizingly detached. It had assumed instead a position of leadership within the Non-Aligned Movement.

Soviet perceptions

Soviet analysts from Lenin on have viewed Latin America as a "dependent" continent. Yet, as mentioned previously, the Soviets did not consider it to be a genuine part of the Third World either. This was because of the nature of Latin American regimes, their close ties with the United States, and the existence of a large bourgeoisie. When Latin America began to assume a new position in the Third World during the 1960s, most Soviet analysts remained unaware of this change. For example, a typical 1966 article noted the potential for closer ties between Africa and Latin America but asserted that this had yet to materialize.[3] Similarly, through the early 1970s, whenever Latin

America took the same position at the UN as Asia and Africa, the Soviets interpreted this simply as the region's anti-North Americanism.[4]

In the early 1970s the first serious Soviet study of Latin America's role in the NAM was made. The author, R. A. Tuzmukhamedov, asserted that whereas the Asian states had played the leading role in the movement during the 1950s, and the African states had done so during the 1960s, the 1970s were becoming a Latin American era.[5] He considered Latin America's membership in the NAM to be very positive, since "life has shown that nonalignment facilitates anti-imperialism."[6] Already a US military installation on Easter Island had been expelled.[7] Nevertheless, the author remained concerned that Latin America might merely be using the movement as a lever to force economic concessions from the capitalist world, rather than being genuinely interested in restructuring the international system.[8] Tuzmukhamedov, arguing that the Latin American states could not be a member of both the NAM and of the OAS and the Rio Pact, concluded that "Latin America was on the verge of becoming a part of the nonaligned movement, but was not a part of it yet."[9] Klochkovskii, in an article examining the "new economic order," noted that although "developing countries have started to attack the basis of the economic domination by imperialism,"[10] Latin America, because of its greater dependence on capitalism and because its elite groups had links with foreign capital, was the least able to resist imperialism and was therefore different from the rest of the developing world.[11]

Soviet suspicions that Latin America was not truly committed to the causes of the Third World and to the NAM intensified during the late 1970s, when several leftist regimes in the region fell from power. For example, in an article analyzing Ecuador's foreign policy during the military regime of the 1970s, G. Z. Tanin accused the regime's nonaligned foreign policy of being an opportunistic scheme, designed more to improve Ecuador's terms of trade with the imperialist powers than to bring about change in the international system. As evidence, he cited the fact that Ecuador joined OPEC only in November 1973, when OPEC's power was immense, and that by 1978, when the oil market had become "soft," Ecuador abandoned its nationalist oil policy.[12] Further, despite its strong rhetorical support of the developing world, Ecuador (the world's largest banana producer) had destroyed a banana cartel by refusing to join it.[13] Tanin concluded that although Ecuador continued to make progressive gestures, such as supporting Panama's claim to the Canal Zone and an end to the embargo against Cuba, Ecuador's anti-imperialist policy, as a practical matter, had ended in 1976.[14]

In a similar vein, M. L. Chumakova observed that although Brazil since 1974 had reoriented its foreign policy away from the United States and toward greater identification with the rest of Latin America, Africa, and the Arab world, these changes merely reflected Brazil's need to find additional economic partners in the changing global economic situation. She contended that for all President Geisel's rhetoric, Brazil continued to court the imperialist powers.[15] According to Chumakova, Brazil was attempting to follow a two-track policy: while continuing to expand its ties with the nonaligned countries of Africa, Latin America, and the Levant, it also continued to guard its "special relationship" with Washington – as was illustrated by the (1975) mutual consultation accord negotiated with Henry Kissinger.[16]

Perhaps the strongest doubts about the impact of Latin America's participation within the Non-Aligned Movement came from Anna Matlina, who asserted that Latin America was heavily dependent on industrial exports and could not survive without the MNCs' distribution networks. Thus, she agreed with Glinkin's notion[17] that there were severe limits on Latin America's ability to challenge the imperialist order.[18] She stated that although various Latin American regimes might favor rhetorical confrontations with imperialism to bolster their legitimacy, the cornerstone of these regimes remained their ties to the United States.[19] Matlina concluded there could be no genuine shift in Latin America's global orientation without prior changes in the domestic governments of Latin America and that "the search for a new international order may yet become the opium for the masses of the Third World."[20]

Although most Soviet analysts were not convinced that the Non-Aligned Movement benefited greatly from Latin America's participation, others felt that Latin America's association with the Third World was helping the region to break free of US hegemony. V. N. Nikolaev noted that since the NAM's 1970 Lusaka conference the movement had become Latin America's main forum in which to confront the United States and other imperialist powers over such issues as the Panama Canal and the Falkland Islands.[21] Nikolaev asserted: "The growth of Latin American participation within the non-aligned movement undercuts the historic domination of the region by the United States in the economic, political and military spheres."[22] He claimed that the growing Latin American affiliation with the movement raised US fears about a possible Latin American withdrawal from the Rio Pact.[23] Similarly, Juan Cobo asserted that Latin America's increasing involvement with the Third World permanently reoriented Latin America's policies. Since the first Latin American delegations participated in the 1961 conference the region's foreign policy had become progressively more independent of the United States, having given Venezuela the impetus to forge OPEC.[24]

This positive assessment was echoed by A. Khrunov, who asserted that given Latin America's level of development it might help other developing countries to bypass imperialist monopolies. As an example, Khrunov cited the oil exploration carried out in Africa and Iraq by Brazil's Petrobras.[25] He did, however, concede that not all Latin American attempts to establish close economic ties with developing countries were fruitful. For example, Mexico's efforts to increase trade with Asia and Africa had failed because Mexico could not compete in either price or quality with the developed world. Nevertheless, Khrunov stated that Latin America's role within the Non-Aligned Movement was a fact of contemporary reality and had great potential.[26]

In conclusion, most Soviet analysts clearly remained suspicious of Latin America's newfound interest in the Non-Aligned Movement. The prevailing attitude was that most of Latin America, with its multinational-affiliated bourgeois regimes, had little interest in actually undermining the capitalist system but was rather using the movement as a forum to extract better economic terms for itself.

Another prevailing theme was Moscow's irritation with Latin America's insistence (along with the majority in the Third World) on dividing the world into "rich" and "poor" countries – and including the USSR among the "rich." Almost all Soviet analysts complained that it was unjust and even pro-imperialist for Latin America to insist, as it did, that all developed countries, including the USSR, donate 1 percent of their gross national product toward the development of the Third World. In general, Moscow's support for a new international economic order declined after UNCTAD VI in 1980, when the USSR responded to Third World demands for a fairer distribution of wealth among the "rich" and the "poor" nations, by demanding that the elites of the Third World should first carry out domestic redistributions of domestic wealth. Other Soviet analysts accused Third World elites of conspiring to appropriate, for themselves, the benefits of the new international world order, in much the same manner as, it was argued, they had appropriated the wealth of their own countries.[27]

Thus, although some Soviet analysts welcomed Latin America's involvement in the Third World as yet another manifestation of the growing antagonism between the United States and its southern neighbors, most remained cool and unenthusiastic about Latin America's growing involvement in the Non-Aligned Movement, even during the early 1970s, when leftist regimes dominated large parts of the continent.

4   Soviet views on Latin America's regional integration

The idea of Latin American unity is as old as the region's independence. Latin America's founding fathers, especially Bolívar, envisaged either one huge Spanish-speaking state, stretching from Mexico to Argentina, or an alternative of no more than three states.[1] Although Bolívar's dream failed to materialize, and the four viceroyalties of Spanish America fragmented into eighteen separate states, the idea of unity has nevertheless continued to evoke a response throughout Latin America.

During the nineteenth century, the Latin American states periodically revived the idea of regional unity when they perceived a threat of foreign aggression. Four congresses were called in response to, for example, fears that Spain might attempt to reintroduce colonialism in the hemisphere. The absence of concrete results at these conferences, and of exterior threats to the territorial integrity of the Latin American states after 1865, resulted in declining interest in political unity.

Unlike the idea of political unity, the notion of economic unity did not emerge until after World War II. The lack of economic intercourse within Latin America can be attributed in part to the continent's vast physical scale and the impassable terrain separating different areas. Furthermore, the region's infrastructure obstructed the development of inter-Latin American trade, since any economic development that had occurred was designed to serve a specific foreign market – usually European or North American.

A basis was laid for expanding trade among the region's republics when several larger states undertook an "export substitution" policy during the Great Depression. Combined with Latin America's isolation from industrial centers during World War II, this resulted in substantial diversification of the region's economies. Implementation of regional integration, however, did not occur until the 1960s, despite the earlier formation of the Economic Commission for Latin America under UN auspices.

Soviet attitudes toward Latin America's efforts at economic integration primarily hinged on assessments of whether greater integration would enhance the region's global standing and, therefore, lessen its dependence on the United States. This chapter not only discusses evolving Soviet attitudes but considers which models of regional integration were favored by the USSR for Latin America and why, as well as the Soviet prognosis for future integration efforts in the region.

The Latin American Free Trade Association and the Central American Common Market

Both the Latin American Free Trade Association (LAFTA) and the Central American Common Market (CACM) were organized in 1960 and expanded during the early 1960s. Both sought to expand inter-Latin American trade and reduce the region's dependence on the developed nations, primarily on the United States. Yet the prevailing attitude in Moscow was hostility toward both organizations: any Latin American efforts to enhance economic integration would serve primarily to enhance the presence of foreign multinational corporations, and the interests of the associated local elites, and thus deepen regional dependence on imperialist powers – primarily, on the United States.

Although LAFTA's declared goal was the promotion of a Latin American economic presence in the world, most Soviet analysts responded to the group's formation in the same negative terms that they responded to the creation of the European Common Market. They saw in both an attempt to establish large economic units that would enable US monopolies to take advantage of the emerging economies of scale. In fact, LAFTA (unlike the EEC) never proved to be more than an internal tariff preference system meant to encourage regional trade. An early attack on the concept of regional integration in Latin America came from Zoia Romanova, a prominent analyst associated with the Institute of World Economy. She stated that the entire notion was devised by the creators of the Alliance for Progress, who saw in such integration an opportunity for US corporations to penetrate the emerging manufacturing sector of the region as well as an antidote to Latin American nationalist aspirations.[2] Successful integration, although it might enhance the region's economic independence, would certainly strengthen capitalism and especially the power of the large bourgeoisie in Argentina, Brazil, and Mexico.[3] On a more positive note, however, Romanova predicted that a unified Latin America would trigger sharper "inter-imperialist" competition between Europe and the United States over Latin America – which would be a welcome development.[4]

N. Iudanov concluded that LAFTA would both fail to increase Latin America's independence and enhance US dominance. He blamed the region's monocultural economic model on historical US opposition to regional integration and claimed that the United States had attempted to frustrate any such effort by using its MNCs. Iudanov believed that the United States had shifted its position and now supported LAFTA because of the MNCs' emerging need for greater economies of scale.[5]

Although most Soviet analysts saw in LAFTA a Trojan horse created by US multinationals and aimed at consolidating US economic hegemony, Anatolii Shul'govskii was a notable exception. He viewed integration as "the answer to the region's economic needs"; an effort "without the United States, and virtually against the United States."[6] Shul'govskii also noted that Latin America's growing economic power as a result of integration had stimulated interest in France and other European countries, which were carefully following the growing rift between the United States and its southern neighbors.[7] He attacked those who claimed that regional integration would yield gains for the pro-US elites. Instead, he observed, it was the old landed oligarchy that continued to favor "Pan-Americanism," while the emerging bourgeoisie was far more interested in Latin solidarity and was naturally hostile to the United States.[8]

Perhaps Gvozdev displayed the most typical Soviet attitude. Gvozdev asserted that President Johnson supported LAFTA because he believed that it would help the United States to check growing Soviet prestige in the area. Gvozdev pointed out that LAFTA's leaders were almost exclusively mainstream economists, such as Felipe Herrara and Carlos Sanz de Santamaría, both of whom were associated with the Inter-American Development Bank and the Alliance for Progress. Thus, Gvozdev observed, it was natural that LAFTA's prime objective was to enhance the presence of foreign capital in Latin America.[9] According to Gvozdev, the United States supported LAFTA only to enable US corporations to operate on a continent-wide scale. Gvozdev predicted that LAFTA would disintegrate because of the growing tension between the larger states – such as Brazil and Argentina, which benefited most from the customs union – and the smaller, least developed states – such as Ecuador, which actually lost from the undertaking. Gvozdev concluded that the only way to bring about the regional integration of Latin America was to change the region's political system.[10]

By the early 1970s the expectations of LAFTA's members had not materialized, largely because of disagreement among member states as to which goods ought to enjoy the lowered tariffs. A postmortem article by N. Zaitsev, then deputy director of the Latin American Institute, asserted that LAFTA had never amounted to much and that the inter-American share of the region's overall trade showed no significant increase since the group's formation. According to Zaitsev, LAFTA's sole accomplishment was to increase MNC power, since lower tariffs had enabled foreign corporations to bypass states controlling their activities by moving their operations to those countries where there were no controls at all.[11] In his opinion LAFTA had failed to be an effective vehicle for regional integration because it had reflected the interests of MNCs and affiliated elites instead of the needs of Latin American independence.[12] In another article he noted that more than half of all industrial exports generated by LAFTA had been manufactured by the MNCs.[13] Zaitsev further stated that Latin America's situation was not analogous to that of Western Europe, where he conceded that economic integration had indeed resulted in greater independence from the United States. Zaitsev attributed this success to the fact that European countries, unlike those of Latin America, were developed and had a large bourgeoisie dependent neither on the direct presence of US corporations nor on foreign credits. Zaitsev, however, had also come to credit Latin American efforts at integration with having a strongly anti-imperialist character.[14]

By the early 1980s, LAFTA was essentially defunct, and most Soviet analysts concluded that it had accomplished little except to allow the US presence to expand south of its border. Among those with a more positive reading were E. V. Lyvkin, who, although he conceded that LAFTA had aided US expansion, believed that this had resulted in the displacement of the local bourgeoisie, thereby leaving a lasting legacy of anti-Americanism among the region's most relevant political elite.[15] Lev Klochkovskii, director of the Latin American Institute's economics department, wrote that LAFTA had succeeded in stimulating trade within Latin America. He further stated that greater trade and cooperation among members in various coproduction schemes had significantly advanced regional industrialization, a development that in turn resulted in less trade with the capitalist world. Klochkovskii blamed LAFTA's disintegration on its failure to satisfy the demands of less developed members for a more equal distribution of benefits.[16]

CACM, unlike LAFTA, was a genuine common market that included all Central American states. By 1965 almost all tariffs among its member states disappeared. A substantial increase in trade developed, especially in industrial goods, and inspired a massive increase in foreign investment in the region.

The USSR perceived the apparent success of CACM, and the emerging closer political ties among the Central American states, in the most sinister light. Not only did Soviet analysts view CACM as a vehicle for the expansion of the North American economic presence, but, more significant, they labeled it a US attempt to create a right-wing bloc aimed at suppressing national liberation movements in the region, and serving as a praetorian guard against Cuba. A. Kartsev charged that CACM was not intended to serve the interests of the region's peoples, nor was it really an economic organization but rather a political-military union established to serve as a gendarme of the United States.[17] Kosarev, Matlina, and Sergeev agreed, noting that Washington hoped to create a rightist political alliance to goad Cuba. They further warned that, although Latin Americans might view integration as a tool to resist imperialism, in reality an integrated Latin America became a more attractive target for imperialist penetration.[18] Lev Klochkovskii, however, asserted that the vast industrial growth of the region's industrial base generally contributed to the well-being of Central America. He also made the case that inter-imperialist rivalry was increased, and US hegemony decreased, because much of the massive influx of foreign capital (triggered by the existence of the common market) was from other than US sources.[19]

When CACM started to lose its effectiveness, beginning with the "football war" (which broke out after a soccer match between Honduras and El Salvador in the summer of 1969) and during the early 1970s, most Soviet analysts welcomed the development and considered the organization's collapse a step toward a greater – not lesser – role for Central America in the international arena. Moscow had never viewed either CACM or LAFTA as a mechanism by which Latin America could enhance its international political role, along the lines of the Arab League or the Organization of African Unity. Rather, both efforts were criticized for being yet another means to deepen the region's semi-colonial relationship with the United States.

The Andean Pact

Whereas the Soviet attitude toward CACM and LAFTA alternated between coolness and hostility, the Andean Pact came to be perceived by most Soviet analysts as a genuine vehicle for Latin American freedom from imperialist domination. The charter of the Andean Common Market, usually known as the Andean Group or the Andean Pact, was signed in 1969 by Bolivia, Chile, Colombia, Ecuador, and Peru; Venezuela joined in 1973. The group was initially formed as a subregional organization within LAFTA. However, in the Bogotá Declaration of 1966, the group's leaders made known their disappointment with LAFTA's slow progress and committed themselves to integrating their economies substantially. The policy that emerged during the early 1970s was to limit the presence of foreign capital and implement a centrally planned "command economy."

From the very beginning the Andean Pact was different from any of its predecessors. Unlike LAFTA, which was dominated by the pro-capitalist regimes of Brazil and Argentina, the two leading members of the alliance were Peru and Chile, both of which at the time were ruled by leftist regimes committed to ending Latin America's role within the capitalist economic structure. One radical innovation was the emphasis on centrally planned "directed economies" (*dirigismo*), which would assign areas of economic specialization to each member and centrally control the activities of foreign capital.

Given the stated goals of the Andean Pact, it was hardly surprising that Soviet analysts saw this effort to attain economic integration in a different light from its predecessors. According to Oleg Konstantinov, the Andean Pact, through its uniform policy toward foreign capital, enabled pact members to pursue a rigorous anti-imperialist policy and become a model of development to other Latin American countries.[20] G. S. Efimova and A. A. Lavut made a more cautious assessment. Although they hoped that the pact's policies would result in greater regional trade and the reduction of the North American presence, they cautioned that the United States and the EEC were intensifying their efforts to penetrate the larger market.[21] As if to underscore their anxiety, the authors claimed that part of the struggle against imperialism for Latin American communists was the struggle to prevent the usurpation of regional integration by imperialism.[22]

The unified policies of the Andean Pact limiting multinational activities in the region, as well as the wave of nationalizations in Bolivia, Chile, and Peru, consistently earned the praise of the Soviet media. Yet some analysts remained altogether skeptical about the viability of Latin American integration. In one of the sharpest critiques of Latin American integration S. Mishin asserted: "The work of existing regional and sub-regional groups (LAFTA, the Andean Pact and others) does not yet exercise any appreciable influence on the economic development of Latin American nations."[23] Mishin went on to argue that most of the economic conferences held by the Latin Americans were fruitless.[24] He credited efforts at political integration with even less success than those intended to promote economic integration and thus stated that it was unrealistic to expect the latter to lead to the former.[25] He concluded that so long as the region was polarized between those states seeking greater integration and independence and those seeking to nourish ties with the United States, Latin American integration was impossible.[26]

The 1973 coup in Chile and the consequent reorientation of that country's economic policies (along the market-oriented lines of the so-called "Chicago model") was viewed by Soviet scholars as a severe setback for the Andean group. Its political configuration was significantly altered as Chile came under the right-wing Pinochet regime, and, according to Lavut, political changes in Bolivia had further contributed to a serious weakening of the organization.[27] When Chile announced its decision to leave the pact, the Soviets welcomed the news. As the Soviet news agency TASS put it in 1977, Pinochet's Chile had always acted as a fifth column in the service of imperialism within the pact and now the remaining members would be able to pursue their goals more effectively.[28]

The Soviet media continued to remain sympathetic to the Andean Pact, even as the demise of the leftist regimes in Bolivia, Chile, and Peru, along with the inclusion of capitalist Venezuela, began to alter the pact's structure and aims. For example, *Pravda* hailed the pact's decision to create a domestic automobile industry, which it felt would be a blow to US automobile monopolies as well as yet another step toward Latin America's political independence.[29] Similarly, in an article commemorating the tenth year of the creation of the Andean Pact, *Pravda* proclaimed that "the process of limiting the activity of foreign capital was continuing" and that despite the "subversive activity by US monopolist circles ... they cannot halt the profound changes which are taking place in Latin America."[30]

Less popular journals with narrower readership, however, were less flattering. For example, V. Sudarev noted that the intrinsic weakness of the Latin American bourgeoisie had enabled the MNCs to double their economic presence in the Andean region in less than ten years.[31] He further stated that despite the pact's anti-imperialist rhetoric, its real aim was to find a better niche within the capitalist division of labor, as demonstrated by the creation of economic commissions with the EEC, Japan, and Spain.[32] He emphasized how the Andean Pact – never a revolutionary body – had moved further to the right when its leadership passed from leftist Chile and Peru to pro-US Colombia and Venezuela: insisting on a "representative democracy," asking for a "special relationship" with the United States in 1979, and supporting Washington during its dispute with Cuba over "Mariellito" refugees who began arriving in the United States illegally in 1979.[33]

By the early 1980s, Soviet analysts started to realize that the decline in the prices of primary commodities on the world market, the general deterioration in Latin America's terms of trade with the outside world, and the subsequent deepening of the debt crisis were all forcing a retreat in the Andean Pact's economic policies. Most analysts recognized that it was now unrealistic to expect regional integration to displace in a substantial way the presence of foreign capital. Dependence on foreign investment therefore was bound to continue for a long time.

Lyvkin, in an article reviewing the role of foreign capital in the Andean Pact, conceded that the dire economic straits in which Latin America found itself had forced the pact to raise the levels of repatriation of profit by MNCs from 14 percent of the capital invested to 20 percent and to make other concessions as well.[34] Although clearly disappointed at this forced retreat from the pact's original goals, Lyvkin felt that the experience of the Andean Pact was generally positive, since it had focused the attention of the rest of Latin America on the activities of foreign capital on the continent.[35] Although Lyvkin accepted the pact's economic need to make further accommodations with foreign capital, he was less sympathetic to the change in the region's political posture. Writing in a book edited by Glinkin and Sizonenko, he noted that the Chilean coup and subsequent departure from the pact had initially made the group less tolerant of rightist dictatorships, as illustrated by its united opposition to the Somoza dictatorship.[36] With the demise of the military regime in Peru (1980), the subsequent border clashes between Peru and Ecuador, and the pact's deteriorating economic position, the group's political cohesion and its ability to resist US pressure had been weakened. Consequently, the pact had been compelled to be more pliant concerning Washington's demands, as manifested by its support of the US-backed junta in

El Salvador.[37] Thus, Lyvkin concluded, an alliance among Latin American states was both possible and desirable, but only when there were no contradictions among the members' political, economic, and social doctrines.[38]

Although the USSR did not completely write off the Andean Pact as an effective vehicle toward greater Latin American independence from imperialism, the great expectations held by some Soviet analysts had clearly failed to materialize. To those who would argue that Soviet support for the Andean Pact was less indicative of Moscow's support for regional integration and more so of its support for the leftist regimes of Bolivia, Chile, Ecuador, and Peru, a couple of facts should be pointed out: The USSR continued to support the Andean Pact even when Allende, Lara, and Velasco passed from the political scene. Moscow continued to express support for the pact well into the 1980s, when both Velasco and Allende were gone by 1976 and pro-capitalist Venezuela had joined the pact as its most powerful member in 1973.

Other groupings

In addition to CACM, LAFTA, and the Andean Pact, other efforts were made within Latin America to facilitate regional integration. Two of these were (1) the Amazonian River Group, comprising Brazil and several other countries along the Amazon River, and (2) the Cuenca del Plata group, comprising the countries along the Río de la Plata and its tributaries (Argentina, Bolivia, Brazil, Paraguay, and Uruguay). Both integration schemes received scant attention in the Soviet media. The first was viewed by the Soviets as a Brazilian effort to restrain Venezuelan attempts to dominate, economically, its weaker Andean partners, such as Bolivia, Colombia, Ecuador, and Peru. The second was considered nothing more than a mechanism to regulate the rivalry between Brazil and Argentina in an area that each traditionally viewed as its natural sphere of influence. A review of the literature devoted to these pacts, considered vehicles for Brazilian expansion, reveals an interesting absence of the hostility manifested toward LAFTA and CACM.[39]

In contrast, the formation of the organization of the Latin American Economic System (SELA) in 1975, an attempt to create a new economic order in the region, received lavish praise in the Soviet media. *Pravda*'s Leonid Maksimenko saw in the new organization "one more proof of the growing aspiration of the Latin American countries to unity of action to defend their national interests" and tied SELA's birth to the vote by the OAS foreign ministers a few days earlier to lift the economic embargo against Cuba.[40] *Izvestiia*, commenting two months later, called the creation of SELA "a challenge to the neo-colonialist principles on which the OAS is based."[41] The main reason that Moscow welcomed SELA was that this organization included Cuba and excluded the United States. However, although Moscow welcomed the increasing integration of Cuba into Latin America, there was little expectation among Soviet analysts that SELA would actually facilitate greater Latin American independence from the industrialized West.

In conclusion, by the early 1980s Soviet analysts started to perceive almost any integrating effort, even if led by rightist Brazil, as an effort to diminish the region's subservience to the United States and Western Europe. In what amounted to a postmortem on regional integration, I. K. Shermet'ev stressed that most Latin American integration schemes failed because of the wide disparities among the members' levels of economic development, the disruptive role of the multinationals, and the lack of working-class support for integration.[42] His analysis concluded with the belief that SELA's less ambitious agenda and greater flexibility gave it a greater chance of success; however, its "technocratic nature," and the lack of proper attention to the "class content" in the undertaking, made real success unlikely. Zaitsev, despite his previous doubts about Latin American integration, noted that although the Latin Americans underestimated the difficulties entailed by economic integration, even the existing integration gave Latin America a greater voice at the UN and the Group of 77, which "enabled Latin America to have a more cohesive position in its dealings with the United States, the EEC, and Japan."[43] Zaitsev concluded that it was vital to support Latin American integration, since it encouraged intrabloc dependence, which limited the power of the industrial West.[44]

Finally, it is interesting to note that, shortly before Brezhnev's death, some Soviet analysts started to question the wisdom of Moscow's support for Latin America's economic integration. N. Zinov'ev noted that the major outcome of Latin America's integration efforts was not an increase in the region's political independence *vis-à-vis* the United States, but rather a greater tendency toward self-sufficiency in the region, which limited the USSR's ability to compete in Latin America's markets.[45]

5 Soviet conclusions regarding Latin America's ability to conduct an independent foreign policy

Although by the early 1980s Latin America had clearly ceased to fit Stalin's description of a "collection of US satellites," it was equally clear that Latin America had yet to find a new niche in the international system. Soviet analysts recognized that despite Latin America's increased efforts to loosen its chronic dependence on the United States, either by expanding its regional integration, by establishing closer ties with other centers of the developed capitalist world, or by assuming a leading role within the Third World, none of these efforts was sufficiently successful to offset the region's dependence on the United States.

But did economic dependence preclude the ability to conduct an independent foreign policy? To decide that such was not the case would be a significant departure from the traditional Soviet-Marxist line, which insisted on purely economic determinism. It can be considered unusual that Karen Brutents noted that although the Third World countries continue to hold a:

> dependent and exploited position in the world capitalist economy [which] . . . defines their relation to imperialism . . . nevertheless they [the Third World countries] ought to be characterized on the whole as anti-imperialist and anti-colonial, capable of limiting the influence of imperialism.[1]

The Academy of Sciences held a conference; the root issue was whether Latin America's global posture had truly changed or whether it remained the same, albeit camouflaged with outbursts of nationalistic and anti-US rhetoric. A landmark article by Anna Matlina adhered to the latter position. The prominent analyst asserted that Latin America's development had relied on direct foreign investment and so deepened the region's dependence on foreign corporate interests.[2] She further dismissed the independent foreign policy positions of the Latin

63

American regimes as declaratory rhetoric, designed to enhance their legitimacy, without actually confronting capitalism.[3] Soviet analysts were divided into two camps: One, led by Glinkin and Shul'govskii, asserted that Latin American states – despite their dependence on the United States – were increasingly able to conduct independent foreign policies, because growing economic multipolarity opened numerous alternatives for economic partners. Another, led by Maidonik, Kloch-kovskii, and Matlina, claimed that Latin America's economic depen-dence on the United States ensured that any diplomatic assertiveness was almost entirely a rhetorical exercise, rather than a substantive departure from the region's traditional position.[4]

Glinkin, in the lead article, called it "vulgar economism" to analyze the region's foreign policy strictly in terms of its economic situation.[5] Glinkin felt that a deep-seated change in Latin America's orientation had been proved by twenty years of assertive policy,[6] and he argued that since Latin America was no longer isolated from the rest of the world, "the era of automatic alliance with [the United States] is over."[7] Glinkin proclaimed that any country's foreign policy was determined by the aspirations of the various classes within a society and that since Latin America's policy reflected the aspirations of its nationalist bour-geoisie and the demands of the proletariat, one could reasonably expect a truly independent foreign policy.[8] Shul'govskii echoed these views but was skeptical about the genuineness of Latin America's challenge to the United States. Suggesting that some Latin American states had established ties with the USSR so that they could claim their foreign policies had an "anti-imperialist 'tilt,'" he stated that the only genuine anti-imperialist policy was to embark on a "noncapitalist path of development."[9]

Other analysts joined in giving Latin America credit for a more assertive and independent foreign policy. According to A. V. Fadin, this development proceeded from the greater opportunities that resulted from the demise of the bipolar world (and the emergence of such new "poles" as OPEC and the Arab world) as well as from more clashes between the continent's nationalistic political elites (both left-wing and right-wing) and multinational corporations.[10] Iakovlev ob-served that Latin American states generally had more progressive foreign than domestic policies. Unlike Matlina, Iakovlev felt that grow-ing industrialization had pushed countries such as Brazil toward greater confrontation with imperialism out of both the changed self-interests that economic development had induced and the emergence of new anti-imperialist social classes (both the nationalist bourgeoisie and the growing proletariat).[11] Nevertheless, he concluded that only two kinds of Latin American states were able to conduct truly independent foreign policies: those that followed a "noncapitalist orientation" (Cuba and Grenada) or those that were heavily developed, such as Argentina, Brazil, and Mexico.[12]

V. N. Dmitriev noted that those Latin American states that possessed large state sectors had developed a high degree of acumen in exploiting inter-imperialist schisms to their own benefit. Thus, despite continuing economic dependence on the West, Latin America was increasingly improving its capacity to conduct an independent foreign policy and to confront the West on major international issues in a unified manner. This had been illustrated, for example, by Latin America's stance during the Falklands War and by López Portillo's foreign policy.[13] Whereas US economic pressure had once been able to force Latin America to retreat from a confrontation with the United States, by the mid-1970s such pressures merely forced Latin America to diversify its trade away from the United States, as shown by Mexico's oil and natural gas export policy.[14] Dmitriev concluded by observing that Latin American states consistently pursued an anti-imperialist policy and called for "a new world order."[15]

On the other side of the issue was Anna Matlina. Although she conceded both Latin America's ability to confront the West with "one voice" and its attainment of an "autonomous" foreign policy, which at times enabled it to extract concessions within the capitalist division of labor,[16] she stressed that "given Latin America's economic dependence on the US, sooner or later all Latin American states run into a barrier which limits the freedom of their foreign policy."[17] Moreover, she declared that Latin America's goal, in reality, was a modernized version of dependent imperialism.[18]

Professor Totskii of the Odessa State University snubbed Latin America's record, observing that even Mexico could not conduct a foreign policy as independent as some of the smallest states of Europe, given the nature of Mexico's capitalism and its economic dependence on the United States.[19] He and Maidonik seemed to agree that the newly found Latin American diplomatic independence was more a matter of appearance than substance. According to Totskii, Latin America's apparent diplomatic assertiveness – of which the United States was "indulgent"[20] – was nothing more than a sinister effort to cover up domestic repression and regional imperial ambitions.[21] Maidonik conceded that Latin America had gained some strength *vis-à-vis* the United States in both the political and economic spheres but stated that its "field of dependence" on the United States was continuing to expand, albeit in different forms.[22]

The views of Matlina, Totskii, and Maidonik were echoed by Klochkovskii, who noted that Latin America's chances of conducting an independent foreign policy were severely curtailed by its economic dependence.[23] He argued that the appearance of an independent Latin American foreign policy was often aimed at calming domestic strife within Latin America, rather than at challenging imperialism.[24] Further, the global economic downturn during the late 1970s and early 1980s had forced Latin America to back away even from its rhetorical position demanding a "new economic world order."[25] Dabagyan would not even refer to Latin America's foreign policy as "anti-imperialist," since he believed that, with the exceptions of Cuba and Grenada, all of the region's regimes linked their survival to the preservation of the existing world order.[26]

Sudarev went further, stating that the Latin American states were practicing a hypocritical, "deliberately declaratory foreign policy," the main purpose of which was to gain the approval of the masses, especially given the existing socioeconomic stress.[27] He added that Latin American states often made radical declarations merely to draw Washington's attention. Thus, when López Portillo embarked on a policy supporting the Sandinista regime in Managua, he was mainly concerned with increasing his importance to Washington, rather than with changing the international order.[28]

There was, therefore, no consensus in the Soviet political community regarding the question of whether the Latin American states were indeed capable of conducting a truly independent foreign policy. Yet even if Moscow had been convinced that the Latin American states were genuinely asserting an independent foreign policy, it is hard to see what benefits the USSR would have expected, other than the isolation of the United States in the international arena. As noted earlier, Moscow had little expectation that Latin America would play a major role in the existing international order, given its social structure and declining economic significance. As will be discussed, there were many compelling reasons why the USSR during much of the Brezhnev era chose not to get more involved in Latin American affairs – skepticism about anti-US rhetoric most probably serving as an inhibiting factor. Nevertheless, since most Latin American states were willing to undertake a declaratory anti-US foreign policy, the USSR was able to attain modest diplomatic gains, regardless of Latin American motives.

Part II

Soviet perceptions of Latin American social structures

Introduction

Latin America, although a part of the Third World, has several characteristics that make it unique among developing continents. Unlike Asia and Africa, Latin America is basically dominated by a single linguistic and cultural pattern. However, the belief that all Latin American countries are identical because of the predominance of the Iberian languages and Catholicism is, of course, incorrect. Nevertheless, with the exception of the Arab world, Latin America is unique in its cultural communality.

Latin America's level of economic and social development certainly makes the region a part of the Third World. As part of the global economic periphery, it relies on the export of primary commodities and the import of capital and industrial goods. Yet Latin America is far more developed than Africa and most of Asia. As a result of significant industrial development, some initiated as early as the 1930s and further accelerated during and after World War II, Latin American society is far more developed, with an older and a more distinct urban population than that of most developing regions. Thus, while much of Latin America still retains its traditional social structure of latifundism, parts of the continent are now heavily industrialized, and a large proletariat and middle class have entered the Latin American political panorama.

Unlike most of the Third World, where the majority of the existing states are less than fifty years old, almost all Latin American states attained their independence by the 1820s, and thus the tradition of a nation-state is more established in Latin America than in many other parts of the world. Latin America's long political independence and a rather developed social structure produced an assortment of well-established political parties, reflecting various social strata. These parties have provided at least some elements within Latin American society with a means to articulate their political demands and, thus, have served as a mechanism, however inadequate, to effect some peaceful political change. As the region's political reality has changed, the power and position of these parties have often changed as well.

Given the martial tradition introduced into Latin America by the Spanish conquistadors, and the bloody wars by which most Latin American states attained their independence, the region's military establishments have been an active political force from the very start. After World War II, however, the political position of some armies became increasingly ambiguous because of changes in Latin America's social configuration. Whereas the military had traditionally been identified with the latifundist class, it often became divided between left and right and in some cases advocated reformist policies.

In addition, the Latin American peasant class, historically inert politically and often separated from the rest of society by race and religion, became increasingly active, with peasant guerrilla warfare becoming endemic in several countries on the continent.

The church, an institution that has played a political role in Latin America since the discovery of the continent, and that historically was one of the most traditional institutions, in the late 1950s also started to reflect the changes and tensions pervading the region's political life. The Latin American church today is a divided institution, with some segments preaching traditional obedience to the existing social order and others openly supporting Marxism-Leninism and wars of national liberation. Similarly, the region's large and varied labor union movement, with membership in the millions, has affiliations ranging from anarchist–syndicalist groups, to Marxist-Leninist unions, to groups affiliated with the AFL–CIO.

Given the flux in Latin America's key social institutions and the rapid transformation of the correlation of forces among the various Latin American social groupings, a growing number of Soviet observers started to devote a great deal of attention to these changes. A lively debate developed as to what the changes in Latin America meant for the continent's potential transformation to a "noncapitalist path of development," and as to whether these changes warranted a reassessment of the strategy of the USSR and pro-Moscow communist parties in the hemisphere. The following section examines changing Soviet (and Latin American communist) perceptions of these institutions during the Brezhnev years and considers the impact of such evolving attitudes on Soviet policy toward the region. Although it is dangerous to generalize about a continent as vast as Latin America, especially given its varied levels of development, it nevertheless seems that the strong cultural affinity throughout the continent allows some profitable generalizations to be made.

6 The Latin American church

Latin America is the most Catholic of all continents. All states have overwhelmingly Catholic majorities, and if the current demographic trends continue, by the end of this century more than half of the world's Catholics will be Latin Americans. The church's role in political life has always been a significant aspect of Latin America's social configuration since America's discovery was first financed by "Isabella the Catholic." As in most parts of the world, the church was long identified with the most conservative stream in political life, supporting, for example, the imposition of serfdom on the Indian population of the New World and the introduction of African slaves. During the Latin American wars of independence, the church hierarchy remained loyal to the Spanish crown, thus clashing with the regimes of the new republics. When some Latin American states entered a liberal phase in the second half of the nineteenth century, the church opposed all reforms in a confrontation that in some cases led to the formal separation of church and state and confiscation of church lands. During most of the twentieth century the church remained, by and large, a conservative body in alliance with the latifundist (landowning) class, preaching obedience to the existing order and opposing social reorganization.

Yet despite its consistently conservative, if not reactionary position, the Latin American church was hardly ever a monolithic body. The lower clergy in particular often sided with revolutionary, anti-establishment political currents. Bartolomé de Las Casas, the first priest and later the first bishop in the New World, spent most of his later life leading a crusade defending the rights of the Indians and of the African slaves. Although the Latin American church hierarchy remained devoutly monarchist, the Mexican war of independence was started by two country priests named Hidalgo and Morelos. Other priests, such as Camilo Henríquez and José Simeón Canas, are often cited as fostering the humanistic and revolutionary traditions of Latin America.

In addition to the divisions within the Latin American church as a whole, the churches of various countries varied greatly in their adaptability to change. For example, in Mexico the church opposed the 1910 revolution and consequently was stripped of its lands, its priests forbidden to wear their cassocks outside the church. In contrast, the Brazilian church proved far more adaptable, with Cardinal Leme supporting Getúlio Vargas' *Estado Novo* in the 1930s and Cardinal Câmara leading the opposition to military repression in the 1960s.

The traditional Soviet attitude toward the Latin American church was one of implacable hostility. Numerous Soviet books and articles characterized the church as a bulwark of reaction and anticommunism, a supporter of the most reactionary latifundist forces on the continent and an institution that at times flirted with fascism. Beginning in the mid-1950s, however, various developments prompted reevaluations of the Catholic church in Latin America. The first such stimulus came in 1955, when Pope Pius XII ordered the Latin American church to increase its support for educational institutions, labor unions, women's groups, and other civic organizations. However, the initial remaking of the church's posture was dismissed by most Soviet analysts as nothing more than "popular capitalism" aimed at blocking the advance of communism.[1]

Not until the emergence of the "activist church" following the Second Ecumenical Council in the Vatican (Vatican II) was a true debate triggered about the Latin American church and its "progressive" potential. The church, called on to identify with the poor, sponsored an emerging mass grass-roots organization. Given the Soviet policy of supporting broad coalitions opposing right-wing regimes (as well as the precedent set by France, where the communist party cooperated with "worker-priests"), it was likely that the Soviets would endorse cooperation between the church and communists in opposing the existing regimes. Yet Soviet analysts and allied communist parties were divided in their perceptions of the real goals, and the depth of commitment, of the "new" church: Was the church's strategy aimed at real change in Latin America, or was it a tactical move aimed at "letting off steam"? A further concern was whether the activist church, if indeed keen on social change, would compete with the communists for influence within the same political constituency.

The emergence of the activist church and the initial reaction (1962–66)

Soviet analysts usually date the appearance of the activist church from two events in 1962: the convocation of Vatican II and the appearance of an article in the Chilean Jesuit magazine, *Mensaje*, which called for church involvement in a revolution leading to a complete break with capitalism. The initial Soviet reaction to Vatican II was cautious and noncommittal, and political literature continued to attack the Latin American church. For example, a veteran Soviet journalist described the Latin American church as a reactionary body endowed with fabulous wealth while the masses of Latin America languished in misery.[2]

The Chilean church drew particular fire. Iosif Grigulevich, the doyen of Soviet students of the church, charged the church with resorting to unfounded scare tactics during the 1964 elections, in which the Christian Democrats defeated Marxist Salvador Allende by a very narrow margin. He concluded that the Chilean church supported reforms only in order to undercut the communist–socialist alliance.[3] A similar observation was made by Orlando Millas (of the Chilean communist party) in his post-1964 election analyses. According to Millas, the Chilean church had to show interest in the social problems of the poor to ensure a Christian Democratic victory: Such concern "by no means implies that differences and antagonism disappeared or that old prejudices have ceased to exist." Rather, "US circles are exerting a strong pressure on the Chilean church," which remained tied to the Alliance for Progress reformist approach.[4]

Despite his reservations, Millas felt that the Chilean church was moving in the right direction, as it increasingly voiced "faith in man and his capacity to change his life along progressive lines."[5] Nevertheless, the communist party of Chile was still convinced that the church remained a reformist rather than a revolutionary body. The party leader, Luis Corvolán, reminded his readers in an article in *Pravda* that the goal of the church was "not to foster revolution, but to prevent it."[6]

This rather cool response to the activist church by Soviet analysts and Latin American communists significantly warmed with the appearance of the so-called "Leftist Activist Church." Its intellectual genesis can be traced to a 1962 article in *Mensaje*. However, it was the political actions of Colombian priest Camilo Torres and the archbishop of Recife, Dom Helder Câmara, that brought the leftist church to the attention of Soviet and Western analysts. A Jesuit priest, Torres publicly declared that the only way to save Latin America was by waging a war of national liberation against imperialism and adopting socialist principles. These rather radical views drew an enthusiastic response from the Soviet press. Some journalists argued that Torres' movement was rapidly engulfing large segments of the Colombian religious community and threatening to bring down the entire structure of the traditional church.[7] Similarly, Dom Câmara's attacks on the capitalist system and US imperialism, and his defense of human rights under attack from the military regime in Brazil, won "Câmara the Red" significant attention and admiration in the Soviet and communist press.

The disintegration of church unity and the Soviet response (1966–78)

Confronted by the competing pressures of 1962–66, the Latin American Catholic church became divided, and its once apparently unified position on social questions totally disintegrated. Delimiting Christian opinion were extremist minority groups. The upper crust of the church remained firmly conservative, carrying on the tradition of opposing any and all change that in its view was "communist" in nature. For example, Cardinal Rossi of Brazil in 1964 had hailed the armed forces' overthrow of President Goulart as deliverance from communism. Similarly, the Argentine church supported the coup led by General Juan Onganía in 1966.

Extreme leftist groups, at the other end of the church spectrum, often supported guerrilla warfare and "wars of national liberation" in a manner reminiscent of the Latin American "ultra" leftists. Members included such priests as Camilo Torres in Colombia, who called for an immediate war of national liberation. Also included was Archbishop Câmara in Brazil, who urged Christians to accept socialism (in the words of the *Manifesto of the Bishops of the Third World*, which he helped write) as "the form of social life which best meets the exigencies of the present and the spirit of the Gospel."[8] In Argentina extreme leftists clustered around the magazine, *Cristianismo y revolución*, which advocated the acceptance of the doctrine of wars of national liberation as part of the Catholic theology.[9] The Jesuits led the cause of radical church activism in Chile.

The largest segment of the Latin American clergy was a moderately reformist group that supported substantial reorganization of the existing order but was unwilling to endorse violence or socialism. This position was expressed at the 1966 conference of Latin American bishops at Mar del Plata. In their concluding manifesto the bishops stated that they believed the gaps between rich and poor should be narrowed and that society should cease to be divided into these two layers. However, they pushed for reforms that would not clash with the legal system of the state. The bishops also reaffirmed the church's support for private property.

This fragmentation of the Latin American church caused considerable consternation among Soviet and communist analysts, who maintained an implacable hostility to the right wing of the church but were uncertain how to respond to its leftist and moderate wings. They generally welcomed both activist groups, since both represented a weakening of the traditional, and remarkably durable, authoritarian system. Yet skepticism prevailed that the church was not sincerely committed to social change but rather was indulging, for instance, in bourgeois reformism akin to the Alliance for Progress. Such reform, it was feared, might slow the march toward a "non-capitalist path of development" by pacifying some of the masses.[10] In addition, there was persistent anxiety that leftist radicals were more closely aligned with Maoists, Castroites, Trotskyites, or other ultra-leftists than with the Soviet version of Marxism.

Thus, during most of the late 1960s and early 1970s, Soviet and communist analysts continued to challenge the authenticity of church progressivism while acknowledging that there was some basis for hope of a future social transformation. Roque Dalton (of the Salvadoran communist party) contended that the entire reformist movement of the Latin American church was a creature of West European churches, directed from a special center located in Louvain, Belgium,[11] and that the church's calls for reforms were less than sincere: "The advocates of 'aggiornamento' even go so far as to condemn certain fundamentals of the capitalist system without, however, attacking the bedrock of the capitalist mode of production–private ownership. Consequently, condemnation of this kind can also be used as a tactical means to perpetuate the capitalist regime."[12] Dalton also accused the activist church of being supportive of the US-inspired Alliance for Progress.[13] Although somewhat more sympathetic to the leftist church, which advocated revolution, he cautioned that the leftist Catholics' anti-imperialism did not make them communists. Although they accepted popular revolution as "possible and politically justified," Dalton noted that "they formulate their own views regarding revolutionary tactics, which often diverge from those of the communist parties."[14]

Yet despite his serious reservations concerning the moderate and the leftist church, Dalton felt that the position of the church was sufficiently promising to warrant closer dialogue and cooperation with it: "However, even such attitudes in respect to capitalism, although profoundly contradictory, would have been utterly inconceivable in the past . . . Communists and Catholics can unite to build Paradise on earth, leaving aside the question whether Paradise exists in heaven."[15]

Like Dalton, Mikhail Andreev attributed increased church activism to the large inflow of priests and funds from North America and Western Europe, and he believed that the church's newfound "social consciousness" was an effort to "let off steam" rather than to support genuine reform.[16] However, Andreev also noted that the church's political power was rapidly expanding; the number of Christian Democratic parties in Latin America has risen in a ten-year period from three to twenty; and "the role of the church in the labor unions cannot be underestimated, its membership is now in the millions."[17] Andreev concluded his article by observing that the church, nevertheless, was increasingly a divided body – the opinions of its membership covering the spectrum of Latin American opinion, from the latifundists to the communists.[18]

Iosif Grigulevich, in a 1968 study of the Latin American church during the preceding decade, severely contested the genuineness of the "reform" church and accused it of "relying on 'Christian' models to give these reforms an anti-Marxist character."[19] He stated that the church had shifted from "negative anticommunism" to "positive anticommunism" by calling for a "revolution with 'freedom' thus protecting the interests of the rich."[20] Even so, Grigulevich noted some basis for hope in the movement's future direction, by observing that the Chilean Jesuits had realized that the continent no longer had the time for an evolutionary transformation. Thus by 1967 the Chilean church had become fully identified with the Third World, as its "progressive" and "revolutionary" wings grew most rapidly.[21]

V. P. Andronova (with the exception of Grigulevich, perhaps the most noted Soviet student of the Latin American church) observed that the Colombian church – historically ranked among the most reactionary in South America – had become politically marginal. Indeed, she stated, it had largely ceased to be relevant to almost any of the Colombian political players. It had lost the support of such political allies as the religiously devout peasant and the Christian Democratic party because it had failed to adapt to new realities (unlike the Brazilian or Chilean churches): the peasants now saw no contradiction between Christianity and guerrilla warfare; the Christian Democrats, although preferring class harmony, supported land seizures by the peasants and increasingly took an anti-US and anticapitalist position. The church hierarchy, however, besides opposing land seizures, was drifting away from the ideals of Vatican II and excommunicating those who attacked capitalism.[22] Andronova concluded that the only relevant and survivable segment was the left wing of the church, which increasingly engulfed large parts of the lower clergy and lay leadership, and that a tactical alliance with this segment was both possible and desirable.[23]

In contrast, Grigulevich posited that by 1970 the Chilean church placed greater importance on responding to the aspirations of the masses than on clinging to an anticommunist position. According to Grigulevich, the church had no alternative but to disassociate itself from the former Frei administration, which had failed to fulfill any major hopes of the masses. It thus gave full support to Allende once he was elected.[24]

In perhaps the best Soviet study of the Latin American church in the decade following Vatican II (*The "Rebellious" Church in Latin America*), Grigulevich crystallized the Soviet perception of the Latin American church. He stated emphatically that the church's involvement in the social affairs of the continent had become irreversible: "Social revolution is the propelling force of the Latin American Church within both the conservative and progressive camps."[25] However, despite the appearance of genuine progressive elements, the church overall was attempting to follow a reformist path that would prevent any real transformation of social relationships in the region. Grigulevich also noted that although the Vatican II declaration aimed to block "totalitarian" ideas, its real goal was to hamper the communists.[26]

Although Grigulevich agreed with other Soviet observers that the Jesuits were more outspoken and daring than the rest of the church because they answered directly to the pope rather than to local bishops, he reminded readers that Friar Vakemans (the Belgian leader of the Chilean Jesuits) called upon the regimes of Latin America and the United States to conduct a "revolution from above."[27] He further pointed out that President Kennedy had viewed the church as a natural ally of the Alliance for Progress; his successor, Lyndon Johnson, along with Robert Kennedy and Henry Cabot Lodge, supported Vatican II as an antidote to Marxism.[28] The calls for partial agrarian reforms by Latin America's bishops at the 1966 Mar del Plata conference and for social reorganization by the Jesuits were both meaningless, since both parties insisted on legal means, which did little more than legitimize the existing system.[29] Thus, unlike Dalton and others, Grigulevich praised Torres as a living bond between the church and the revolution but saw in Câmara a sinister plot against Marxism. Grigulevich stated that Câmara's support for "nonmaterialistic" Marxism was a concealed assault on the socialist system; that Câmara's council of "Third World" bishops, which referred to the Third World as the modern-day proletariat, was nothing more than a trick to distance the Latin American masses from socialist states.[30]

Grigulevich found the Vatican somewhat more progressive than Latin America's clerics but noted that, even there, definite limits confined the degree of support for progressive forces. For example, when it was discovered that US Maryknoll missionaries were aiding Guatemalan rebels, the Curia put pressure on the order to end its involvement.[31] Grigulevich of course recognized the progressive forces within the Latin American church – as manifested by the establishment of Torres chapters throughout Latin America, the support of the Peruvian church for the progressive policies of General Velasco, and the letter signed on the eve of the Medellín conference of Latin American bishops (June 1968) by 1,000 Latin American clerics who supported violent struggle against right-wing oligarchy and foreign multinationals.[32]

Nevertheless, Grigulevich ended his book on a pessimistic note by concluding that the Latin American church was not only unrevolutionary but was actually sliding back from even its modestly progressive position of the early 1960s. He explained his pessimism on the following grounds: (1) The pope, who had supported progressive change in the Latin American church, was now restraining its activist elements. (2) The bishops who attended the Medellín meeting had clung to certain notions of the conservative right, and their very moderate document was a disappointment to the progressive forces in the church. (3) Although once supportive of "national development," the church had reverted to cooperation with imperialist instruments, such as the Inter-American Development Bank. (4) Although the church took a very harsh position regarding the followers of Camilo Torres, it remained silent when priests were repressed by rightist regimes.[33] Grigulevich concluded his book with the observation that although Pope Paul's attempt to turn the church to the right did not slow the radicalization of some segments of the church,[34] "by and large the church remains the tool of the exploiting class."[35]

Although representative of mainstream Soviet opinion, Grigule-vich's rather pessimistic views were by no means universally shared either by Latin American communists or other Soviet analysts. In a book written by the Argentine communist, J. Rosales (*Los cristianos, los marxistas y la revolución* [Buenos Aires 1970]) (reviewed by Grigulevich in the Soviet press), the author concluded that the Latin American church was on the verge of a historical split between the old-line Western-oriented bishops and the "Third World"-oriented, strongly anti-imperialist church. In reality, Argentina did not have one church but two. The author drew his rather optimistic view of the prospect of a progressive church from the fact that even the reactionary Argentine church was undergoing a rapid change within its lower ranks and from his belief that a small, progressive segment of the church was struggling side-by-side with the Marxists.[36]

Similarly, authors Koval', Semenov, and Shul'govskii asserted that there had been a fundamental change in the church and, unlike Grigu-levich, saw in the Medellín conference an open challenge to capitalism and imperialism.[37] These authors saw the church both as a serious partner in the revolutionary process and as a potential "bridge" between Marxists and other groups "during the transformation to socialism."[38] They pointed to a significant shift toward Marxism in the Central American church – traditionally known for its reactionary publications – which had called on believers to study Marxism in the church publication *Estudios centroamericanos*.[39] The authors concluded, "Marxist-Leninists attribute great importance to the changes in the position of the Catholic church and call for greater contacts with believers."[40]

It should also be noted that while most analysts were warming to trends within the Catholic church, some were increasingly concerned about the spread of Protestantism and African sects in Latin America, representative of the conservative view. Although abuses of power had motivated Brazilian Protestants to speak out in defense of human rights and Chilean Protestants to support Allende's nationalization of the mining industry,[41] there was a worrying spread of fundamentalist Protestant and African religious sects. As articulated by author E. F. Grushko, these sects had created a class of "apolitical poor" among the recent migrants from rural areas to the urban slums, thus neutralizing a class that logically should have been the vanguard of the struggle for social transformation.[42]

Soviet and communist assessments of the Latin American Catholic church's progressive potential received a considerable jolt after the collapse of the Allende regime in September 1973. The event signaled not only the defeat of an experiment in peaceful social transformation in Latin America but also the general defeat of popularly elected regimes in all of Latin America. Allende's fall left only Colombia, Costa Rica, Mexico, and Venezuela with regimes that were relatively stable and democratic. In the harsh repression that was imposed throughout the continent, almost all political institutions, such as labor unions, political parties, and the free press, were obliterated. Only the church retained its structural integrity. Moreover, unlike in previous decades, it refused to support dictatorships – even when faced with threats – and emerged as the focus of opposition to the military juntas.

In a startling reversal, Grigulevich, who had placed so little confidence in the church, praised the Chilean church for its demonstrated loyalty to the Allende regime. Grigulevich contrasted this with the efforts of Eduardo Frei and the Chilean Christian Democrats to undermine the Allende regime and induce the coup. The church had attempted to stabilize the regime by mediating between Allende and the opposition parties. Later, although Cardinal Enriques had remained silent during and immediately after the coup, the church openly attacked the Pinochet regime once it launched its campaign of terror.[43]

The communist reappraisal of the church was formalized in the Havana Declaration of the Latin American communist parties, in which the participants referred to the church as a "fighter for the people" and to its leftist component as an indispensable element in the struggle with imperialism.[44] Sebastián González of the Chilean communist party echoed this position when he asserted the significance of the church's role in the face of Pinochet's destruction of many Chilean political institutions and increasing reliance on nationalism as a source of legitimacy: "Chiming with mass sentiment, the Catholic church has come out against chauvinism, against excessive and rapturous praise of the motherland which is turned into an idol, against fascist attempts to describe active opponents of the dictatorship as 'anti-patriots' . . . and last but not least against fascism's denunciations of 'foreign' ideologies."[45]

González called for an alliance between the communists and the church, saying that "the main trends in Chilean life suggest that such unity is possible." He further emphasized the urgent need for an alliance, given "fascist attacks on the Catholic church because a large part of it condemns the violations of human and social rights."[46]

Luis Corvolán's earlier charges that the Chilean church was hindering progress and supporting conservatism were now superseded by

Corvolán's ringing endorsement of the church and the prospect of cooperating with it. Corvolán asserted that Vatican II and the bishops' meeting in Medellín had set the church on a path defending the rights of the oppressed, and he declared the Chilean communist party's "full solidarity with the church of Chile."[47] He stated that the perception of the church as a reactionary body was dated, noting that the church had initially opposed the bourgeoisie but later joined it; now the church shifted from opposing socialism to supporting it.[48] Corvolán also called on the church and the Marxists to cooperate in all spheres.[49]

As before, however, not all Soviet analysts were as optimistic about the church's progressive potential as those just cited and as the Latin American communists. The latter increasingly warmed to the church as military-backed regimes sprang up throughout the hemisphere. A primary criticism was that the church was not a revolutionary force, since it was still part of the establishment. For example, Grushko acknowledged that the Latin American church had shifted from fascism and was playing a positive role, but he labeled the Medellín position "a classic bourgeois position which does not challenge the position of the ruling class."[50]

After dismissing the mainstream of church-inspired reformism, Grushko asserted that the only real revolutionary component of the Latin American church was the leftist segment which called both for a struggle against the current system and for the installation of socialism.[51] Even so, however, the leftist church contained elements antithetical to Soviet ideology, according to Grushko. He warned that it insisted on a "third way" (between capitalism and socialism), along with a nationalist orientation evocative of ultra-leftism.[52] Finally, Grushko reproached the leftist church for the lack of scientific method evident in its simple division of the world into "rich" and "poor" nations. He concluded: "Church socialism has nothing in common with scientific socialism."[53]

Karen Khachaturov, a Soviet analyst who wrote mainly on ideological issues, denied that the Latin American church was reacting to some new ideological moral revelation and stated that it was instead pursuing its own interests: It had thrown its support behind the Christian Democrats only as a tactical move to preserve some degree of its eroding influence among the masses. Yet Latin American clericism, he continued, had sunk to such a low point that only in Venezuela and Chile did the Christian Democrats amount to a viable political force; thus the church in the rest of Latin America had to shift further to the left. Nevertheless, Khachaturov conceded that the overall shift in the church's position should be considered a blow to US imperialism.[54]

Thus, by the end of the 1970s, both Soviet and communist analysts felt that the shift in the church was fundamental and real. Latin American communists saw in the church a potential long-term ally in their struggle to bring about socialism in Latin America. But though impressed by the shift occurring within Latin America, Soviet analysts remained acutely aware that church activism might yet result in a successful reformist model or, worse yet, in the strengthening of the "ultra-left." They thus preferred to see the church strictly as a tactical ally of the communists.

The pontificate of John Paul II and the retreat from activism (1978–82)

The death of Pope Paul VI in 1978 and his replacement by John Paul II (John Paul I having died less than two months after taking office) initiated a serious reassessment of the Vatican's attitude toward the activist church. The pontificate of John Paul II created a new stratification. During the pontificate of Paul VI the Catholic church was split along the lines of a moderate pope, relatively conservative bishops, and moderate to leftist clergy. The new pope now represented the most conservative element within the church, the bishops occupied the middle ground, and much of the lower clergy "tilted" to the left more than ever before. A rightist backlash was also beginning to emerge, which, combined with the presence of a more conservative pope, led analysts to reevaluate Latin America's chances of progressive reform.

V. P. Andronova maintained that church support for such change was still an open question, recalling what she termed the tactical moves of the Brazilian church during the previous twenty years.[55] The church position in such key countries as Argentina, Colombia, and Guatemala, she reminded readers, had not changed at all. Now, in her opinion, the reactionary backlash was threatening the expansion of reformism, already having manifested itself in the Latin American bishops' Puebla declaration of 1979 – a far less progressive document than the Medellín declaration had been.[56] Andronova did not belittle the positive changes of the 1970s linked to "liberation theology": the church had for the first time tied its theology to a social doctrine, and support for liberation theology had moved beyond the lower clergy to include some bishops; the objective analysis by which liberation theology studied the condition of the masses was strongly influenced by Marxism, and broader segments of the church were becoming pro-socialist; and the church had finally broken with regimes in power.[57] However, Andronova felt that there was a danger of overstating the church's position and that the progressive tendency within the Latin American church had probably reached its outer limit.

Grigulevich stated that the church was indeed continuing and expanding its progressive trend, despite John Paul's success in forcing a retreat from the Medellín positions.[58] For example, the Chilean church continued to oppose Pinochet, the Nicaraguan bishops were opposing Somoza and calling for "dynamic" class struggle, and Archbishop Romero called on the pope and the US administration not to send aid to the regime in that country.[59] The church's role in undermining the Somoza regime, in fact, was generally regarded as an important break with the church's traditional position. Yet Grigulevich also warned that the church's role should not be exaggerated: the church was radicalized in many of its segments, but it was not a revolutionary force and it would not play a central revolutionary role as Islam did in Iran.[60]

N. S. Konstantinova, in agreement with Grigulevich's view that the church was continuing its leftward shift despite the new pope's conservatism, pointed to Brazil as an example. Fearing the total loss of its spiritual authority to the Marxists and various Protestant sects, the Brazilian church, Konstantinova asserted, was by 1983 totally committed to progressive social reorganization. It had joined the vanguard of the struggle for Brazil's democratization. Konstantinova emphasized that, despite constant pressure from John Paul II, the Brazilian bishops had remained adamant in opposing Puebla's whitewash of Medellín, and she contended that most segments of the Brazilian church not only accepted "liberation theology" but ardently advocated it.[61]

Although a minority within the Latin American church, supporters of liberation theology offered to the Marxists a comparable methodology of analysis and shared belief in class struggle as a legitimate form of liberation. Given this, Andronova concluded that the leftist church, despite its murky understanding of class differentiation, was a valid partner to a revolutionary struggle.[62] Nevertheless, Andronova maintained that the church as an institution feared real social transformation and that, despite its rhetoric, it remained a bourgeois-reformist institution committed to legality and harmony among the classes rather than to revolution. She pointed to clashes between "democratic" elements in the church and Allende in Chile and the Sandinistas in Nicaragua.[63] Warning that the conservative backlash in the church should not be underestimated, she noted the election of Rafael Trujillo (a Jesuit allegedly linked to the CIA) as the secretary of the council of Latin American bishops[64] and believed that right-wing elements in the church had played a role in ousting Allende.[65] According to Andronova, the mainstream Latin American church, which blamed both capitalism and Marxism for the prevalent social strife, was no friend of genuine progress.[66]

Thus, Soviet attitudes toward the Latin American church underwent a significant and continuous evolution during Leonid Brezhnev's eighteen years in power. The era when Soviet analysts automatically referred to the church as a pillar of either oligarchy or fascism receded into history. Most Soviet analysts became convinced that the church had broken its historical alliances with Latin American regimes and become a potent political force intent on bringing some kind of reform to the continent.

Although some Soviet observers remained skeptical about the depth of the church's commitment to real reforms, and others were concerned that the leftist church was more akin to the ultra-leftist Maoist groups than to the Soviet version of Marxism, the Soviet perception of the Latin American church became increasingly positive during the last four years of the Brezhnev era. There was a general accord within Soviet writings that the church's political activism, despite all its shortcomings and in the face of reawakened conservatism, was a real positive development. The majority agreed with Andronova's statement that the church since the 1970s had ceased to be an integral part of the ruling establishment. Thus, by virtue of this transformation, the church – even if its commitment was limited to bourgeois reformism – could no longer both retain its ties with its constituency and support the traditional oligarchy. In short, although the church had earlier been a conservative force committed to keeping the political system closed to the vast masses of the continent, by the late 1970s it had become irreversibly tied to the notion of expanding political participation – a development that all Soviet and communist observers welcomed.

Soviet attitudes toward the Latin American church underwent a significant and continuous evolution during the eighteen years that Brezhnev was in power. The era when Soviet analysts automatically referred to the church as either a pillar of the oligarchy or of fascism receded into history; nor did Soviet diplomats repeat Stalin's question as to "how many divisions does the pope have?" Summarizing Soviet perceptions, one could quote Grushko, who stated that the "Latin American church, with its ideology, retains a deep imprint on the national psyche of the continent." With few exceptions, most Soviet analysts became convinced that the church's political mainstream had permanently broken away from its historical allies in Latin America, and that it now represented a potent political force bent upon bringing some kind of reform to the continent. The role of the church in undermining the Somoza regime, especially after 1978, was an important break with the church's traditional position. The fact that the clerics Miguel D'Escoto and Ernesto Cardenal provided the Sandinista regime a substantial amount of administrative talent, as well as a source of legitimacy both within Nicaragua and abroad, was not lost on Soviet observers interested in Latin America.

While the direct policy implications of the Soviet perception of the church are difficult to pinpoint, both Prime Minister Kosygin and Foreign Minister Gromyko visited Pope Paul VI; Gromyko called on Pope John Paul II. Latin American churchmen such as Câmara did visit the USSR, and the Latin American Institute within the Academy of Sciences launched several (generally positive) studies of the church. Meanwhile the concept of cooperation between the communists and the church shifted the unthinkable to almost standard fare in Soviet and communist writings.

7　The Latin American armed forces

The Latin American armed forces,[1] with the exception of the church, represent the oldest and the most enduring political institution on the continent. From the very onset of national existence the armed forces have played a key political role. Given the weakness of all other state institutions in much of Latin America and the armed forces' historical predisposition to such a role – gained during long and bloody wars of independence – this was only natural. In addition, the Iberian tradition, by which the armed forces perceived their mission as one of both defending the country from external threat and guarding the nation's destiny and integrity, left a deep imprint on most of Latin America. The presence of Prussian military training missions during the first decade of this century further reinforced this intellectual rationalization of a political role. Today, that role is confirmed, as the armed forces remain the only national institution holding together countries that are spread out across vast, impassable territories often divided by language, race, and culture.

Historically the Latin American armed forces have been identified with the most reactionary politics. Traditionally the officer corps was staffed by white criollo landed gentry, primarily concerned with preserving their status. This preoccupation was constantly manifest, from the time that Simón Bolívar (the founding father of the region's military tradition) spent his final years trying to protect the criollo elite from the "dark" masses of negroes and mestizos,[2] to the infamous slaughter of 30,000 peasants by El Salvador's General Maximiliano Hernández Martínez in 1932, which was intended to preserve the country for the "fourteen leading families."

Historical contempt (1964–68)

Because almost all of Latin America's commissioned officers had received some military training in the United States, and also in light of the history just mentioned, Soviet analysts traditionally perceived the armed forces as creatures of the Pentagon. Through the early Brezhnev era Soviet analysts consistently asserted that the armed forces defended the interests of US multinationals and the Latin American oligarchy – and that this pillar of the existing order had to be destroyed along with the oligarchy if Latin America was ever to free itself from the shackles of imperialism.

Adaptations in US policy during the period of the Alliance for Progress reinforced this view, especially when the United States shifted from its earlier position of not tolerating military coups in Latin America. US support for the El Salvadoran military coup in the spring of 1963 led analyst Anatolii Shul'govskii to assert that US recognition of the Salvadoran junta represented a major policy shift. He felt that, although the United States was no longer willing to rely on military caudillos in the mold of Batista (Cuba), Trujillo (Dominican Republic), or Odría (Peru) as a basis of its support, it assigned to the armies of Latin America an institutional mission of sustaining the existing order in the hemisphere.[3] Alfredo Castro of the Brazilian communist party called the Brazilian military coup of March 1964 against the leftist regime of President Goulart a victory of the bourgeois classes rather than a return to caudillismo. It was made possible by "a change in the social forces" by which some of the urban bourgeoisie had joined forces with the military "to prevent the upsurge of the popular movement." Castro noted that "the leaders of these forces had the backing of US imperialism."[4]

It should be noted that the Soviet characterization of the Latin American armed forces as the praetorian guards of the existing order in the hemisphere was applied both to politically active armies, such as those of Argentina, Brazil, and Central America, as well as to apolitical armies, such as that of Chile. Soviet analysts often quoted Lenin's claim that there was no such thing as an apolitical army: differences in the activeness of Latin American armies simply reflected the stability of the regime in question. Yet with regard to Asia and Africa Soviet analysts often viewed the armies as the vanguard of political change, and they felt that this progressive posture resulted from the officers' lower middle-class origins. In Latin America, Soviet perceptions remained unchanged,[5] despite far greater class differentiation than in the rest of the Third World, and despite the fact that most of Latin America's officer corps were of lower middle-class origins.[6] Neither the key role played by military-ruled Brazil in the Inter-American Force policing Santo Domingo, nor the Argentine Onganía regime's massive assault against Marxists and communists, raised Soviet expectations that the Latin American military would assume a comparable vanguard role.

Some Soviet analysts perceived the Brazilian coup of 1964 as a watershed, which marked the defeat of progressive forces in the hemisphere and a major victory for the US multinationals and Latin American oligarchy.[7] According to one noted student of Brazilian affairs, the coup and resulting military dictatorship dealt "a severe blow not only to the democratic forces in Brazil but also to the liberation movement throughout Latin America."[8]

Traditional Soviet distrust of the Latin armed forces ran so deep that, when Francisco Caamaño and his "constitutionalist" followers revolted in order to restore the leftist regime of Juan Bosch of the Dominican Republic, the Soviet press openly questioned the sincerity of the rebels.[9]

The growing number of US military missions throughout Latin America, along with the introduction of a US "counterinsurgency" strategy emphasizing the "internal mission" of the Latin American armed forces, only confirmed historical Soviet perceptions. Nor did the emergence of a large middle class in some Latin American countries, which strongly affected the composition of the officer corps, or significant changes in the training and orientation of officers alter Soviet attitudes. Thus, even before the rightist coup in Brazil in March 1964, and before the Johnson administration's adoption of the Mann Doctrine (according to which the Latin American armies were viewed as the key instrument in sustaining US influence in the region), the Soviet media saw in the Alliance for Progress a US attempt to move the Latin American body politic to the right by the militarization of these societies.[10]

Soviet policy toward the Latin American armed forces (1964–68)

In contrast with Soviet recognition during the mid-1960s of the Latin American church as a potential ally, the USSR made no effort to establish even a dialogue with the Latin American military. Although visits by Soviet military delegations to developing capitalist countries had become commonplace since Marshal Zhukov's visit to India in 1955, and, in fact, Soviet military delegations visited such staunch pro-US countries as Morocco and Iran, there is no record of military exchanges with, or visits to, even such Latin American countries as

Mexico and Uruguay, with which the USSR had enjoyed long and cordial relations. After the reestablishment of diplomatic relations between Chile and the USSR in late 1964, which resulted in a Soviet grant of $57 million in credits to Chile, not even a minimal dialogue with the Chilean armed forces was attempted. This was despite the latter's apolitical nature and a history of support for leftist forces going back to the 1930s.

Furthermore, the Soviet Union declined to take advantage of an opening by which it could help arm Latin American forces. Primarily responding to the $75 million limit imposed by the US Congress on weapons exports to Latin America, the Argentine-inspired "Plan Europa" attempted to diversify the suppliers of weapons away from the United States. During the Egyptian weapon procurement crisis in 1955, when the West refused to raise its exports of weapons above $37 million, the situation had resulted in a "Czech" offer of weapons worth $250 million[11] and an intimate relationship between the USSR and the Egyptian armed forces. No such arrangement emerged in Latin America.

Although there is no definitive explanation as to why the USSR clearly invested little interest or effort in establishing any kind of relationship with Latin American military institutions before 1968, several reasons can be offered. Some Soviet analysts asserted that because of its rigid, class-based analysis, the USSR failed to recognize the unique role of the military establishments in the Third World and thus was slow to respond to the progressive winds within those armed forces.[12] Given the history of Soviet support for Chiang Kai-shek before 1927 and Moscow's embrace of the "progressive" military regimes of Nasser (Egypt, 1955) and Qassim (Iraq, 1958), however, this appears incorrect. The explanation that the USSR was anxious to avoid friction with the United States over Latin America, a region peripheral to Soviet interests, also does not appear likely. Although the USSR was exceedingly careful not to provoke the United States after the Cuban missile crisis, a mere dialogue with the Latin American armies, similar to the USSR's dialogue with the armed forces of NATO or other pro-Western countries in Asia and Africa, would probably have engendered little risk of a US–Soviet confrontation. The best explanation is that the USSR eschewed a relationship with military institutions that it perceived as representing a monolithic, US-trained praetorian guard, dedicated to defending the interests of the Latin American bourgeoisie and US multinationals. Given this perception, the USSR may have felt that such a relationship, while unlikely to be particularly fruitful for the

USSR, might exacerbate the already tense relationship with Moscow's only ally in the region, Cuba.

Euphoria and caution (1968–75)

During the early hours of 3 October 1968, Peruvian armed forces, led by General Juan Velasco Alvarado, took control of the country in a bloodless coup and launched Peru on a path of confrontation with the United States and the existing economic order in the hemisphere. The initial Soviet reaction was that the coup was just another takeover engineered at the Pentagon.[13] Radio Moscow described the new regime in Peru as "gorillas who established in the country a regime of ferocious military dictatorship."[14] Even when it became clear that President Velasco was anything but a friend to the United States, the Soviet press continued to question the Peruvian junta's intention to carry out the promised nationalization of foreign capital. *Pravda*'s chief South American correspondent wearily noted: "Time will tell how consistently the new Peruvian regime will follow its line of defending the country's national sovereignty."[15] A reevaluation was soon to occur, however, and in later years Soviet analysts would view the coup as a watershed in the political position of the Latin American armies.

The emergence of a leftist military junta in Peru bent on curtailing the role of US capital (Peru successfully nationalized large segments of US investment), changing the country's patterns of social organization, and reorienting Peru's international orientation, profoundly shook traditional Soviet assumptions regarding the Latin American armed forces. In addition, leftist military regimes emerged in Bolivia, Ecuador, and Panama (the Panamanian military regime demanding sovereignty over the Panama Canal) and the Chilean army had not only respected the election of Allende but provided vital backing to his regime during the critical winter of 1972.

A major debate ensued in the Soviet media over whether the Latin American armed forces were undergoing a major reorientation parallel to that of the Egyptian forces after 1952. Unlike Egypt, where the leftist officers had formed a mass party, the Arab Socialist Union (and unlike Syria and Iraq, where the armies joined forces with the Ba'ath parties), in Latin America the armies embarked on profound institutional reforms without creating a mass political movement.

Thus, the emergence of "revolutionary armed forces" in Latin America raised the following questions: (1) Were the armed forces capable of carrying through a fundamental reform in Latin America? (2) What was the depth of the armed forces' commitment to genuine reforms, given the fact that those armies were creatures of the United States? (3) What were the inherent limitations to reforms carried out by the armies?

The optimist school

Soviet reevaluation of the Peruvian military establishment (and those of several other Latin American countries) responded, in particular, to the adamant position of the Peruvian junta regarding the presence of US capital in that country (especially the nationalization of the Exxon subsidiary, IPC), the establishment of diplomatic ties with Cuba and the USSR, and the fundamental agrarian reform initiated by the armed forces. Even before it became clear that the Velasco regime intended to institute major reforms, some Soviet analysts noted that the nationalist position of the Peruvian armed forces was undermining the 1947 Rio Pact, which tied the Latin American armed forces to the United States.[16] The rash of nationalizations affecting US-owned concerns in Peru and Bolivia sufficiently impressed the USSR for it to include a statement in the communiqué of the International Conference of Communist and Workers' Parties noting "democratic" trends within the Latin American armed forces.[17]

Juan Cobo, of the Latin American Institute, who initially reacted to the coup in Peru as a US-inspired *putsch*,[18] by 1970 was describing the Peruvian armed forces as the vanguard of anti-imperialist social reforms, whose model was bound to affect not only the leftist army of Panama but even the right-wing military regimes in Argentina and Brazil.[19] The belief that the Peruvian example was bound to spread to other Latin American armed forces was by no means unique to Cobo. Yurii Antonov, a noted scholar of Brazil, stated that the "anti-American mood had penetrated all Latin American armies."[20]

Changed attitudes toward the Latin American armies soon forced an ideological readjustment in the Marxist dogma toward armies in general. Without entirely abandoning the doctrine that armed forces are a tool of the social order that created them, Soviet analysts claimed that the military represented society as it is. Thus, changes in social balance and social forces within a country were bound to be reflected within the armed forces. To prove the correctness of this assessment, Soviet analysts resurrected the predictions of Friedrich Engels – that the institution of universal conscription in Europe would change the armies' composition by filling their ranks with peasants and workers and that the armies' political stand would change in consequence.[21]

This new explanation was soon echoed by several Soviet analysts. Cobo, in his article, "The Peruvian Phenomenon," stated: "The role played today in Peru by the armed forces is neither an accidental aberration nor an inexplicable paradox. It is a manifestation of the changes taking place in Latin American society as a whole."[22] Rubén Souza of the Panamanian communist party stated that, given the social change in Latin America and consequent anti-Americanism, even the Brazilian army would have to respond to the change in the social balance of power and adopt an anti-American posture.[23]

By 1971 the initial ambiguity that typified the Soviet response to events in Peru was brushed aside, and most Soviet and communist observers accepted the "Peruvian way," albeit with reservations, as the most probable road toward transformation. The topic of the role of the military in Latin America had also become sufficiently important to be addressed in the pages of *Kommunist*. According to Boris Ponomarev, the armed forces "assume the role of the arbiter of national life . . . The appearance and the strengthening of revolutionary-democratic feelings within the armed forces may accelerate the process of revolutionary development."[24] Although Ponomarev warned that armies can play a reactionary role as well, he observed the growing strength in certain Latin American countries of "a new type of officer who is a progressive nationalist."[25]

For the first time since it started publication, *Latinskaia Amerika* presented an in-depth analysis of the Latin American armed forces in an issue dedicated entirely to this topic. Anatolii Shul'govskii, in the lead article, noted that a prolonged alienation of the Latin American armies from the United States was occurring. He cited, among other reasons, that: (1) the "internal war" assigned by the United States to the Latin American armies under the Alliance for Progress clashed with the armies' sense of professionalism; (2) the Latin American military-industrial complexes viewed association with the United States as a guarantee for perpetual dependence on, and accelerated "brain drain" to, the United States; and (3) the growth of the armies' role in the economic management of the hemisphere, in part inspired by the Alliance for Progress, brought the armies into a direct clash with the multinationals.[26]

In addressing the issue of the armies' class-consciousness, Shul'govskii challenged the traditional Marxist maxim that the armies would defend their class interests. He noted that most Latin American officers were of middle-class origin, a class that had been undergoing a process of radicalization for a long time. Thus, Fidel Castro's middle-class origins did not prevent him from playing a revolutionary role. Shul-'govskii was content that the armies of the region were alienated from both the bourgeoisie and the oligarchy: "The military no longer sees its interests as identical to those of the current political system."[27]

Writing somewhat less optimistically in the same issue of *Latinskaia Amerika*, N. S. Leonov emphasized that the army's middle-class prejudice against workers and peasants, and the lack of the latter's participation in shaping the new state, placed inherent limitations on army-inspired reforms.[28] Iu. A. Antonov observed that, despite progressive elements, the behavior of the armed forces was conditioned by its fear of the lower classes – a fear that at times motivated even some in the Brazilian military to support elements of populism in order to retain some public backing.[29] Juan Cobo and G. I. Mirskii, in their contribution, saw the situation as analogous to Nasserite Egypt, where lower middle-class officers, driven by hatred of colonialism and the local elite's association with foreign influence, were pushing the country to break with the capitalist system.[30] Silvio Mendaundua, a Cuban contributor, saw the radicalization of the Peruvian armed forces as an opening to an array of many exciting possibilities.[31] Mendaundua's remarks were significant, given Cuba's adamant hostility toward Latin America's armies in the past.

By late 1971 praise for the Peruvian and other Latin American forces had become the new dogma in Moscow. Anna Matlina, addressing the issue of the military in Latin American politics in her highly regarded book on reformism in Latin America, although still negative in her general assessment of Latin American armies, described the events in the Dominican army (1965) and the posture of the Peruvian army after 1968 as "brilliant" examples of some new tendencies.[32] Even the Soviet armed forces' newspaper, *Krasnaia Zvezda*, which rarely dealt with Latin American issues, joined the chorus by stating that "the progressive character of the actions of [the armies of] Peru, Bolivia, and the army of Chile show the patriotic mood of the officers expressing the will of the masses, and using their support to allow social and economic transformation."[33]

Enthusiasm about Peru reached such a pitch that Shul'govskii equated Juan Velasco with the liberator Sucre.[34] The Peruvian shift away from the traditional position of most Latin American armies convinced the USSR that there had been a significant diminution in the United States' ability to control events in Latin America. Radio

Moscow gleefully observed that the United States could no longer rely on the army to suppress leftist regimes in Latin America.[35]

The euphoria emanating from Moscow was shared by some Latin American communists. Jorge del Prado, the leader of the Peruvian communist party (PCP), stated: "The process of change in Peru was anti-imperialist, and anti-oligarchic from the outset . . . irreversible and far-reaching."[36] His enthusiasm for the military-led "revolution" was so great that del Prado was willing to bestow on it Leninist legitimacy: "By virtue of our Marxist-Leninist analysis we the Peruvian communists hold that the change now in process affects the socioeconomic structure, that is, possesses revolutionary content."[37] It should be noted, however, that a key reason for del Prado's optimistic view was that the military regime had made the PCP the sole exception to its ban on political parties.

Changing perceptions even induced a revision of the historical billing given the armed forces of Peru. Any past attention paid by Soviet analysts had concentrated on the fact that most of the Peruvian army's officers were trained in the United States and supported the country's traditional elite. A 1970 history emphasized that Peru's army had always stressed its Indian roots and had shown its progressive nature as early as 1959 when it called for the expulsion of IPC.[38]

The high point of euphoria regarding Peru came in 1972–74 (despite the 1971 fall of the leftist military regime in Bolivia and the 1973 ousting of Allende, which will be discussed later). Shul'govksii asserted: *"It is the position of the armed forces that will determine the long-term development of Latin America"*[39] (emphasis in the original). He echoed del Prado's statements that, despite the Peruvian officers' denials that they were Marxists, their actions had a "revolutionary content."[40] In describing his perception of the Peruvian military, Shul'govskii stated: "A new era of a revolutionary-proletarian and national liberation-oriented army is helping to shape our epoch."[41] The Peruvian communist party, which had become increasingly associated with the Velasco regime, upgraded its designation of the regime from "national-patriotic" to "national-revolutionary" in its September 1972 congress.[42]

Although both Soviet and communist analysts often expressed distress that the Peruvian armed forces were acting in a technocratic manner and not relying on the workers and peasants, by January 1973 del Prado was hopeful that "the military government's attitude to other parties or movements is changing for the better . . . The government displays respect for the communists and cooperates with them indirectly in revolutionary projects."[43] Furthermore, he observed that although the revolutionary path in Peru was somewhat unusual, it did correspond to the unique circumstances of the country and was, therefore, legitimate.[44] In defending Peru's military regime, del Prado challenged the standard communist maxim that the political orientation of the military is determined by its "social origin." He asserted the primary importance of the "historic moment" in which the army finds itself institutionally – and in the case of Peru the "historic moment" favored the army's support for class struggle.[45]

The prospect of the Peruvian army's playing an avant-garde role genuinely excited some Soviet analysts such as Shul'govskii, who in the past had been outraged whenever "gorillas" took power in Latin America. Now he scoffed at the idea of the army "going back to the barracks," asserting that those who favored an "apolitical" army were reactionaries attempting to restore the previous status quo.[46] Shul'govskii went on to assert that the communists never viewed the army as either their permanent enemy or the eternal guardian of the existing order in Latin America; it was bourgeois slander to assert that the communists could not cooperate with the army.[47]

Although Peru was at the center of Soviet analysis of the "progressive" military in Latin America, developments in the armed forces of Chile, Bolivia, Ecuador, and Panama also attracted Soviet attention. The Chilean armed forces, traditionally the most "Prussian" and least politically involved army in the Americas, not only tolerated the election of a Marxist president but ignored the provocative murder of General René Schneider and continued to support the Allende regime. In 1972, when the Allende government was shaken by numerous strikes led by the truckers, the armed forces under General Prats agreed to accept several cabinet posts and to restore order in the country at a time when the regime's disintegration appeared imminent. Although there was little serious analysis of the Chilean armed forces, the Soviet press often praised the Chilean army for supporting the "will of the people."[48] In addition, Luis Corvolán, perhaps the most stalwart representative of the Soviet line in Latin America, repeatedly praised the army as a pillar of Chilean democracy.

Soviet analysts also gave a favorable reading to events in Bolivia, where Generals Ovando and Torres were pursuing an "anti-imperialist" path (which, among other things, included the nationalization of the operations of Gulf Oil and the expulsion of Peace Corps volunteers). Politburo member Mikhail Suslov, in a keynote address celebrating the 53rd anniversary of the October revolution, accorded equal significance to events in Bolivia and in Peru under Velasco and in Chile under Allende.[49] As it had done for Velasco's regime, the communist party gave its total support to the military regime of Ovando–Torres. The first secretary of the Bolivian communist party assured General Torres that the masses (presumably led by the communists) would tilt the balance within the armed forces in Torres' favor.[50]

In addition to praising the military regimes of Bolivia, Chile, Panama, and Peru, the USSR, as well as local communist parties, gave credit to the "patriotic-progressive" military regime of Ecuador, led by General Lara, and the regime in Honduras led by General Oswaldo López Arellano.

The pessimist school

Despite the dominant optimism about the potential role of the armies in Latin America, a less sanguine minority group in Moscow persisted in expressing its doubts about whether the "leopard would be able to change his spots." A number of Soviet analysts took this dimmer view of the prospects of a military-led social transformation in Latin America, but the group was nevertheless rather assertive in its views and sufficiently well-connected to state those views in the most influential publications, such as *Kommunist* and *World Marxist Review*.

As early as 1968, when most Soviet analysts were increasingly drawn to the "Peruvian Phenomenon" and saw a growing institutional alienation between the US armed forces and those of Latin America, Iurii Eliutin asserted that this rift was bound to mend. Eliutin attributed the rift to the United States' refusal to supply modern weapons to Latin America – and not to a leftward ideological turn by the Latin American armies. These armies had therefore turned to Europe but, Eliutin contended, would resume their ever-growing cooperation with, and dependence on, the United States after President Nixon's agreement to sell them weapons.[51]

Konstantin Tarasov, in a study of the US–Latin American military relationship, stressed that the Latin American armies had very little elbowroom to oppose the United States – the main source of their budgets.[52] Regarding the "Peruvian Phenomenon," he asserted that "the program of Peru's military, thus far, did not go beyond the framework of bourgeois democracy."[53] In early 1973 he stated that a break between the Latin American armies and the United States was all but impossible, since the bonds between them extended to the entire configuration of Latin America's military training, supplies, and economic and technological cooperation.[54] Tarasov argued that the

industrial development in Latin America since World War II, along
with the emergence of military-industrial complexes in Latin America,
had deepened the regional armies' dependence on the United States,
since no Latin American military-industrial complex could survive
without US backing.[55]

Furthermore, not all analysts shared the view that the social origin of
the officer corps was irrelevant. V. N. Selivanov, an analyst who
generally wrote for Soviet armed forces publications, stated that once
officers entered the military hierarchy, they became servants of the
bourgeois ruling class.[56] Although he acknowledged that events in
Peru should give pause to those who made mechanical assumptions
about Latin American armies, he concluded that these armies
remained "a vital link in the US imposed 'Inter-American' system,
fulfilling their role as the defender of the capitalist system and oppres-
sor of the people of the continent."[57] He was joined in his skepticism by
A. Aleksin, who characterized the military as an insular "caste" remote
from the masses and an inherent danger to reformists.[58]

Three prominent Latin American communists, L. Padilla, J. Laborde, and E. Sousa, highlighted that no military government had yet
"set the objective of a socialist revolution." They attributed this to the
fact that "the movement is led by the bourgeoisie not the proletariat . . .
The military regimes are not stable, the leaders of the *petite bourgeoisie*
vacillate under public pressure."[59] Despite nationalist feelings among
some officers, the authors cautioned that "the armed forces of Latin
America are tied to the Pentagon's apron strings . . . and therefore it
has never been clearer that the future of the revolutionary process
depends on the workers and the people. They should not bank too
much on the victory of the nationalist trends in the armies."[60]

Even such relatively optimistic analysts as Cobo and Mirskii warned
that although the military of Latin America might be willing to remove
various economic obstacles and carry out some social reforms, all this
was done in order to preserve the general social order. Ultimately the
army *"opposes social revolution with every means"*[61] (emphasis added).
Similarly, V. Tikhmenev cautioned that the leftist military regimes
were not a "vanguard party" that would obviate the need for a communist social revolution.[62]

The disbelief of some Latin American communists in the likelihood
of military-led social transformation in the hemisphere was strengthened by the fall of Torres' leftist regime in Bolivia in 1971. Regardless of
the Bolivian communists' support for the regime, Padilla noted, not all
of the "progressive" forces were willing to put their support behind

the junta: "The lack of unity among the workers and the people on the significance and the prospects of the alliance with the military who came to power prevented the formation of a genuinely popular government."[63] Furthermore, Padilla declared that Torres was never a Marxist-Leninist but a bourgeois politician trying to correct the mistakes of Ovando, who had been "a compromiser and a defeatist."[64]

Soviet policy toward the Latin American armed forces (1968–75)

The traditional Soviet notion that Latin American armies were the ultimate defense of the latifundists and the foreign multinational corporations had been replaced with a new notion on which both the optimists and the pessimists could agree: these armies, like the societies in which they originated, were complex institutions containing "progressive" as well as "reactionary" elements. Soviet observers as diverse as Shul'govskii and Tarasov agreed that the armies had become the new ideological battlegrounds in which "reactionaries" could prevail (as in Brazil) or "progressive" forces might win out (as in Peru). Thus, by the late 1960s, for the first time since the USSR started to devote attention to Latin America (and despite ample historical precedents of progressive tendencies in the Latin American armies dating to the 1920s), the armies of the region began to be seen as a potentially progressive factor. Consequently, the USSR expanded its ties with countries governed by leftist military regimes as well as with the armed forces of countries that retained civilian regimes. It even attempted to create an institutional relationship with armies that were currently the leaders of right-wing regimes.

In those countries where leftist military governments were in power, the USSR embarked on a program of substantial foreign aid. For example, with regard to Peru, Moscow agreed to upgrade significantly Peru's vital fishing fleet, to build a new fishing complex ranging from port facilities to fish processing plants, and, in principle, to undertake the Olmos hydroelectric-irrigation project (which would have dwarfed the high dam at Aswan, built by the Soviets between 1955 and 1964). Aside from economic aid, the USSR gave Peru more than $150 million worth of military aid,[65] the first such aid granted by Moscow to any Latin American country other than Cuba.

Military and economic aid was accompanied by overtures to institutional relations between the Soviet armed forces and their Peruvian counterparts. Thus, in June 1972, Peruvian Chief of Staff Montero-

Rojas visited Moscow at the invitation of Defense Minister Grechko.[66] Within a few months Air Marshal Kutakhov visited Lima,[67] to be followed by General Sokolov, the future Soviet defense minister.[68] While Soviet and Peruvian generals were visiting each other's countries, the navies of both countries also exchanged visits. As a result of this intensified relationship, by late 1973 the first Soviet-made T55 tanks started to arrive in Peru, along with Soviet instructors.[69]

In the case of Bolivia the USSR agreed to carry out a systematic geological survey of the country so as to weaken Bolivia's dependence on the geological findings of the multinational mining concerns.[70] To reduce Torres' dependence on US firms, and to increase Bolivia's export earnings, Moscow agreed to build tin-smelting facilities that would enable the country to export processed tin rather than ore.[71] The most interesting demonstration of the Soviet belief that leftist military regimes were likely to be both long-lasting and friendly to the USSR was Moscow's apparent plan to build a satellite tracking station in Bolivia.[72] Although Soviet aid to the military regimes of Bolivia and Peru was small compared with assistance to Cuba, Egypt, or North Vietnam, Latin America's share in total Soviet credits granted to foreign countries rose from 2 percent in the mid-1960s to 25 percent a decade later.[73] Aside from Chile (under civilian Marxist government) the other major recipients of those credits were Bolivia, Brazil, and Peru, all of which were governed by military regimes.

The USSR spared no effort in cultivating the Chilean armed forces which, despite their respect for the elected regime of Allende and their subsequent support, maintained close ties with the United States and the Inter-American Defense Board and continued to rely almost entirely on the United States as a source of military equipment. Not only did the Soviets attribute central importance to the political role of the Latin American armies, they also recognized that the ultimate survival of the Chilean regime depended on the goodwill of the armed forces. Thus, the Soviets waged the ideological battle for the Chilean armed forces through offers of cheap weapons and strenuous efforts to establish an institution-to-institution relationship between the Soviet and Chilean armies.

According to unconfirmed reports in 1971, the USSR offered Chile between $50 million and $300 million worth of weapons, so as to end Chile's overriding reliance on the United States.[74] The USSR issued numerous invitations to Chilean officers and welcomed a visit by the Chilean navy cadet vessel to Vladivostok.[75] Shortly thereafter, a

Chilean Air Force delegation visited the USSR at the invitation of Air Marshal Kutakhov;[76] Admiral Corneje, commander of the Chilean navy, spent a week in Moscow at the invitation of Fleet Admiral Gorshkov.[77] In September 1972 Marshal Kutakhov visited Chile,[78] and he was reported to have offered Chile twenty-five MiG 21 jets for a token price of 6.5 million pounds sterling.[79] In May 1973 the Chilean defense minister and chief of general staff, General Prats, visited Moscow and met Defense Minister Grechko and Prime Minister Kosygin. According to the official Cuban press agency, Kosygin offered Chile's army substantial weapon transfers.[80]

The Soviet impression was that the Chilean armed forces maintained their existing loyalty to the Allende regime. The collapse of a rightist military coup in Chile in July 1973 brought the following reaction from Moscow:

> An important role in crushing the attempted coup was played by the Chilean armed forces, loyal to their patriotic duty. Fascist ideas were spread in the barracks and there were attempts to break military discipline and provoke clashes with left-wing patriotic forces. The army rejected all the advances of the right-wing plotters and took an active part in disarming the handful of traitors whom the fascists won over for their anti-government plot . . . Life itself convinced the Chilean military that left-wing forces were the faithful defenders of the nation's interests.[81]

Even in the case of Ecuador, where the leftist military junta showed little warmth toward the USSR, a military delegation of the Ecuadoran armed forces was invited to Moscow and hosted by the deputy chief of staff, General Ogarkov.[82]

As noted, efforts to cultivate Latin American military establishments were not restricted to countries with leftist regimes. Although Soviet analysts often viewed Argentina's military as the vanguard of "fascist gorillas," relations between the USSR and General Lanusse's regime improved notably and revived various trade agreements that had been moribund for a decade or more.[83] Institutional contacts were also initiated with other Latin American armies, both politically inactive and even right-wing. In the summer of 1972, the Colombian training ship *Gloria* visited Leningrad, carrying cadets whose affiliations ranged from the leftist armies of Peru and Ecuador, to the neutralist armies of Colombia, Mexico, and Venezuela, to right-wing establishments of the Dominican Republic and Paraguay.[84] Similarly, the Soviet training ship *Borodino* visited Rio de Janeiro in late 1972, extending an invitation to the Brazilian navy to pay a port call in the USSR.[85] A year later the *Borodino* visited Cartagena, Colombia, and Veracruz, Mexico, prompting a visit to Odessa by Mexico's *Chihuahua*.

While these exchanges were unexceptional, they are significant because, until the 1970s, the USSR had no contact with the Latin American armies. Even during World War II, when Brazil actually dispatched an expeditionary force to Europe and fought as an ally of the USSR, there is no record of any Soviet attempt to befriend the Brazilian armed forces. That the USSR plunged into an ideological battle for the political orientation of the Latin American armed forces testifies to the Soviets' recognition that these forces were not, as they had once imagined, the homogeneous tool of imperialism and that their tolerance was essential to any political transformation in the region.

Transition (1975–77)

Because during 1975–77 many assumptions about the Latin American armies began to crumble, this period can be designated as one of transition. Yet, perhaps out of inertia, Soviet analysts continued to ignore developments. Understandably, the fall of the Torres regime in 1971 had a minimal effect on the Soviet perception of the Latin American armed forces. Given the historical volatility of Bolivian politics and the covert Brazilian intervention to oust Torres, it was hardly surprising that Soviet students of the Latin American armies refused to generalize from the Bolivian experience. The few comments made by Soviet or communist analysts explained Torres' fall in terms of his failure to establish a mass party based on workers and peasants, which represented a failure to develop a political base with which to face future travails; the fact that the Bolivian military was never fully united behind Torres; and Torres' small chance of survival once Brazil, along with the CIA, decided to undercut his regime. Within weeks of Torres' fall, his regime's existence was all but forgotten in the Soviet Union.

It is far more surprising that the bloody coup carried out by General Pinochet did not provoke a reevaluation of the Latin American armies. In fact, the prevailing attitude in Soviet political literature was that the coup had occurred because the Chilean army had been provoked by certain ultra-leftist elements in the Allende government rather than because the army was unprogressive in its nature. Although Professor Gonionskii, chairman of the Soviet–Latin America friendship association, called for a reevaluation of the political role of the Latin American armies,[86] there was little if any response.

The first analysis of the Chilean military to be written after the coup was by Shul'govskii, who asserted that the coup was not pre-destined.[87] He recalled how the Chilean army had weathered the murder of General Schneider and how General Prats, by agreeing to become Allende's interior minister, had given the regime the prestige and authority of the army when Allende's political fortunes were at a nadir. Apparently, Shul'govskii rejected the notion that the coup was brought on by the army's natural inclination and felt responsibility rested with the Allende regime's ineptitude – manifest in the rapidly declining living standards of the middle class with which the army had identified[88] – and the army's growing fears that ultra-leftists within the Allende government were increasingly threatening the army's insti-tutional integrity.[89] Nor did Shul'govskii become overly pessimistic about the future role of the Latin American armies. Despite the Chilean tragedy, he argued, the Latin American armies could not remain solely a tool of the exploiting class, if only because of the changing social origins of both the officers and the enlisted men.[90]

Similarly, the major Soviet postmortem[91] rarely blamed the demise of the Allende regime on the armed forces as an institution, but rather on the inept economic policies of Allende and the provocative actions of the ultra-left within the government. Mikhail Kudachkin, the chief of the Latin American section of the Central Committee of the CPSU, observed: "The Chilean communist party repeatedly unmasked the traitors and the provocative role of the MIR which by its irresponsible seizures of small private enterprises and lands pushed a significant part of the middle class into the camp of the reaction, facilitating the implementation of the fascist coup."[92]

An Academy of Sciences study also blamed Allende's economic policies, his inability to build a coalition with the middle class, and his inability to check the provocative behavior of the ultra-left.[93] Some Soviet analysts, such as candidate member of the Politburo Ponomarev (writing with the benefit of hindsight), felt that the Allende regime should have denied traditional opponents power levers such as the army.[94] Tkatchenko accused Allende of failing to understand properly the class nature of the Chilean army, thus failing to see who was loyal to him and who was not.[95] Similarly, H. Neuberg of the Latin American Institute in Rostock (GDR) felt that the Chilean communists had not done enough to cultivate the progressive elements in the army.[96]

The Latin American communist parties manifested similar divisions in their attitudes toward the military after Allende's fall. While Peru's del Prado continued to believe in the progressive nature of the region's armed forces, other Latin American communists felt that such optimism might be misplaced. Alvaro Delgado of the Colombian communist party sounded the alarm by stating: "The military putsch in Chile is seriously affecting the political scene in Colombia. Militaristic and anticommunist tendencies have grown stronger ... Now no constitutionally formed civilian government in Latin America is safe from the rightists' putschist propensities."[97]

Soviet reluctance to criticize the Chilean army, and to propose that Allende should have destroyed the existing army and replaced it with a "democratic" one, may be explained in the following manner. The Soviet Union maintained close ties with the Peruvian army, and the Portuguese army supported the communist-led revolution of 1975. Thus, advocating such a course would have been awkward at best.

Although Velasco's fall from power in 1975 finally provoked a major reassessment of the Latin American armed forces' revolutionary role, the initial Soviet reaction revealed a belief in Moscow that the palace coup reflected merely a change of personnel rather than ideology. Only after the ascent to power of General Morales Bermúdez did the USSR realize that Velasco's fall signaled more than a change of leadership. Thus Shul'govskii, writing on the eve of the coup that ended the Velasco era, asserted that the Peruvian armed forces, as an institution, increasingly accepted the influence of José Carlos Mariátegui (the founder of the Peruvian communist party) and the concept of class struggle.[98]

The Soviets' persistently positive attitude toward the Latin American military was further manifested in their reaction to General Videla's coup against the presidency of Isabel de Perón of Argentina. S. A. Kazakov, in the first major analysis of the Argentine coup, noted that unlike the past, when the armed forces had proceeded to attack the communists upon seizing power, General Videla actually sought the support of all other parties, including the communist party.[99] Furthermore, although the Argentine armed forces had been among the most ardent supporters of the Pentagon-inspired "National Security" doctrine, which pitted the army against its own people, the current leadership saw as its main mission the protection of the Argentine people from imperialism.[100] Kazakov's apologia for the Argentine armed forces reached absurd heights when he alleged that one of the reasons that the army had rebelled against the regime of Mrs. Perón was that it was outraged by the crusade of the anticommunist alliance (the AAA) led by López Rega – Perón's sorcerer, lover, and minister of the interior.[101] Even the highly cooperative policy toward multinational corporations pursued by finance minister Martínez de Hoz was dismissed by Kazakov as temporary sop to the right.[102]

The Soviet perception that Latin American armies were well on their way to breaking their traditional ties with the United States, and were playing an increasingly progressive role in the hemisphere's politics, continued until early 1977. In one of the latest testimonials to this perception, Piotr Shiblin, reviewing US–Latin American military relations, observed:

> The process under way within the [Latin American] armed forces shows that the inter-American military-political system has developed serious cracks. The Latin American armed forces have not escaped the laws governing social and economic development. New elements are emerging on the political scene. The ranks of the armed forces formerly recruited from among illiterate downtrodden peasants are now replenished by workers and representatives of the middle classes with higher levels of political awareness. The officers are no longer a separate caste ... A segment of democratic-minded officers is emerging, who, far from shunning their own people, are prepared to fight for their interests.[103]

Shiblin concluded that democratic officers had emerged in the armies of Chile, the Dominican Republic, El Salvador, Panama, Peru, and Uruguay.[104]

Disappointment and new realism (1977–82)

The USSR's realization in 1977 that the Peruvian experiment had ended caused a major Soviet reassessment of all Latin American armies. In a special conference organized by the Latin American Institute, most speakers, who had previously expressed great hopes for the Latin American armies, now confessed that they had misread the situation. Thus, Shul'govskii opened the conference:

> Many of us thought that the revolutionary regime in Peru could bring about the opening of the political system to the masses and expand the base of its progressive institutions ... Almost all of us were moved by the sight of tens of thousands of workers demonstrating their support for the revolutionary regime. We often ignored the obvious weaknesses of the regime. *We were dizzy with success*[105] (emphasis added).

Yet Shul'govskii refused to write off the armies completely, asserting

that internal divisions generated elements that could play a constructive role. His minimal goals for Latin American communists were that
they should have sufficient ties with the army to prevent fascism.[106]

A. Glinkin, although no longer anticipating revolutionary behavior
from the Latin American armies, saw long-lasting effects in their destruction of the notion of "continental defense" for the region, in favor
of defense against "economic aggression." This weakened US hegemony in the hemisphere.[107]

G. I. Mirskii, one of the first Soviet scholars to study the political role
of the armed forces in the "Third World," and in the past one of the
mcst enthusiastic supporters of the "progressive military," noted that
the main goal of those armed forces was to carry out a modernization of
their societies. Since most of Latin America lacked a middle class to
modernize the country, the armies invariably drifted toward reliance
on the multinationals.[108] Mirskii rejected the former Soviet belief that
the lower middle-class origins of the Latin American officer corps
would make these officers sympathetic to the masses: An officer's
behavior was determined by where he was trained, not by his class
origin. The experience of Peru and Portugal had shown that these
officers shifted to the right when faced with a truly revolutionary
threat. Concluding that "no army can be a substitute for a political
party," Mirskii added that the most the left could hope for was a split
within the armed forces when a revolutionary situation was at hand.[109]

Juan Cobo observed that despite its leftist rhetoric, the Peruvian
army had aimed to preempt and not to promote the left.[110] Despite its
lower middle-class origins, the Latin American officer corps was highly
socialized, with few links with the masses. Furthermore, since there
was no stress on the institutional structure of the Latin American
armies (unlike Russia in 1917), it would be incorrect to expect the army
to disintegrate or to play a revolutionary role.[111]

An even more pessimistic assessment of the Latin American military
was voiced by Khenkin, who claimed that the progressive mood of the
Latin American armies had peaked during the "Tenentes" uprisings in
Brazil during the early 1920s and that as Latin America became more
developed its armies were becoming more and more regressive.[112]
Sergo Mikoian observed that although the Latin American armies were
cohesive, elite institutions, the economic reality of the continent was
such that despite such symbolic gestures as the rejection of US military
aid, leftist military regimes were compelled to accommodate the
United States.[113]

In his concluding remarks to the symposium Shul'govskii noted that despite the obvious setback in Peru, it was premature to declare a Latin American *Thermidor*. The fact that the Latin American armies craved change, according to Mirskii and Cobo, was a positive development in itself, regardless of the military's elitist and corporatist nature.[114]

Latinskaia Amerika, which in its editorial policy had been generally sympathetic to the progressive trends within the region's armed forces, became increasingly critical and less sanguine. In an attack on the Latin American armed forces, reminiscent of Soviet attitudes during the 1950s, the French Marxist, Alain Joxe, contended: "If the peoples of Latin America are ever to attain their 'second independence' they must first break the resistance of the military establishments . . . whose officer corps remain organically tied to imperialism."[115] Anna Matlina, in her examination of "military revolutions," asserted that actual revolutionary action, even in Velasco's time, had been less real than it seemed. Even in the early 1970s, she observed, the army had remained a corporatist institution and the "aristocratic" navy and air force had never supported reform.[116] Thus, at the height of Velasco's anti-American campaign (1971), 278 Peruvian officers had been training in the United States in counterinsurgency tactics, and US investment in Peru had reached a new record of $800 million.[117]

Soviet perceptions of the Latin American armed forces (1977–82)

The collapse of the leftist regimes in Bolivia, Ecuador, Panama, and Peru, along with increasing difficulties experienced by rightist military regimes, especially in Argentina, Brazil, Guatemala, and Uruguay, induced a change in Moscow's perception of the Latin American armed forces. Past beliefs that the armed forces could permanently impose their political will on any Latin American country were losing credibility. The defeat of Somoza's national guard by a coalition of guerrillas brought to an end the traditional Soviet position that a guerrilla force could not defeat a cohesive army, and it in fact resulted in the rehabilitation of Che Guevara's military doctrine.[118]

Although Soviet analysts did not revert to their old perception of Latin American armies as a tool of the Latin American oligarchy and US imperialism, they perceived a decline in both the armies' revolutionary potential and their coercive ability. Thus Soviet analysts were unimpressed when a junta of junior officers ousted the dictatorship of General Romero in El Salvador in 1979 and launched agrarian reform as well as nationalizations in the banking and insurance industries. In fact, the Soviet reaction was largely negative, and the coup received none of the praise that had been heaped on Generals Ovando, Velasco, Torrijos, or Lara when they adopted similar measures.

Similarly, by 1979 Soviet analysts revised their once optimistic impressions of Brazil's economic achievements, which had led them to assume that the military regime would hold power for a long time to come. Instead, they viewed the Brazilian military as a beleaguered institution, groping for a way out. A. A. Sosnovskii asserted that by late 1981 the Brazilian army had two choices: either to remain in power and thus risk social turmoil, which might threaten its institutional coherence; or to attempt to withdraw from politics while leaving behind a nonthreatening bourgeois regime.[119]

Nor was the outlook for other military regimes much brighter. In the wake of the Nicaraguan revolution A. A. Sukhostat stated that the defeat of the Nicaraguan national guard scared all military regimes, thereby causing even such repressive military regimes as those in Chile and Uruguay to push for change from above in order to preempt the left. Linking the military's physical and intellectual exhaustion with attempts at restoring bourgeois-democratic regimes, Sukhostat nevertheless maintained that the forces of the left were no longer willing to settle for a return to a status quo ante.[120]

By the late 1970s and early 1980s, therefore, Moscow considered the Latin American armed forces to be neither a source of potential reform nor a permanent obstacle to social change. Consequently, Soviet policy toward the Latin American military establishments changed. In the post-1977 period virtually no military intercourse with Latin America occurred. The intensive courting of Latin American brass by the USSR was clearly over.

As late as January 1979 S. A. Sergeev voiced the fear that a guerrilla uprising in Nicaragua might result in a repetition of the 1932 *matanza* (which had destroyed the Salvadoran communist party), and he spoke of a delay of a possible revolutionary transformation. He stated outright that Somoza's national guard could not be defeated by a guerrilla force.[121] Yet the defeat of Somoza in July 1979 caused the Soviets to swing to the other extreme, asserting that the Nicaraguan experience could be repeated in El Salvador. Even after the defeat of the "final offensive" in El Salvador, the Soviet media continued to state that the Latin American armies were exhausted and that victory by the guerrillas was inevitable, albeit not immediate.[122]

The Soviet perception of the Latin American military that emerged during the last days of the Brezhnev era was that the Latin American armies were a new ideological battleground that the communists must try to split and perhaps co-opt. The central role assigned to Latin America's military in previous Soviet writings, however, was now discarded and the army assigned a lesser role. No longer did the Soviets hope that the region's armies would play a leading role in the hemisphere's progressive transformation; however, neither did they view the armies as a permanent pillar of the right, unchangeable and undefeatable.

8   Latin American labor unions

The proletarianization of Latin America began almost at the instant Columbus landed on the continent. The development of a vast mining industry in Spanish America, and later the introduction of an export-oriented plantation economy, created a substantial proletariat in the Americas well before the emergence of similar phenomena in much of Asia and Africa, and even parts of Europe. Increased European immigration during the latter half of the nineteenth century and early twentieth century, along with the economic impetus given the hemisphere by World War I, helped create an enlarged proletariat in parts of Latin America by the time the Bolsheviks seized power in Russia in 1917.

The presence of large proletarian populations in Latin America facilitated the establishment, by Comintern operatives, of communist parties in Argentina, Chile, Mexico, Uruguay, and other countries within a few years of Russia's October revolution. At the same time as the Comintern was expanding its operations in the hemisphere in the early 1920s, a Latin American labor union movement was emerging. By 1925 various communist parties had managed to make inroads in this movement,[1] and until well after World War II the communist-dominated unions would play a significant (although not always successful) role in the hemisphere's political struggles. In fact, Latin America proved to be a testing ground for strategies that would be attempted in Europe – domination of labor unions by relatively small and insignificant communist parties and Soviet use of communist-dominated unions as a policy instrument (for example, in France, Germany, and Italy).

The first major Soviet attempt to use Latin American labor unions as an instrument of policy occurred in 1927, when the Comintern instructed communist activists to block the shipment of foodstuffs to Britain from Argentina during the 1927 "war scare." When Luis Penelón, the leader of the Argentine communists, refused to comply, he was ousted from the party.[2] Apart from trying to undermine imperialist interests in Latin America, communist-controlled unions sought to "debilitate the capitalist system" and "unmask treacherous reformist leaders." In pursuit of these dual goals they launched a series of strikes and uprisings, which usually ended tragically. Between 1925 and 1932 the communist unions (belonging to CSLA [Communist Syndicates of Latin America], a member of the Profintern [the trade union agency of the Comintern]) launched the following major strikes: nitrite workers in Chile in 1925 (3,000 dead); port workers in Guayaquil, Ecuador in 1925 (500 dead); banana workers in Colombia in 1928 (4,600 dead); and peasant strikes in El Salvador (10,000 dead).[3]

With the promulgation of the "popular front" doctrine by the Seventh Comintern, which urged communists to cooperate with other "progressive" forces, the Latin American communist labor unions entered a series of alliances with other nationalist unions. In January 1936 they formed the hemisphere-wide union of the CTAL (Confederación de Trabajadores de América Latina), whose growth was so phenomenal that by 1953 it was by far the largest labor organization in Latin America, representing between 6.8 and 8 million workers.[4] Since the communists had managed to secure early and total domination of the union, the CTAL's policies closely followed those of the Profintern and the Soviet Union. Thus, after opposing any Latin American involvement in the European war until 1941, the CTAL responded to Germany's attack on the USSR by urging all Latin American regimes to help in the war effort. It was willing to cooperate with such right-wing leaders as Somoza in Nicaragua.[5]

However, just as rapidly as it had grown, the CTAL was reduced to total insignificance by 1962. With communist activity banned in much of the region after the onset of the cold war, two competing unions had emerged: the AFL–CIO-affiliated ORIT (Organización Regional Interamericana de Trabajadores) and the church-affiliated CLASC (Confederación Latino-americana de Sindicalistas Cristianos). When the CTAL's Chilean branch (under instructions from the Prague-based WFTU [World Federation of Trade Unions]) proposed unification with these unions, it met with rejection by all potential partners, which further isolated the CTAL from the mainstream of the Latin American labor movement. By 1964 the CTAL's membership was reduced to fewer than 2 million members, of whom 1.5 million were Cubans.[6] Under such circumstances the WFTU ordered the dissolution of what was once the most powerful communist trade union outside the USSR.

After almost thirty years of activity the CTAL was dissolved in January 1964, only months before Brezhnev became general secretary of the CPSU. Similarly, before the Brezhnev era began, the Latin American leftist labor movement suffered another major blow. In March 1964 the largest Latin American network of urban and rural labor unions collapsed without offering any resistance to the military coup in Brazil.[7] Since the communist-inspired unions in Brazil by 1959 controlled such key urban unions as those of the dockworkers and metalworkers, in addition to 250,000 peasant leagues, their defeat was particularly traumatic to the communist movement.[8]

Thus the Brezhnev era began, with little Soviet interest in the Latin American labor movement that had once played a significant role in the USSR's regional priorities. Although most Soviet analysts upheld the labor movement's importance in undermining the presence of US and multinational corporations, during the Brezhnev era few expected the Latin American communist movement to reestablish a powerful force similar to the CTAL. These attitudes were first manifested during the conference of the Pro-Moscow Latin American Communist Parties, held in Havana, November 1964. The goal that the delegates of the Latin American communist parties and the CPSU assigned to the labor movement in their final communiqué was remarkably minimal: "To develop the spirit of solidarity within the Latin American proletariat by promoting labor protests in all enterprises and bringing these to the attention of the World Federation of Trade Unions."[9] The Comintern had once viewed Latin American labor unions as the prime tool for bringing down the capitalist system; by 1964 communist expectations were limited merely to unspecified "labor protests." Furthermore, throughout the 1960s and early 1970s Moscow viewed the "reformist" Latin American labor unions as little more than an oligarchical tool for co-opting and controlling the working class.

In a special volume issued by the CPSU, N. N. Razumovich articulated why it would be folly to expect much revolutionary activity in the foreseeable future from the area's proletariat, even though Latin America was by far the most developed region of the developing world. The labor movement, although embracing more than 30 million workers, was split and therefore weak, owing to these facts: (1) Bourgeois-reformist governments had granted various concessions to workers' demands and thus dampened class conflicts. (2) More than 75 percent of the region's workers were newly arrived from the countryside and thus lacked the essential class solidarity. (3) The most qualified workers in the hemisphere were often employed by the multinational corporations and formed a "labor aristocracy," which was better trained and better paid. Thus instead of becoming the avant-garde, they often became a co-opted part of the status quo forces. (4) The various labor unions were split ideologically and were often controlled by status quo institutions, such as the church or the PRI (Partido Revolucionario Institucional) party in Mexico.[10]

In their analysis of the structure of the Latin American labor movement Kondrat'eva and Danilevich agreed with Razumovich's assessment. They further stressed that however misguided the Catholic labor movement might be when it insisted on a "third way" (neither capitalist nor Marxist), the Catholic union position responded to nationalist cravings in the region and thus undercut socialist-oriented unions.[11] The authors applauded the efforts of the Latin American communists to establish a hemisphere-wide union such as the CTAL but felt that the accomplishment of such a goal was bound to take a long time.[12]

Latin America lacked the conditions that would enable class-consciousness to develop, according to the conclusions of a statistical study by the Institute of World Economy. The study, which examined the demographics of the region's labor force, noted that although class divisions made Latin America more similar to Europe than to Asia and Africa, the region's employment pattern was different. More than a third of the region's proletariat was either self-employed or worked for very small enterprises.[13]

The Soviet view that Latin America's labor unions were no longer a significant revolutionary force, however, was by no means unanimous. B. I. Koval' (director of the Latin American section at the Institute of the International Workers' Movement) and B. I. Merin asserted that the Latin American labor movement was increasingly shifting from economic to political issues and that, in some countries, the movement had become a factor in the national liberation struggle.[14] L. Pegusheva, a prominent labor specialist in the Latin American Institute, agreed with Koval' about the shift toward political issues, as demonstrated by the ousting of US corporations from Peru. Pegusheva felt that Latin American labor unions (except those affiliated with "the CIA-connected" ORIT) were anti-imperialist in nature and their sole weakness was lack of unity between Catholics and socialists.[15] She also asserted that the AFL–CIO had increasingly penetrated the unions' leadership and steered the region's labor toward capitalism and reformism.[16] Ermolaev and Shul'govskii lamented that the labor union leadership's vacillation between *"petit bourgeois nationalism"* and ultra-leftism – both of which served the interests of the ruling classes – had hindered greater cooperation between the movement and the communists.[17]

Although all Soviet analysts expressed satisfaction that Latin American labor unions showed increasing readiness to defend their countries' sovereignty against Wall Street's intrusions, Soviet frustration with the unions mounted. As disappointment deepened over the behavior of labor movements during the leftist presidencies of Velasco and Allende, this frustration peaked. As one analyst complained, Peruvian labor was too often syndicalist, lacking class-consciousness and political maturity, and thus succumbing to both reformist and ultra-leftist impulses that often undercut the progressive policies of the Velasco regime.[18] Exasperation with the Chilean movement reflected Chile's unique position in historical Soviet perceptions.

Unlike the rest of Latin America, where the communists had lost their grip over the labor movement shortly after World War II, in Chile the communist party continued to dominate the labor federation (CUT). For almost a quarter of a century Moscow had treated CUT as a model labor union. By 1971 it comprised 40 percent of Chile's workers. It had demonstrated a symbiotic relationship with the Allende regime: in 1970 it was CUT that had threatened a general strike should the right-wing deny Allende his electoral victory; Allende had appointed a communist activist in CUT as his minister of labor and invited East European instructors to improve the union's organization.[19] When it became clear that segments of CUT had been involved in some of the most damaging strikes that swept Chile during Allende's final days, the Soviet media was understandably disappointed.

Maukukhin called on the Chilean communist party to spare no effort to preserve the unity of CUT (that is, communist control), which he felt was increasingly undermined by Christian Democratic infiltration from the right and the ultra-leftist MIR from the left.[20] Pegusheva criticized the political immaturity of CUT, which had failed to make the necessary shift from "economism," formerly essential for dealing with the Frei regime, to the "politicism" essential under Allende.[21] She concluded that the Chilean experience proved that tight political and ideological control was needed for labor unions to be politically effective.[22]

Some Soviet analysts were so disappointed by CUT that they called for an alliance with the Catholic church to preserve the anti-imperialist nature of the Chilean labor movement. Kondrat'eva asserted that no democratic labor movement could be effective without active participation in a progressive alliance with Catholics and other anti-imperialist forces. Such cooperation was appropriate, she explained, because since 1971 the Catholic unions had dropped their narrow "syndicalist" orientation and had increasingly become the defenders of social reorientation.[23] Kondrat'eva's statements reflected a major change in the Soviet attitude toward the Catholic labor movement, which in the early 1960s had been accused of splitting the labor movement by advocating "yellow reformism."[24] By the mid-1970s Moscow accepted that, although the Latin American labor unions lacked revolutionary content, they played an important role in raising class-consciousness.

The unsettling situation in the Latin American labor movement prompted several indigenous efforts by communists to rebuild a unified, communist-dominated labor union similar to the defunct CTAL. CUT activists managed to organize a labor conference in Brazil in January 1964, which resulted in a new leftist trade union federation (CPUSTAL). Its main goal was the struggle against imperialism, capitalism, and the oligarchy.[25] Although a 1967 accord with the Prague-based WFTU promised training for the CPUSTAL's cadres and political guidance,[26] the CPUSTAL never lived up to the expectations of its founders or the USSR. By the early 1970s Soviet analysts were increasingly critical, charging that the CPUSTAL had failed to reach out to the nonunionized workers and the rural proletariat. The Catholic unions were far more successful at this, according to Soviet analysts,[27] and it was the Catholic unions, rather than the CPUSTAL, that were invited to attend the 1969 Moscow conference of trade unions.[28] The 1975 Declaration of Havana of the Latin American communist parties openly conceded that its labor organizations had failed to break the dominance of *petit bourgeois* ideology within the labor movement.[29]

In a major article analyzing the ideological problems facing the region's labor movement, Shul'govskii pointed to serious problems that prevailed over the superficial ripeness for ideological progress in Latin America – home of 40 million proletarian workers and more than 500,000 communists. Segments that should have been the cutting edge of the proletariat (such as the miners in Bolivia or the rail workers in Mexico) viewed themselves as an "elite." They refused to associate themselves with the rest of the workers, preferring to settle for *"petit bourgeois* economism."[30] Shul'govskii complained of erratic behavior, which alternated between "reformism" and politically ineffective "juvenile ultra-leftism." He illustrated his point with the Córdoba labor uprising in Argentina, which had succeeded in ousting the Onganía military regime in 1969 but then failed to adopt a scientific socialism. Instead, Shul'govskii asserted, they had immediately drifted to ultra-leftism, which alienated the masses and allowed the reactionary forces to reassert themselves.

Vizgunova, in an analysis limited to the Mexican labor movement, concurred with Shul'govskii's conclusion that the split in the proletariat between a highly educated technological elite and a mass of first generation "peasant workers" appeared to breed "economism" and "reformism." Nevertheless, Vizgunova felt that the economic crisis that had gripped Mexico since 1974 was giving impetus to the emergence of a "class-based" trade union movement.[31]

The pervasive Soviet pessimism regarding the revolutionary potential of the Latin American labor movement was clearly articulated in a volume published by the Latin American Institute under the title, *The Working Class and the Revolutionary Process in Latin America*.[32] In the lead article, Shul'govskii asserted that "the development of class-consciousness among the workers of Latin America is not occurring without defeats, reversals and deformations due to a variety of negative influences."[33] Complaining that the progressive labor movements had lost their links with the rank and file, he stated that "divisions within the various labor unions made it unlikely that unions would be able to play a revolutionary role."[34] Merin noted that although much of the strike activity was directed at the imperialist presence in the hemisphere, the region's labor unions were acting in a "syndicalist manner," even when dealing with such progressive regimes as Velasco's. Kondrat'eva asserted that for Latin American labor unions to be effective, they would have to draw on the most educated and capable workers (those employed by the MNCs), a task so far beyond the local communists and their trade unions.[35]

As Marxist-Leninist groups failed to create much more than a fringe labor movement, and Soviet frustration grew, Soviet analysts increasingly called for coalitions with other labor movements that had greater peasant support. S. M. Khenkin's belief that the proletariat should never allow itself to be isolated from the progressive elements of the bourgeoisie[36] was echoed by Pegusheva. According to Pegusheva, although many of Latin America's trade unions had been created by the ruling class to control the labor movement, the labor unrest of the late 1960s and early 1970s proved that those unions were more than marionettes of the ruling elites and could be useful.[37] In addition, they served as a catalyst that raised the working class's political consciousness.[38] In another book she asserted that events had forced even the

ORIT federation, which sought to fight communism and socialism, to drift to the left and that it had developed a progressive wing.[39]

In a review of the state trade unions in Latin America during the 1970s, Pegusheva claimed that most Latin American labor unions were weak, parochial, and paternalistic and that the rise of military regimes and state capitalism had resulted in either the weakening or the co-optation of the labor movement. Nevertheless, even weak unions played an important role in making the masses politically sensitive.[40] Her only concern was that the growing politicization of workers frequently produced "anarchist-syndicalist" tendencies.[41] However, she maintained that even if the Latin American labor movement did not follow the correct Marxist line, it had political utility for progressive causes.

Similarly, P. P. Iakovlev wrote that, despite the movement's defects, the Latin American labor unions had forced the region's regimes to adopt a progressive foreign policy. As examples, Iakovlev noted that the trade unions had prevented Latin American governments from sending troops to Korea during the war there, forced the Mexican government to adopt a "peace-loving" foreign policy, and prevented the formation of SATO (NATO's southern counterpart).[42] More recently, the labor movement had pressed Latin American governments to accelerate the nationalization of foreign MNCs, support SALT II, and demand better terms for debt repayments.[43] This positive theme was echoed by Stroganov, who noted that even such right-wing unions as those affiliated with ORIT had taken a strong stance against the Pinochet and Somoza regimes and opposed the policies of President Reagan in Central America.[44]

Thus, to Soviet disappointment with the performance of the CPUSTAL (which the Soviets openly labeled a failure by 1985)[45] and CUT was added a persistent note of regret that no significant communist following had been created in the countryside. This failure became a particular source of consternation after 1979, when Moscow dropped its emphasis on a "peaceful transition" to socialism in Latin America and began supporting the notion of guerrilla warfare in the countryside – a consequence of the Nicaraguan success. Soviet policy toward the Latin American labor movement during the 1970s and 1980s sought first to merge all labor unions in a united front against the existing economic and political order. When Moscow's relentless calls for such a front failed to generate any significant response from the Catholic or ORIT-affiliated unions, the USSR made a concerted effort to establish relations with right-wing unions. Even in their disappointment with the region's labor unions, however, the Soviets by the mid-1970s had come to believe that the unions played an important role in raising class-consciousness while forcing regional regimes toward a confrontation with the imperialist presence and advocating a progressive foreign policy. Although the Latin American labor movement was no longer expected to play the revolutionary role accorded it by Marxist doctrine, the region's labor unions were nonetheless credited with a progressive role that would ultimately hasten the transfer toward "noncapitalist" development.

It should be noted that there is a school of Western thought that believes the USSR lost interest in the Latin American labor movement and, to a lesser degree, in the region's official communist parties. Proponents of this position attribute diminished interest to disillusionment with the "peaceful road" after Allende's collapse and the embracing of wars of national liberation in Latin America after the Sandinista victory. Thus, according to this view, the USSR is currently far more interested in rural guerrilla groups than in basically nonrevolutionary bodies, such as the mainline labor unions.[46]

9   Bourgeois political parties

Throughout the Brezhnev era the Soviet attitude toward the "reform-ist" parties in Latin America evolved in connection with the changing realities of the region. (This chapter centers around parties perceived by the Soviets as reformist, since the Soviet posture toward the political right wing was consistently negative.) Although some of the region's many states followed different paths of development, three phases emerge as key in the history of Soviet reassessment of Latin American bourgeois parties.

Initially the debate focused on whether these parties wanted only to "update" the status quo or whether they could be considered allies in a political and social transformation. As military rule swept the region they were evaluated as a potential partner against the fascist threat. With the fall of many military regimes and the victory of the Nic-araguan guerrillas, their importance to the communist cause would diminish.

Soviet perceptions and policy toward Latin American bourgeois parties 1964–70

The Soviet attitude toward bourgeois political parties of Latin America was hostile during the early Brezhnev years for several reasons. First, the historical relationship between the Latin American "reformist" political parties and the communist parties was tense and highly competitive. Although the communists had cooperated with several progressive parties – such as the Videla regime in Chile, the Vargas regime in Brazil in its early phases, the Perón regime in Argen-tina, the revolutionary coalition that preceded the PRI party in Mexico, and the Batista regime in Cuba – such cooperation had ultimately resulted in a break between the two groups, with the communists invariably weakened. An almost instinctive suspicion manifested itself

119

in both Soviet and communist writings about Latin America's reformist parties. Distrust ran so deep that when Brazil's leftist President
Goulart sought communist backing, the Soviets suspected that he was
seeking to use his friendship with the Brazilian communists and the
USSR merely as leverage to extract greater help from Washington.[1]

Second, from 1964 until roughly 1974, bourgeois regimes were cooperating with Kennedy's Alliance for Progress. As the emphasis of the
alliance was generally perceived by the Soviets to be one of establishing bourgeois regimes led by the middle class, this cooperation further
provoked the suspicion that progressive parties were an instrument of
the United States, intended to "renovate" capitalism in Latin America.
Consequently, the debate in the Soviet media centered on whether
these parties were genuinely keen to restructure the region's political
system or interested merely in "updating" the status quo. Thus, after
the communist uprising in Venezuela, the Soviet press repeatedly
referred to the country's president, Betancourt, as a bloody dictator.[2]
Other leaders of reformist parties, such as Fernando Belaúnde Terry of
Peru, were often branded as weak-kneed compromisers, willing to
yield to the demands of the right whenever faced with a challenge.[3]

Third, the Soviet attitude toward bourgeois political parties was
complicated by Soviet ambivalence about whether to support Cuba's
"export of revolution" or "peaceful coexistence." The popular belief is
that Moscow lost all interest in the "export of revolution" shortly after
the 1962 Cuban missile crisis and that by the time Brezhnev ascended
to power, Soviet policy was to support "peaceful coexistence" in Latin
America. In reality Moscow continued to support the concept of the
"export of revolution," albeit with decreasing enthusiasm, until at
least 1966, when the communist insurrection in Venezuela was totally
defeated. Given the USSR's official – or, at least, rhetorical – support
for revolutionary change in Latin America, it is hardly surprising that
the USSR was less than friendly to those parties that epitomized
capitalist "reformism."

As the Soviet media during the 1960s continued to cast Latin
America's progressive parties in the role of updating the existing
political and social structure through cooperative reforms, it was
unlikely that Moscow would attempt to cultivate a relationship by
which these parties would cooperate toward a communist transformation of the region. Further, the belief that Latin America was ripe for
revolutionary change was so strong that several Soviet analysts openly
questioned the need to come to any accommodation with the bourgeois political parties. S. Semenov, writing in 1964, asserted that the

conditions for revolutionary transformation were better in Latin America than in postwar Eastern Europe and significantly superior to those in Asia and Africa.[4] He felt that capitalism in Latin America was totally discredited. In addition to pointing to the imminent bankruptcy of capitalism, Semenov questioned the sincerity of the Christian Democratic party in calling for the abolition of capitalism.[5] In Semenov's opinion, the party's resort to a pseudo-reformist platform signaled an attempt to save itself and the capitalist system from political irrelevance.[6]

V. P. Beliaev also challenged the anticapitalist rhetoric of the Christian Democratic party. He noted that the party was led by the traditional Latin American elite and that some of its leaders, such as Haya de la Torre of the Peruvian APRA (Alianza Popular Revolucionaria Americana), continued to see benefits in the imperialist presence in the region.[7] Beliaev concluded that even though the growth of the Christian Democratic party was directly attributable to the disintegration of the old reformist parties, it was committed, as its predecessors had been, to "evolution."[8]

Grigulevich expressed his low opinion of the Christian Democratic party by calling it a "clericalist" party that supported the status quo, despite some positive foreign policy positions and promises of agrarian reforms. Therefore, it would be naive to expect much from this party. "The contemporary history of Latin America is replete with cases of radical leaders who enjoyed the trust and support of progressive forces, but once in power betrayed the national interests and became tools in the hands of imperialism and domestic reactionary groups."[9]

In a major analysis of Latin America's reformist parties, Alvaro Delgado labeled the region's wave of reformism as a feeble attempt to forestall revolution, which the bourgeoisie dreaded and could not afford.[10] Given the perceived limited objective of the Latin American reformist parties, Delgado warned that it would be a mistake to confuse these parties with those of Asia and Africa: "The African reforms are aimed chiefly at non-capitalist development, whereas those in Latin America are designed to buttress capitalist regimes in countries subjected to the influence of imperialist capital which more than ever is not *combated but reinforced* by the 'reform' schemes approved at Punta del Este"[11] (emphasis in the original).

Although the USSR extended a $57 million line of credit to Chile, the media continued to attack the style of reformism undertaken by the Christian Democratic Frei regime (1964–70). Disappointment in Frei's performance became almost unanimous in the Soviet press as his term in office passed its midpoint. E. V. Kovalev noted that whereas Frei might have intended to carry out some structural reforms, in reality he had failed in every major sphere: His agrarian reform was a sham, since he failed to distribute land even to a fraction of the peasants; his effort to gain control over the copper mines resulted in Chile's paying huge reparations to the multinationals without breaking the country's dependence on them; and his attempted banking reform was a non-starter, since Frei feared that he might offend foreign capital. According to Kovalev, the only peace that was truly important to Frei was peace with large capital.[12]

I. Zorina, an eminent student of Chile, asserted that, despite support for the Christian Democratic party from all layers of society, the leadership and hence its ideology were totally bourgeois. Thus its only genuine goal was to hasten the expansion of capitalism in Chile, primarily by attracting foreign capital.[13] Writing in early 1971, Zorina noted that Frei's sole political achievement was that with the emergence of the Christian Democrats, extreme right-wing segments of the rural oligarchy had ceased to play a major political role. She concluded that Frei's failure to restructure the basic social and economic configuration of Chile proved that bourgeois parties had neither the will nor the ability to bring about real change.[14]

However, not all in the Soviet political community denied the potential of bourgeois parties to accept social reform. Some analysts envisaged a transformation to socialism by which regimes led by *compradores* (middlemen between foreign imperialism and native business) would give way to a national bourgeoisie, which the communists ought to support.[15] According to Herbert Dinerstein's description of the Soviet viewpoint, which is somewhat simplistic as a generalization, the Latin American middle class was considered deserving of encouragement, since some parts of it "suffer more from America's dominance than they gain from being its agent."[16] As one example, Semenov urged the Latin American communists to enter a broad coalition with the Christian Democrats,[17] whose growing revolutionary wing, he felt, was bound to lead to greater anti-imperialism and hostility toward the United States.[18]

It was evident, however, that the Soviet political community was divided over the correct response to nationalist-reformist regimes in the hemisphere. For example, Delgado asserted that reformism led by the national bourgeoisie was actually dangerous to social transformation: "The peril of pseudo-reformism derives first and foremost from its propensity to delude the masses."[19] Kiva Maidonik, representing perhaps the most Castroite attitude within the Soviet academic community, asserted that the collapse of the Bosch (Dominican Republic), Goulart (Brazil), Illia (Argentina), and Paz Estenssoro (Bolivia) regimes demonstrated the shallowness of the reformist movement.[20] Any prolonged alliance between communists and bourgeois parties was impossible and undesirable, Maidonik argued, since this could scuttle revolutionary transformation at a time when it might be at hand.[21]

Maidonik's statements drew an angry response from V. I. Ermolaev, who stated that Latin American reformism had a rich political history since the turn of the century and that reformist parties led by such leaders as President Cárdenas of Mexico and President Vargas of Brazil were able to satisfy the nationalist cravings of the Latin American people.[22] He further argued that generalizations could not be drawn from Cuba (whose political parties he acknowledged to be bankrupt by the mid-1950s) and that the lessons of Cuba had been learned by the reformists no less well than by the communists of the region.[23] Maidonik was wrong to accuse the reformist parties of being counterrevolutionary, Ermolaev charged, given their hostility toward imperialism and multinational corporations.[24]

When Salvador Allende was elected in Chile in 1970 against the opposition of the Christian Democrats, some Soviet analysts considered that reformist parties were no longer essential for any change in the region's political structure. An article by Mikhail Kudachkin, chief of the Latin America group of the Central Committee of the CPSU, asserted that as the current progressive strides in Chile and Peru indicated, there were new forces operating in Latin America and that the "reformist parties are bankrupt."[25] He declared that the Latin American reformist bourgeoisie now realized that it could neither deliver the needed change nor postpone the inevitable. Referring to the experiences of President Belaúnde in Peru and President Frei in Chile, he concluded that the era of reformism was over.[26]

Thus, with the collapse of reformist regimes in Argentina, Bolivia, Brazil, Chile, the Dominican Republic, Peru, and Uruguay, and the emergence of either right-wing or left-wing regimes (in Bolivia and Peru), the prevailing Soviet attitude toward those reformist parties was clearly disdainful if not hostile. Yet throughout the 1960s there had been no discernible difference in Soviet policy between those Latin American states governed by Christian Democrats and those governed by right-wing military regimes. For example, as noted, in 1968 the USSR gave Frei's Chile a credit line of $57 million. A year earlier Brazil had received $100 million, despite its harsh right-wing political posture. In fact, the level of Soviet economic activity in Brazil was significantly greater after the Brazilian "revolution" of 1964 than during the Goulart period (increasing from $60 million in 1963 to $100 million in 1966).[27] Furthermore, the USSR expanded its ties with military-ruled Brazil and right-wing Colombia even as it delayed establishing ties with reformist Costa Rica and shunned Venezuela because of a communist uprising there. Nor did a commitment by a reformist regime to bourgeois democracy guarantee that Moscow would not aid communist rebels, as the case of Venezuela in the early 1960s showed.[28] Similarly, communist parties remained reluctant to enter into any sort of coalition with the reformists, usually treating them as a front for imperialism and capitalism.[29]

Soviet perceptions and policy toward Latin American bourgeois parties (1973–80)

The collapse of the Allende regime in 1973 represented the high point of a process that had been under way in Latin America for more than a decade. In reacting to the overthrow of bourgeois-reformist regimes, the Soviets initially attributed this phenomenon to the failure of these regimes to perform the tasks assigned to them by the United States under the Alliance for Progress, which thus prompted the United States to "instruct" regional armies to revolt.[30] Soviet analysts had further concluded that the narrow social base of the regimes that were ousted made them easy prey to the military. Most Soviet (and Western) analysts felt that the armies would follow the time-honored practice of returning to their barracks once order was restored. The establishment of permanent military regimes in Argentina, Brazil, and Peru widely dispelled this idea. Since in most cases the various armies not only stayed in power but also often waged an "internal war" against the left, the notion that a military coup need not pose a major obstacle to the activities of the left was no longer valid.

The collapse of the Allende regime illustrated to many in the Soviet Union that even regimes such as Allende's, with the organized support of millions, could be toppled in a military coup with relatively little effort. Further, the events in Chile illustrated how dangerous it was for the left to isolate itself from bourgeois parties. As parts of Latin America came under military rule, the Soviet academic community was obliged to reassess the historical Soviet attitude toward the reformist parties in Latin America and to consider whether they could be a useful partner in breaking the right's monopoly of power.

A more flexible reassessment was aided by changes in the orientation of both the European Christian Democratic and Social Democratic parties. After World War II, the European Social Democrats had drifted to the right, in various cases renouncing all notions of class struggle. The European Christian Democrats, led by De Gasperi and Adenauer, pronounced the struggle with communism as the most important task at hand. Given these attitudes it is hardly surprising that the USSR's attitude toward the Latin American offshoots of these parties was less than enthusiastic.

By the mid-1970s, however, the posture of both groups began to change. The dissolution of colonial empires reoriented Europe's foreign policy away from confrontation, and toward cooperation, with Third World nationalism.

Less dependent on the United States in the wake of Willy Brandt's *Ostpolitik*, the Social Democrats and Christian Democrats became increasingly distanced from America on issues pertaining to the Third World. Both parties criticized the United States' 1965 invasion of the Dominican Republic as well as the US role in the war in Indochina. Regarding the Arab–Israeli dispute, the Social Democrats – once passionate supporters of Israel – by 1974 were insisting on a more "equidistant" position. For example, in the wake of the 1973 Arab oil embargo, the United States advocated a hard line with the Arabs and OPEC, but Europe's Christian and Social Democrats favored an "Arab–European" dialogue.

Both the changes within Latin America and the changes in orientation within the Christian and Social Democratic movements impelled a new Soviet attitude toward reformist parties. After 1974 it became clear to Soviet and communist observers that the only immediate alternatives to bourgeois democracy in Latin America were harsh right-wing military regimes, which totally precluded any possibility of social transformation. Thus, coalitions, or minimal cooperation, with the bourgeois reformist regimes gained currency in Soviet political literature. The questions increasingly asked by the Soviet media were: (1) What was the true aim of the reformist parties in Latin America? (2) What were the motives of the European "mother parties"? (3) What were the prospects for cooperation between the communists and the reformists?

In one of the earliest Soviet analyses of changes within the German Social Democratic party, A. Veber asserted that the Social Democrats were attempting to rid themselves of the stigma of colonialism and thus were willing to support some progressive initiatives throughout the developing world.[31] He viewed their efforts as little more than a public relations act. In Latin America, according to Veber, the Social Democrats were courting such unprogressive elements as Peru's APRA and had therefore lost the support of most progressive forces in the region.[32]

K. M. Obyden, however, believed that cooperation between the Social Democrats and communists in Latin America was both desirable and possible.[33] This was because of a serious change in the Social Democrats' orientation toward the national liberation struggle, brought on by disillusionment following the fall of Allende.[34]

Zorina, writing in the Academy of Sciences' postmortem of the Allende regime, asserted that one of the regime's biggest mistakes was its failure to cooperate with the Christian Democratic party – the only "guarantor" acceptable to the middle class and able to secure its support. Although Allende's efforts to come to terms with the Christian Democrats had been close to consummation on several occasions, the ultra-left had dashed this hope by attacking the middle class. Thus, she stated, Allende's regime was doomed. Zorina concluded with a warning that any progressive regime that did not include parties of the middle class was risking failure and that only by cooperating with the Christian Democrats could the communists wage a credible opposition to Pinochet.[35]

Dabagyan, a noted expert on Venezuela, felt that a coalition between the communists and reformists was not only not essential but also not desirable and probably not possible. He asserted that the nationalist-reformist parties of Latin America, regardless of their designation, were traceable to APRA, which was a *petit bourgeois* reaction to "scientific socialism."[36] Thus, although these parties might be anti-imperialist, they remained firmly pro-capitalist.[37] Furthermore, fundamental differences made any coalition between the communists and the reformists very difficult, since the reformist parties sought a multi-class party led by the bourgeoisie; the communists, although they welcomed the support of all layers of society, insisted on the proletariat's leading role.[38] Nationalist-reformist parties, in Dabagyan's view, feared basic reform. As examples, he cited Peru and Bolivia, where the reformist parties offered the most resistance to the progressive armed forces.[39] In an analysis of the Acción Democrática (AD) party of Venezuela, Dabagyan warned that despite that party's restoration of ties with the USSR and Cuba, its newly preeminent role in the Non-Aligned Movement, and the nationalization of the oil industry, AD (like all Social Democrats) did not really want to change capitalism but merely to "humanize" it.[40]

Despite persistent doubts about the prospects for collaboration between communists and reformists, Moscow truly believed that the Social Democrats had indeed shifted to a more progressive and anti-imperialist posture. I. G. Sibilev, reflecting this view, which appeared to be the prevalent attitude at the Institute of the International Labor Movement, noted that the Social Democrats had begun a progressive evolution since the 20th congress of the CPSU and by 1970 were totally committed to peaceful coexistence.[41] Sibilev noted that the Socialist International had condemned the Pinochet junta, supported Panama's demands for control over the Panama Canal, and urged the United States to break with military regimes, to reduce the role of the multinational corporations, and to lift its trade embargo against Cuba.[42]

Boris Koval', director of the Institute of the International Workers' Movement, in an article coauthored with S. I. Semenov of the Institute of Social Sciences, stated that the current Social Democratic movement was a progressive movement that had nothing in common with the Social Democrats of the 1920s or even the 1960s.[43] The authors felt that the presence of the Social Democrats in Latin America was beneficial to the continent, not only because of their stress on proletarian democracy and a new world economic order but also because their vast experience in defending workers' interests let them lead the workers' movement without allowing it to drift to the ultra-left.[44] Noting that the demise of military regimes in Greece, Portugal, and Spain had resulted in the ascent of the Social Democrats, they believed the Social Democrats would play a similarly important role in a democratic Latin America.[45] Although the authors warned that the Social Democrats, like all reformists, were an opportunistic party that could not be trusted, they considered it vital for communists to form a united front with the Social Democrats in order to avert fascism.[46]

I. V. Danilevich, also of the Institute of the International Workers' Movement, sided with Dabagyan. He argued that the goal of Latin American Social Democrats was "to fuse the reformist labor movement with the needs of capitalism"[47] as well as to provide an alternative not only to fascism but also to communism. Nevertheless, given the events in Chile, he echoed Koval' and Semenov's conclusion that it was imperative for communists and Social Democrats to cooperate.[48]

Yet some analysts continued to resist the notion that an alliance between communists and Social Democrats was possible or desirable.

Such an alliance could have only limited utility, since the Social Democrats would strive as they had in Europe to become part of the capitalist power system.[49] One author asserted that it would be folly to rely on the Social Democrats, who had actually thwarted a socialist revolution in Portugal in 1975 and would never support a true social transformation.[50]

Acknowledging the counterrevolutionary nature of the social democratic movement, Shul'govskii nevertheless claimed that its resentment of foreign capital in Latin America created a basis for a coalition with the communists. Furthermore, only with the participation of the Social Democrats would a broad front to oppose fascism be possible. Only the simpletons of the ultra-left could believe that the Social Democrats were a tool of imperialism.[51] Koval' was more optimistic. He claimed that the growth of the Social Democratic party in Latin America had taken place entirely at the expense of urban middle-class parties, so the center of Latin American political debate had moved to the left. According to Koval', the Social Democrats of Latin America, unlike those of Europe, had a strong populist and anti-imperialist tradition, which made them ideal partners for the communists so long as the communists retained their own sense of identity.[52]

Maidonik maintained that the Social Democrats served the interests of capital, having consistently tried to abort revolutions beginning in Germany during the 1920s and later in Eastern Europe during the 1940s and Portugal in 1975. Although they called for a "new world order," Maidonik identified their goal as a compromise between imperialism and dependent capitalism; he considered them little more than an adjunct to petty reformism.[53] Similarly, an article in *Kommunist* argued that the Social Democrats chiefly sought to arrive at an understanding of the North–South conflict in order to avert a revolution.[54]

Were Social Democrats different from other reformists? One analyst concluded that they were, because they recognized the workers as a class. Even Dabagyan, who had been known for his low opinion of Social Democrats, confessed that he had been wrong in asserting that they were no different from other reformists. He now believed they were willing to carry out a structural reform in the hemisphere and to rely on the teachings of Marx. This changed position may have reflected a pragmatic calculation, since Dabagyan was predicting that the military regimes in Peru and Brazil would be followed by social democratic governments and since he felt that Mexico's PRI was increasingly acquiring social democratic attributes.[55]

The increasing activism of the Social Democrats in the 1970s had been called by Maidonik a design to complement President Carter's "human rights" policy. It is interesting to note that Shafik Handal of the Salvadoran communist party, while agreeing with this link to Carter's policy (itself intended to isolate the region's revolutionary forces in the hemisphere), still felt that under certain circumstances the Social Democrats could be viewed as allies when faced by the threat of fascism.[56] Unlike most Soviet analysts, who felt that President Carter's "human rights" policy complemented the efforts of the Social Democrats, Atroshenko felt that Carter had launched that policy in order to undercut the Social Democrats. Yet despite his deep reservations that the Social Democrats were likely to split the working class and delay the struggle for national liberation, he also felt that the communists should seek the support of the Social Democrats in their confrontation with fascism.[57]

While the debate over the Social Democrats was becoming increasingly topical in the Soviet media, a similar debate emerged regarding the Christian Democrats, who were also expanding their presence in Latin America. Although Soviet analysts had started to reevaluate their attitude toward the Christian Democrats even before Allende's fall, little was written about that party during the mid-1970s. Despite Soviet praise for Venezuela's Christian Democratic party after its restoration of diplomatic ties with the USSR and its legalization of the Venezuelan communist party, there was little Soviet comment about the Christian Democrats in Latin America between 1975 and 1980.

In 1980, however, Soviet interest grew as the German Christian Democratic party increased its activities in Latin America; Venezuela, buoyed by the strength of its oil-based economy, assumed a regional role and often advocated Christian democratic solutions; and the Christian Democrats were playing a greater role in countries shifting from military regimes toward bourgeois democracy. Soviet analysts constantly questioned whether the Christian Democrats would really attempt to introduce some basic changes in the structure of Latin American societies or whether they were merely Washington's substitute for the crumbling military juntas.

Iuri Gvozdev noted that it was difficult even for Washington to assess the potential of the Latin American Christian Democrats, since their posture was confused and contradictory.[58] Gvozdev linked the resurgence of Christian democratic activity to the Sandinista victory in Nicaragua, after which former Prime Minister of Italy Mariano Rumor had declared that the goal of the European Christian Democrats was to foster pluralism in Central America.[59] Yet it was because Christian

Democratic parties comprised all social layers that their policies lacked consistency: On the one hand they might support noninterference in the Eastern hemisphere; on the other hand, Venezuela's rightist Christian Democrats were increasingly supportive of suppressing the guerrillas in Central America.[60] Similarly, although all the Christian Democrats supported *détente* and peaceful coexistence, many Latin American Christian Democrats still held on to Konrad Adenauer's *Weltanschauung* and embraced the cold war. Thus, they had entered into a coalition with the junta in El Salvador, which made that country into a "laboratory" for testing a combination of reforms and repression in order to defend the existing order in Central America.[61]

Gvozdev, however, did not wish to generalize from the El Salvadoran experience. He wrote:

> Despite differences as regards specific world political issues and the contradictory nature and inconsistency of practical activities, a current is taking shape in Latin American Christian Democracy which truly champions the interests of the overwhelming majority of the population and stands for freedom, justice and democracy . . . It is the influence of the patriotic forces among the Christian Democrats of the Andean Pact countries that prompted them to display effective solidarity with the heroic struggle of the Nicaraguan people against the Somoza tyranny.[62]

Gvozdev believed that "the anti-dictatorship stance of a part of the Latin American Christian Democracy could serve as a basis for cooperation with the followers of Marxist ideology."[63] He praised the determined stance of the progressive Venezuelan Christian Democrats under Rafael Caldera Rodríguez, who had refused to criticize the regime in Grenada and to break with Cuba. In this he was joined by M. M. Gurvits, who felt that the progressive nature of the Venezuelan Christian Democrats, including their tenacity in opposing US domination in the hemisphere, made them the model Latin American party for the 1980s.[64]

Aside from the change in its rhetoric during this period, the USSR warmed somewhat toward those Latin American countries governed by reformist parties. By the late 1960s Moscow had not only stopped supporting the Venezuelan communist insurgency against the regime, it had actually restored ties with it. Similarly, Costa Rica's José Figueres, harshly criticized in the Soviet media during the 1960s, was by 1970 offered much more respect and even visited Moscow at the Soviets' invitation. In fact, until the FSLN took power in Nicaragua in 1979, Costa Rica was the only Central American country with a Soviet embassy. The USSR also restored ties with Colombia, despite continuing communist guerrilla warfare in that country.

Although one can dismiss these improved relations with reformist regimes as part of a general pattern of improved Soviet–Latin American ties after 1968, and although Moscow did expand its diplomatic ties with most Latin American countries, and although the bulk of Soviet credits to Latin America went either to Allende's Chile or to military-ruled Argentina, Brazil, and Peru, nevertheless, there was a qualitative change in the Soviet attitude toward the reformist regimes. Although the USSR's policy toward Latin America remained totally opportunistic, Moscow was willing to be more closely identified with the reformist than with the military regimes of the region. For example, no Politburo members were sent to visit any of the military-governed countries, nor were their heads of state invited to visit Moscow. This was despite close ties between the USSR and both Argentina and Brazil, which were strengthened when these countries defied the US-imposed grain embargo of 1979. In fact the only Latin American heads of state to visit Moscow were Mexican presidents Echeverría in 1973 and López Portillo in 1978, and President Carlos Andrés Pérez of Venezuela in 1976. Similarly, Mexico was the only Latin American country to join the Eastern bloc's Council of Economic Mutual Assistance (CEMA), even though the volume of Soviet trade with Argentina and Brazil was far greater.

Soviet perceptions and policy toward Latin American bourgeois parties (1980–83)

Somoza's defeat in July 1979 definitively illustrated that a revolution in Latin America was indeed possible and that a simple choice between "fascism and bourgeois democracy" might be dated. The prospect of an immediate revolution in Latin America fueled the debate as to whether the Latin American Marxists should seek coalitions with bourgeois reformist parties or whether they should attempt to repeat the Nicaraguan experience.

The issue was raised in a book written by Gornov and Tkatchenko (Gornov, according to Jerry F. Hough, is a pseudonym for Kudachkin, who is the chief of the Latin American section of the Central Committee of the CPSU).[65] The authors stressed that such reformist parties as the Social Democrats arose in order to thwart communism and that they still insisted on a fictitious "third way."[66] Unlike most Soviet analysts during the 1970s, Gornov and Tkatchenko had little belief in the viability of coalitions with the reformists in a confrontation with fascism. The authors stressed that the victory of the Sandinistas resulted from a change in the global correlation of forces and the willingness of the guerrillas to wage a protracted war; the fact that the FSLN had entered a coalition with bourgeois reformists was barely mentioned.[67] Although they conceded that the reformist parties in Chile had moved to the left in response to Pinochet's fascism, the authors stated: "In the struggle to free Chile from tyranny the decisive role must remain firmly in the grip of the working class . . . There is no room for a bourgeois alternative to fascism."[68]

In the final days of the Brezhnev era the debate over the reformist parties and the Nicaraguan model appeared in the pages of *Latinskaia Amerika*, where the nature of the Christian Democratic party was analyzed. S. I. Semenov, chairman of the symposium, stated that an alliance between the communists and the Christian Democrats was useful whenever fascist danger was faced. He concluded, however, that the Christian Democratic party was a bourgeois party and that communists should try to split off the party's left wing.[69] Shul'govskii noted that in recent years the Christian Democrats had veered to the right, as shown by the deletion of calls for a "communal society" from the programs of all Christian Democratic parties and by their treatment in Central America and the Caribbean as a preferred partner of the United States.[70] E. Dabagyan warned that once a threat of fascism was removed, the Christian and Social Democrats would likely join hands to block communist advances.[71] The strongest attack predictably came from Maidonik, who accused the Christian Democrats of following a US line. He noted a parallel between the United States' shift to the right after President Reagan's election and an immediate increasing of reactionary policy in Costa Rica and Venezuela. He further claimed that the Christian Democrats were now courting the multinational corporations. He noted that the Christian Democrats of El Salvador had joined with the military junta and predicted that elements of that party in Chile and Brazil were seeking the same deal with the armies of those countries.[72]

Evgenii Kosarev, deputy director of the Latin American Institute and a past opponent of Maidonik on the issue of Chile,[73] noted that the Christian Democrats of Latin America were a spent force, with no real social base, caught in a contradictory position of trying to please both the local bourgeoisie and foreign capital.[74] Konovalova and Galkin attacked the notion that the Christian Democrats had no social base, defending their past efforts at serious reform and their continuing credibility as a partner to any antifascist coalition.[75] In a similar vein, Kudiukin stressed that, despite their faults, the Christian Democrats might well lead Latin America in its transition from fascism to democracy.[76] V. P. Totskii was less optimistic, observing that the Christian Democrats, once popular for their anti-imperialist stand, had by the mid-1970s become more "Europeanized" and more distant from the masses (in Chile, Brazil, and Venezuela). He pointed to the Brazilian Christian Democrats' refusal to join the church in defense of human rights.

This theme was echoed by Dabagyan, who synthesized the Soviet attitude toward the Social Democrats during the early 1980s. In the last major study of the Social Democrats to be undertaken during the Brezhnev years, Dabagyan claimed that the Social Democrats of Latin America were largely drifting toward the European models that were firmly committed to capitalism, such as that of West Germany,[77] and that in a struggle between capitalism and communism most Social Democrats would side with capitalism.[78] However, he also observed that many of the region's Christian Democrats realized that even the slightest reform might necessitate a revolution (for example, El Salvador's Guillermo Ungo, who started as José Napoleón Duarte's Christian Democratic running mate and later became a leader of the El Salvadoran guerrillas).[79] Dabagyan concluded that a growing group of the Social Democrats – tired of the notion of "democratic socialism," which could not be implemented in Latin America anyway – rejected their previous sole reliance on a "peaceful way."[80] Given this and their 1977 declaration that each party was free to decide whether to cooperate with the communists, Dabagyan felt that there was room for an alliance between those two parties. He argued that although the Social Democrats remained strongly anticommunist, they could nonetheless cooperate with communist parties, especially when faced with dictatorships, such as that in El Salvador.[81] In countries where the Social Democrats were in power, the communists should remain respectful of the country's institutions, since those regimes were tolerant of communism and because "the Social Democrats have as their power base masses which are the reserve potential of a revolutionary force."[82] Nevertheless, Dabagyan observed, communists should be aware that whenever the Social Democrats talked about a change in the international economic order, they were talking not about scrapping capitalism but merely about a greater role for Latin America within that system.[83]

Although there were few overt changes in the Soviet policy toward those countries where either the Social Democrats or the Christian Democrats were in power, a subtle reorientation in Moscow's policy could be detected. For example, in 1981 there was a policy shift in the Chilean communist party, which for years after Pinochet's coup had insisted that the only way to oust the military junta was through a united front against fascism with both Christian and Social Democrats. Together with the ultra-leftist MIR, the communists created the Manuel Rodríguez front, now involved in guerrilla warfare against the regime. A similar development occurred in El Salvador, whose communist party until 1979 had sought a broad alliance with either the Christian or the Social Democrats. Shifting its approach, the party joined several other Castroite groups in a guerrilla uprising. Similarly, the Guatemalan communist party, which as late as October 1979 had supported a broad coalition with the various reformist parties against the military junta, by January 1981 reversed its reliance on a coalition with reformist parties and entered an alliance with other leftist guerrillas.

Soviet policy toward the region's reformist regimes cooled considerably. Thus, both Venezuela and Costa Rica were severely criticized in the Soviet press for their unfriendly attitude toward Nicaragua and for Venezuela's support for Duarte in El Salvador. Whereas Soviet policy had traditionally shown deference to Mexico, recurring criticism was launched at Mexico for its failure to free itself from economic dependence on the United States. The USSR's "nonresponse" to the Contadora initiative, begun by Colombia, Mexico, Panama, and Venezuela, can be viewed as yet another indication of cooling Soviet enthusiasm toward the reformist regimes of the region, as compared with the 1970s. Thus, by 1980 the Soviet belief that reformist parties and regimes were the sole vehicle for ridding Latin America of right-wing militarism was clearly gone. Events in Nicaragua had revived the belief in wars of national liberation.

10 Wars of national liberation or peaceful transformation?

Although the preponderant power of the United States in Latin America played a pivotal role in forming the Soviet perception of the region, and indeed often influenced the extent of Soviet willingness to become involved in the hemisphere's affairs (either itself or through Cuba), it was nevertheless the perception of the domestic correlation of forces that ultimately determined the Soviet prognosis of Latin America's political future. The usual Western analysis of changing Soviet attitudes, which correctly identifies the time periods involved, is weak in that it assigns primary importance to external forces acting on Latin America rather than to regional domestic realities. Thus, the course of Soviet attitudes is characterized as follows: (1) Between 1960 and 1962, when the USSR – buoyant, due to the Cuban revolution – expected a rapid repetition of similar wars of national liberation throughout the region. (2) Between 1962 and 1968, when the USSR was chastened by the confrontation with the United States during the Cuban missile crisis and consequently abandoned the notion of wars of national liberation in Latin America but continued to express verbal support (so as not to be upstaged by China as the world leader of the left). (3) Between 1968 and 1980, when the USSR, no longer concerned by the Chinese challenge and far more interested in *détente* with the United States, cracked down on Castro's efforts to "export revolution" and downplayed its belief in the viability of wars of national liberation. (4) From 1980 to the present, after the collapse of *détente*, after the invasion of Afghanistan by Soviet troops in December 1979, and after the victory of the Sandinistas in Nicaragua, when Moscow ceased to be inhibited by Washington's sensitivities and resumed its support for Latin American wars of national liberation.

This analysis is also mistaken in assuming that Soviet attitudes toward wars of national liberation were well defined and hence, that when the shifts occurred, they were clear and distinct. In reality, Soviet

135

attitudes were far more ambivalent, and the shifts that did occur in favor of either wars of national liberation or peaceful transformation were more a matter of emphasis than an outright substitution of one position for another. Furthermore, as noted in the previous chapter, Third World societies were no longer analyzed only in terms of correlation of forces among various classes but also in terms of their histories, cultures, and political institutions.[1] This chapter illustrates how changes in Soviet perceptions of Latin America's domestic structure influenced Moscow's attitude toward the appropriate methods of social transformation on that continent.

Brezhnev's early years (1964–68)

Brezhnev inherited the problem of responding to the upsurge of revolutionary activity taking place in several Latin American countries, which was largely inspired by the 1959 Cuban revolution. Although the euphoria of the Khrushchev era had faded, along with expectations of a rapid repetition of the Cuban experience, Moscow remained ambivalent as to whether this surge of revolutionary activity had run its course. As the most developed part of the "periphery," was Latin America fertile ground for a basic social transformation, or did it lack sufficient class differentiation to sustain a revolution?

B. I. Koval' asserted that objective conditions made Latin America ripe for a revolutionary transformation and that it could skip *prerastat'*, the usual prerequisite bourgeois phase, and proceed directly toward a socialist revolution.[2] According to Koval', the communists were aware of such favorable conditions and thus rejected the concept of bourgeois reformism, a "diversion" from national liberation.[3] Although he conceded that the Latin American working class had yet to reach maturity, Koval' emphasized that "a national-democratic revolution led by the working class is possible."[4]

Rodney Arismendi, leader of the Uruguayan communists, noted that, despite improved conditions in Latin America, the main task of the Uruguayan communists was to gain the support of the proletarian masses. This proposition posed something of a dilemma in that any attempt to take power via a war of national liberation was fraught with danger, but a communist decision to avoid participation in such an uprising might discredit the party as a revolutionary force. "Hence if to expose an isolated vanguard to the enemy fire and sacrifice the finest revolutionary cadres would be foolhardiness, then retreat and surrender of positions in default of fighting . . . must be regarded as a complete capitulation."[5]

The debate intensified in late 1964 and early 1965, when the authoritative *Kommunist* took up the issue in several articles published almost together – a fact that seems to indicate serious debate within the Soviet elite. The absence of a firm, official line on the issue seems implied by the later appearance of divergent Latin American views in the *World Marxist Review*, published under the vigilant eye of Ponomarev's International Department of the CPSU.

M. Kudachkin and N. Mostovets (both noted Latinamericanologists) took a very pessimistic position, stating that Latin America was not ready yet for a revolutionary transformation: "Under present circumstances, necessary revolutionary changes may be achieved only if all national anti-imperialist forces are united. The achievement of unity is a difficult and lengthy process . . . attempts at artificially 'speeding up' the revolution . . . are destined to fail."[6] The authors also accused those who advocated immediate armed struggle of being "anti-party Trotskyites," whose sole accomplishment was to provoke fascist coups.[7] Kudachkin and Mostovets challenged the advocacy of a prolonged guerrilla war in the countryside and, drawing on the failed 1963 Peruvian rebellions, asserted that "the mass of the workers and the peasantry are not ready for armed struggle."[8] Furthermore, the guerrilla warfare waged by the Venezuelan communists had demonstrated the lack of "broad unity among all opposition forces."[9]

After this rather grim statement *Kommunist* published an article by A. M. Sivolobov (a party cadre with no experience in Latin America), who asserted that the precondition for change in Latin America's social structure was fundamental agrarian reform, itself attainable only with a revolutionary government in power.[10] Sivolobov predicted that "peaceful forms of struggle used by the peasants will change into direct action by the masses,"[11] which was bound to spread throughout the region. He lauded the peasant uprisings occurring in most of Latin America, especially the rural guerrilla warfare in Venezuela and Peru.[12] His emphasis on the role of guerrilla warfare in the countryside bore a striking resemblance to the strategy advocated by Che Guevara.

However, another analysis maintained that the domestic realities of Latin America precluded revolutionary transformation. This major study on Third World prospects for such transformation, published by *Kommunist*, declared: "In most countries of Latin America it is impossible to liquidate dependence on imperialism and foreign monopolies without the uprooting of the existing sociopolitical structure."[13]

Instead of supporting the revolutionaries of Peru or Venezuela, the authors praised such mild anti-imperialist forces as the Brazilian Workers' Party (PTB) and the Chilean Christian Democrats,[14] and they castigated opponents of the peaceful transformation thesis as ultra-leftists who divided the popular masses.[15]

Soviet ambiguity toward armed struggle was again manifest in the *Kommunist* coverage of the 1966 tricontinental conference in Havana. Although armed struggle was a key agenda item, an article describing the conference made no reference to the issue. Yet *Kommunist* subsequently carried an article strongly endorsing armed struggle in Latin America, which stated: "Since the days of Lenin's peace decree, the USSR has defended the people's right to use all means possible against colonial oppression including uprisings and national liberation wars, and continues to defend it."[16]

Latin American communists evinced a similar polarization of attitudes. Pedro Mota Lima, of the Brazilian communist party, emphasized that the local communists must first correctly assess the might of the internal reaction to revolutionary change. Lima implied that thus far the communists had underestimated the strength of the reaction and therefore acted in an adventurist fashion.[17]

Yet José Manuel Fortuny, leader of the Guatemalan communist party during the Arbenz period, felt that the Cuban revolution had provided Latin America with a model of the path toward socialism.[18] He denied any possibility for peaceful revolution, given Latin America's present stage of development and the extra effort that the United States and the region's reactionaries were making to preserve the status quo after the Cuban revolution.[19] Criticizing the Latin American communist parties for not exerting "a constant and effective political influence on the basic sections of the working class,"[20] Fortuny urged the region's revolutionaries not to await a change in objective conditions but to encourage a "leap" toward socialism.[21]

In contrast, Corvolán of the Chilean communist party viewed the Cuban revolution as "proof of the fact that reality plays havoc with preconceived assumptions; serving as a reminder of the folly of generalizing the singular feature of this or that experience."[22] His party intended to continue its tactic of building a broad coalition and pursuing an electoral strategy.[23]

C. Levano of the Peruvian communist party took a position falling halfway between those of Fortuny and Corvolán. He noted that Peru's communist party had strong peasant links and supported the guerrilla warfare waged in the countryside but that it feared an all-out attempt to launch an armed struggle, since there was no revolutionary situation in the country:[24] "It was a bourgeois concept of MIR to believe that a guerrilla war in the countryside can lead to an all-out revolution."[25] Rather, the Peruvian communists considered the uprising an important "catalyzer" for a future revolution, since Peru's road to socialism would probably be one of "armed struggle."[26] Ramón López similarly denied the existence of a revolutionary situation in Colombia, where, despite a guerrilla uprising by some rural peasants, "the bulk of the population is not involved [in the struggle] and has no interest to join it."[27]

Perhaps the best illustration of the prevailing indecision among Soviet and communist officials was an interview with Rodney Arismendi. He observed that the communists faced "the danger of adventurism," on the one hand, and "conservative stagnation," on the other hand.[28] Siding with Cuba in its disagreement with Moscow and with the Chilean communists over the applicability of the Cuban road to revolution to other countries of Latin America, he wrote:

> Certainly, no one can support the idea of exporting revolution from one country to another. However, only a narrow-minded nationalist will fail to understand that every country must have the cooperation of other countries. In that sense the name of Major Che Guevara the fallen hero in the struggle for the liberation of Bolivia has become a shining symbol of the struggle for the liberation of Latin America [sic].[29]

Soviet ambivalence toward wars of national liberation in Latin America combined with the covert nature of Soviet help to such struggles make it difficult to show a direct link between such wars and Soviet foreign policy – but such links did exist. Thus, during the communist insurrection in Venezuela, the USSR not only attacked the Venezuelan regime in the harshest of terms but actually provided modest help to the rebels.[30] Although there is no evidence of Soviet help to the Peruvian guerrillas, the Soviet media were consistently hostile to Peru's democratically elected president, Belaúnde Terry. By the late 1960s, however, the intensity of the debate regarding the appropriateness of Latin American wars of national liberation noticeably declined. Consequently, although Moscow never officially abandoned its support for such wars, the former emphasis was reduced.

This change in attitude stemmed primarily from changes that occurred within Latin America. The defeats of the communist uprisings in Venezuela and Bolivia illustrated the slim probability of repeating the Cuban experience. In Peru, where the armed forces in 1963–65 had repressed a leftist guerrilla uprising, the military shifted toward the left and began a progressive reorganization of society. In other countries, such as Argentina, Brazil, and Uruguay, the recently active urban guerrilla movements were reduced to insignificance by efficient repression and, in Brazil, by an unprecedented economic boom. In fact, despite endemic guerrilla warfare, by the late 1960s Central America was enjoying an extraordinary expansion in its economy, which alleviated some of the social tensions that had triggered much of the unrest.

Brezhnev's middle years (1970–80)

Between 1970 and 1980 the USSR continued to de-emphasize the viability of wars of national liberation. Moreover, prominent Soviet analysts began to advocate a reclassification of Latin America from a Third World continent to the level of southern Europe. More than anything else, the Soviets were responding to Latin America's changing domestic scene. Institutions formerly perceived by the Soviets as pillars of the oligarchical order – such as the church, the armed forces, and political parties – were radically changing and calling for a break with the capitalist model of development. In Colombia, Mexico, and Venezuela a bourgeois democracy was consolidating itself; in Chile the bourgeois democracy had tolerated the election of the reformist Frei in 1964 and of the Marxist Allende in 1970. In such countries as Brazil and Guatemala, where military dictatorships had installed themselves, the middle class grew rapidly and the armed forces appeared far more concerned with the needs of the bourgeoisie than with the interests of the traditional landed elites.

Given these socioeconomic changes, Shul'govskii and others felt that the region should be analyzed more in the terms that Soviet analysts applied to such countries as Greece, Ireland, Portugal, and Spain than in the context of Asia and Africa. Shul'govskii stated that because of rapid changes in the Latin American class structure, the appropriate way to assure social transformation was for the communists to establish alliances with other progressive elements, such as the church.[31] Similarly, a study released by the Latin American Institute asserted that the task of the Latin American communists was to build broad progressive coalitions. The paper, which did not even mention wars of national liberation, observed that the middle class was rapidly shifting to Marxist-Leninist positions and that all layers of the Latin American bourgeoisie were becoming increasingly progressive.[32] In contrast to the 1966 tricontinental conference in Havana, the 1971 conference of the South American communist parties also called for building broad coalitions and cited Chile as an appropriate model for the continent.[33] Going even further, Tkatchenko stated that only broad-based coalition governments were capable of resisting imperialist pressure. He expressed great hopes for the emerging popular fronts in Uruguay and Venezuela and stated that the major danger to these popular fronts was the Maoist ultra-left, which advocated violence and fascist right.[34]

The Soviets adhered to their belief in the correctness of the peaceful road to socialism in Latin America even after Allende's fall in 1973. They attributed Allende's downfall to his failure first to assess the class correlation of forces and thus to manage the economy in a manner tolerable to the middle class. Allende was also criticized for failing to control the extreme left, which had thwarted his efforts at gaining the support of the Christian Democrats. Boris Ponomarev, the head of the International Department of the CPSU, stated that because Allende had failed to control the left and to accommodate the needs of the middle class, he had allowed the working class to become isolated within the society.[35] Even Brezhnev argued that "the Chilean tragedy has by no means invalidated the communist thesis about the possibility of different ways of revolution, including the peaceful way."[36]

In fact, most Soviet and communist observers believed that the peaceful road to socialism remained the most viable approach and that the main danger was a right-wing reaction provoked by the ultra-left. González Mansera of the Venezuelan communist party held that the Latin American masses shared in the belief that wars of national liberation were not the only way to alter the existing political order. He recalled the mass support for his party in the 1960s and said that all Latin American communists should take a lesson from his party's "historic error" of plunging into a war of national liberation.[37] In addition, some Soviet analysts became so enthused about the peaceful road that they implied that regional governments were already pushing their societies in that direction. D. Lozinov stated that the first step toward national liberation was the removal of US corporations in the area and that the existing regimes were ending their presence under popular pressure.[38]

Nevertheless, there were some dissenters. Maidonik asserted that the Chilean experiment had failed because the regime had focused too heavily on the needs of the middle class, not because it had ignored them. Furthermore, Allende had not forced a change in the balance of power within Chile – as any revolutionary should have known, there could be no agreement between the working class and an "unbroken" bourgeoisie.[39] Accepting the Stalinist dictum that class struggle intensifies as the revolutionary process advances, Maidonik stated that "a halfway revolution digs its own grave."[40] In other words, "revolutionary change is possible if all power is in the hands of the working class; and only then can a revolution make economic compromises."[41] He concluded his article with a startling remark: that a peaceful transformation is possible only in countries blessed with such unique conditions as a neutralized state apparatus (one that would not actively oppose a radical state transformation – such as the Czech army in 1948) or encirclement by other socialist states.[42]

Kudachkin, while not rejecting the idea of a peaceful revolution, nevertheless accepted the peaceful way primarily as a first step toward socialism. According to Kudachkin, the greatest weakness of the Allende regime had been the failure of the socialists and communists to agree on how to consolidate power. Such a consensus would have precluded a bourgeois return to power.[43]

Similarly, several leaders of the Latin American communist parties started to dispute the validity of the peaceful road toward socialism. Carlos Luís Prestes of the Brazilian communist party charged that Shul'govskii overestimated both the communists' ability to influence the labor movement in the hemisphere and the power of progressive elements within the movement.[44] Luis Corvolán of the Chilean communist party, who was for years identified with the peaceful road to socialism, by 1978 appeared to have moved closer to Maidonik's position: "Whenever a revolution starts to mark time and goes over to the defensive . . . the correlation of forces eventually changes in favor of its enemies."[45] Corvolán concluded that the communists confused the control of government with the control of power, and he stated that for a revolution to succeed, "The hegemony of the working class and its vanguard are crucial factors."[46]

However, the prevailing consensus among both Soviet and communist observers was that, given the current balance of forces among the various classes in Latin America, there was no hope for wars of national liberation. Thus, Shafik Handal dismissed any advocates of armed struggle as "nihilists"[47] and stressed that the Salvadoran communist party would remain committed to building a broad antifascist coalition with all progressive forces, including the Christian Democrats led by José Napoleón Duarte.[48] Similarly, S. A. Sergeev, in a summary of Soviet perceptions of the internal situation in Latin

America, asserted that 1978 was a year of fundamental change in Latin America – and that new opportunities for social transformation had been created – because in several countries (notably, Brazil) the military had retreated from power. He contended that the capacity of contemporary Latin American armies made armed struggles foolish. The communists should therefore establish a dialogue even with right-wing military regimes; under the present conditions, the communists should also adhere to the peaceful road to socialism and persevere in building broad coalitions.[49]

Soviet perceptions of the "Europeanization" of Latin American politics also continued. As Moscow perceived that Latin America's domestic structure was becoming more similar to Europe's and less like that of the rest of the Third World, the USSR introduced a policy similar to Soviet policy in Europe. Communist parties of the region were urged to imitate the policies of Eurocommunism, by which the communists attempted to gain legitimacy through entering coalitions or supporting left-of-center governments. Whereas during the 1960s the USSR had provided moral and at times even limited material support to certain guerrilla movements in Latin America, by the 1970s the Soviets were almost as aloof toward the Latin American guerrillas as they were toward such European urban guerrillas as the Baader-Meinhof gang in Germany and the Red Brigade in Italy. There is no evidence of Soviet support during this period to any of the various guerrilla movements in Latin America. The USSR did not aid the Sandinista guerrillas in Nicaragua, and it continued to expand its state-to-state relations with Colombia, apparently without aiding its communist-supported guerrilla movement. Similarly, during the 1970s, Soviet commentators and the Chilean communists exiled in Moscow and Rome continued to urge a broad coalition between the remaining Chilean communists and the Christian Democrats, labor unions, and the church in opposing the Pinochet regime, but they shunned the guerrilla activities of the ultra-leftist MIR. In sum, the thrust of Soviet policy during the 1970s was to establish state-to-state relations with as many Latin American states as possible, and no known effort was made to bolster wars of national liberation in Latin America.

Brezhnev's late years (1980–83)

The Sandinista victory in Nicaragua, and the general retreat of right-wing regimes from power in most of Latin America, rekindled the debate between believers in the peaceful road to socialism and wars of national liberation. The apparent consensus of the 1970s was dispelled, as rapid changes on the Latin American scene in the late 1970s and early 1980s inspired a variety of responses. On the one hand, the Sandinistas' victory appeared to illustrate, once again, that armed struggle was the only proven way to socialism. The peaceful route attempted in Chile, or reliance on leftist military regimes, as in Bolivia and Peru, had failed. On the other hand, the climate created by the demise of rightist military regimes in Argentina, Brazil, and Uruguay, along with the modest "opening" in the Mexican political system, allowed the Latin American communists for the first time in decades to try to expand their power base in the open.

To analyze the issue, the Latin American Institute called a conference, published first in *Latinskaia Amerika* and then in a book by the Academy of Sciences. Rodney Arismendi, the only Latin American invited to contribute, rejected the abandonment of the peaceful road to revolution: "Nicaragua does not cancel out the Chilean experience or, in other words, the possibility that peoples of some countries can come to socialism by employing various democratic means without civil wars or armed uprisings. It would be wrong to explain away the Chilean tragedy as just choosing the wrong path."[50] It should be noted, however, that Arismendi accepted armed struggle in principle as appropriate for Latin America; its past failures were a result of poor tactics rather than incorrect doctrine.[51]

Unlike Arismendi, Leonov rejected the peaceful road, because, according to him, a successful revolution implied that the new regime must destroy the existing army. Leonov also rejected any possibility of a broad alliance between revolutionaries and the bourgeoisie.

> Reference is here to unity both of the political forces [from the left forces to the national bourgeoisie] and of the political and military leadership of the revolutionary movement. That is yet another lesson of the Cuban revolution. There can be no full internal unity as long as these leaderships are divided and flaunt their having either military force or political prestige.[52]

Maidonik, while agreeing with Leonov, stressed that a successful revolution demanded the unity of all leftist forces (apparently including the ultra-left).[53]

Shul'govskii, who always claimed that Latin American armies were institutions with revolutionary potential, stated that Cuba and Nicaragua had armies that were unusually "praetorian," and he rejected Leonov's notion that a successful Latin American revolution must destroy the old army, calling the idea "vulgar antimilitarism."[54] Shul'govskii also rejected armed struggle as the only way to revolution in Latin America. He maintained that one could hardly draw such a conclusion from the Nicaraguan experience.[55]

Boris Koval', however, stated that the Nicaraguan experience had validated Guevara's beliefs: (1) Popular forces can defeat a regular army. (2) It is unnecessary to wait until all the conditions for revolution mature, as an uprising can induce these conditions where they do not yet exist. (3) In underdeveloped countries guerrilla war can be carried out in the countryside.[56] It was his acceptance of the second proposition that was most significant. In a major article addressing the prospects for social transformation in the Third World and Latin America in particular, Koval' stated that, in today's world, revolutions tended to "deepen" and "broaden" themselves very rapidly, and thus that there was no need to wait until all the objective conditions were ripe. Revolutions could be introduced even in developing countries, since the time required for a society to mature from one social phase to another was now considerably shorter.[57] Although Koval' continued to endorse the idea of communists entering a broad coalition, his new attitude toward such coalitions was that they were nothing more than tactical first steps.[58] Similarly, Iu. Korolev amended his former advocacy for the peaceful road and declared that it was possible only as a first step toward the working class's consolidation of power – and, even then, only when the communist party had the overwhelming support of the working class.[59]

Somoza's defeat in July 1979 had a profound effect on the communist parties of the entire hemisphere, and particularly on the communist parties of Central America. Both the Guatemalan and Salvadoran communist parties reacted quickly. The Guatemalan party, crushed after the fall of Arbenz and operating in a country with one of the largest middle classes and the most efficient repressive military regimes in Central America, responded that it was unprepared for a confrontation with the regime. Carlos González of the Guatemalan communist party stated that "it is vital to combat all gambles and provocations that may enable the reaction and imperialists to drive the people to even greater calamities ... The ultra-right's [plan] is designed to compel us to resort to adventurism and to divert us from our efforts."[60]

The Salvadoran communist party (PCES) took the opposite view. The PCES reversed its position on a peaceful way and, within months of the FSLN victory in Nicaragua, endorsed the concept of an immediate war of national liberation for El Salvador. Jaime Barrios of the PCES, contributing to the same article in which González' statement appeared, declared: "El Salvador has entered a decisive revolutionary stage."[61] Shafik Handal went further and proclaimed that the PCES was always ready to resort to revolutionary warfare at the right moment, and "the right moment is now."[62]

The debate continued unabated until the end of the Brezhnev era. For example, T. E. Vorozheikina, a student of Maidonik, observed that the role of the Nicaraguan communist party during the revolution was "sad" and that "armchair" revolutionaries accused true revolutionaries of being Maoists or ultra-leftist in order to avoid their revolutionary duty.[63] A more cautious position was taken by M. F. Gornov (as noted earlier, probably Kudachkin), who stated that although events in Cuba and Nicaragua had proved that there could be no change in the social structure without a confrontation with imperialism, such a confrontation could not be carried out without the support of a broad coalition: "The struggle against imperialism is not carried out by the communists alone, but also by other leftists, students, workers, the *petite bourgeoisie* and the middle class."[64] Rejecting the notion that an alliance with other democratic elements should be viewed merely as a tactical first step, Gornov urged communist parties to oppose not only right-wing opportunism, but also the ultra-leftist position that revolutionary steps can be skipped.[65]

On the burning issue of El Salvador, the Soviet academic community divided into two camps. On the one side, Maidonik and Vorozheikina led a group in the Institute of World Economy that asserted that it was possible to repeat the Nicaraguan experience and that the strategy of wars of national liberation could be pressed until success was at hand. On the other side, a group led by Vol'skii and Shul'govskii stressed that, unlike Somoza, who had lost all support at home, Duarte retained the support of the middle class, Washington, and a viable army. Thus the only option open to the guerrillas was negotiation with the Duarte regime that might set El Salvador on the road toward peaceful transformation.[66]

Thus, the closing years of the Brezhnev era witnessed division among Soviet analysts and Latin American communists regarding the prospects for a successful revolutionary transformation of the region and the most promising path toward this goal. The "consensus" that emerged in the early 1980s, therefore, advocated a two-track approach. In the "European" countries of Latin America, where there were large bourgeois classes in power or about to gain power, Soviet analysts and

Latin American communists would maintain support for the peaceful way and persevere in building broad coalitions. In countries where there was no hope for a peaceful transformation, the communists would pursue wars of national liberation, even if this entailed an alliance with the ultra-left.

Thus, Gilberto Viera – leader of the Colombian communists, who had been engaged in guerrilla warfare for more than two decades – agreed to accept the truce offered by President Betancur. Similarly, the Brazilian communist party accepted the existing situation in that country and started to seek alliances with other left-of-center parties. This shift was such a deep break with the party's traditional attitude that it necessitated the sacking of Carlos Prestes, who had led that party for nearly fifty years. A similar tack was taken by the communist party in Mexico, where, as mentioned earlier, the political system was undergoing a somewhat more modest "opening." In addition most Soviet analysts consistently urged the Latin American communists to join hands with the progressive elements of the region's bourgeois parties, leftist church organizations, and other political actors, such as the progressive military and trade unions.

According to the second track of the approach, those Central American armies that remained a praetorian guard of the existing order were to be destroyed. Support for this policy was shown on the eve of the "final offensive" in El Salvador. Kudachkin and Karen Brutents, both high officials in the Central Committee, accompanied Shafik Handal on a tour of several East European countries, Vietnam, and North Korea. The result was a substantial infusion of weapons from those countries. Similarly, the Guatemalan communist party, which had shied away from a war of national liberation as late as November 1979, by 1980 had reversed its position and was willing, at least theoretically, to support a violent revolution. The Chilean communist party, which was credited with pioneering the "vía pacífica" and tenaciously held to this doctrine even after the Pinochet coup, in 1980 broke off negotiations with the Christian Democrats concerning a broad coalition in opposition to the military junta. It now endorsed the concept of armed struggle and entered an alliance with its traditional gadfly, the MIR.[67]

Thus, Soviet perceptions and policy regarding Latin America's potential for wars of national liberation changed during the Brezhnev years in response, primarily, to changes in the regional correlation of forces. Although clearly defined turning points are not discernible, by the end of the 1960s the USSR had assumed a low profile on wars of national liberation. During the 1970s it apparently withdrew any former support for such activities. The success of the Sandinistas in 1979, however, inspired a renewed willingness to pursue guerrilla warfare in those countries considered to be beyond the hope of a peaceful social and political transformation.

Part III

Soviet–Latin American relations during the Brezhnev era

Introduction

Moscow's non-interest in Latin America prior to the Cuban revolution can be attributed to several factors, not the least of which was US influence in the region after World War II. However, it would be simplistic to characterize this influence as the sole basis for Soviet policy, then or later. To begin with, the newly independent states of Asia and Africa in fact monopolized Soviet diplomatic and economic activity in the Third World during the Khrushchev era. Moscow hoped that these new elites, resentful of Western economic and political imperialism, would launch "revolutionary democratic" regimes that would be antibourgeoisie in nature and would practice "positive neutralism" and oppose foreign investment.[1] Latin America's economic dependence on the United States gave rise to no such hopes.

Moreover, the preferred economic models of the USSR and Latin America were incompatible. The Soviet-advocated "import substitution model" – by which Third World nations would develop indigenous industrial capacities so as to substitute locally produced industrial goods for Western imports – had been tried in Latin America in the 1930s and was associated there with inefficiency, technological backwardness, and chronic current account deficits. Only Peronist Argentina, with its antibourgeoisie rhetoric, supported import substitution, signing an isolated bilateral agreement with Moscow in 1952.[2]

The Cuban revolution of 1959 and the reestablishment of diplomatic relations with Brazil in 1961 (which would later deteriorate after the 1964 coup) raised Soviet interest in Latin America but did little to improve Moscow's ties with that continent. More important to Moscow was its ideological struggle with China and its desire not to alienate the maverick Castro regime. Thus, most Latin American states drew closer to the United States as Moscow, pressured by China and Cuba to support wars of national liberation, declared support for Castro's export of revolution. Attempting to impose some degree of discipline on Castro and to unify the political position of all Latin American communists, the USSR called the 1964 Havana conference and consolidated support for the region's freedom fighters. Yet the concept of armed struggle was not universally accepted by Latin American communists, and there is little to indicate that the USSR backed up its rhetorical support for guerrilla wars with any commitment of resources.

In 1964 the USSR reestablished ties with Chile,[3] beginning what would constitute its primary involvement in Latin America during the Brezhnev era – the expansion of diplomatic and economic ties. This was a more pragmatic policy than Khrushchev's in that potential economic gain for Moscow held more weight than a country's "progressive" credentials. Even before Khrushchev was ousted an increasing number of Soviet analysts took an unabashedly Menshevik position, stating that before Latin America could undergo any profound social transformation, the continent would have to experience further capital accumulation that would expand the power of the middle class.[4]

Diplomatic initiatives soon followed with Brazil in 1965, despite its brutal repressions of communists and the fact that it was the sole South American state to participate in the occupation of Santo Domingo. Moscow issued substantial credits to both Chile and Brazil and engaged in diplomatic visits. In 1968, as Moscow was verbally supporting the Colombian communist guerrillas, negotiations began for the reestablishment of diplomatic ties with Bolivia, Colombia, and Venezuela. In addition, Moscow entered into commercial agreements with Costa Rica, Ecuador, and Uruguay.[5] By 1971 the USSR had established diplomatic ties with all of Latin America except the Dominican Republic, Haiti, Honduras, and Paraguay.[6]

Moscow moved with greater confidence in Latin America as the Sino-Cuban alliance weakened and both countries' significance to the communist movement diminished. By 1967 China had drifted into self-imposed isolation, as a result of its "cultural revolution," and within a year Cuba's economy had seriously deteriorated. Yet it was the establishment of leftist regimes in Bolivia, Chile, and Peru that significantly heightened the level of Soviet trade with, and aid to, the region. As stated by candidate Politburo member Ponomarev, "The victory of the Popular Unity bloc in Chile, the progressive struggle in Uruguay and other countries have led us to believe that the revolutionary process there [that is, Latin America] is continuing to develop at a faster pace than in other parts of the nonsocialist world."[7]

However, regardless of the emergence of leftist regimes in the Andean region, Moscow's overall policy toward Latin America did not change as it did toward Egypt after 1954 or toward Ethiopia after the ousting of Haile Selassie. During the early 1970s Soviet policy basically consisted of moderate support for the leftist regimes of Bolivia, Chile, Panama, and Peru and of continued expansions of economic ties with the traditional regimes of Argentina, Brazil, Colombia, Mexico, and Venezuela. Some military aid was also provided.

The Soviet commitment to expanding economic ties with Latin America was manifest in various ways. Whereas in 1968 Latin America accounted for only 0.5 percent of total Soviet bloc credits extended to developing countries, by the late 1970s (notably, after the demise of leftist regimes in Bolivia, Chile, and Peru) the region accounted for 15 percent of these credits, with Argentina and Peru being the first and second recipients of CEMA aid to the Third World.[8] Mexico was granted an affiliated status with CEMA in 1975. In the end, the USSR expanded its trade with almost all Latin American countries – trade that allowed Latin America to enjoy consistent surpluses, as opposed to sustained chronic deficits experienced through trade with the capitalist centers.

Moscow maintained its pragmatic policy approach toward Latin America in spite of the right-wing, brutally anticommunist Argentine regimes of Generals Videla and Viola. Even before the USSR was forced by President Carter's grain embargo to turn to Argentina as a vital source of grain, Moscow did its best to expand ties with Argentina. Despite Argentina's direct support for both the Somozistas and the Salvadoran armed forces, the USSR provided that country with nuclear fuel. Similarly, the USSR participated in Brazil's ambitious electrification program and cooperated with Brazil in a hydroelectric construction program on the Cuanza River in Angola.

At times, however, Soviet policy toward Latin America was contradictory and ambiguous. Thus, during the Falklands War of 1982, the USSR, unlike Cuba, proved unable to capitalize on the waves of anti-British and anti-American feelings sweeping Latin America. Unlike Cuba, Peru, Venezuela, and other Latin American countries, the USSR did not offer any meaningful, prompt assistance to Argentina. Even more curious, Moscow failed to veto a UN Security Council resolution that was far more favorable to Britain than to Argentina.

To conclude this overview of factors impinging on Soviet–Latin American relations through the Brezhnev era, it is important to place this discussion in the context of Soviet–Third World relations. It is true that the USSR made a concerted effort to expand economic and diplomatic ties with South America. It is also true that the successful Nicaraguan revolution led many Soviet analysts to believe that Central America's prospects for a revolutionary transformation were improved. In fact, the USSR did provide some support for the "final offensive" launched by leftist guerrillas in El Salvador in early 1981. However, at no time did Moscow's zeal and interest in Latin America approach its interest in Asia or Africa. The Western hemisphere remained of mostly peripheral concern to Brezhnev's policymakers.

11   Case study: Mexico

Mexico was the first Latin American country, and indeed one of the first countries in the world, to recognize the Bolshevik regime. Mexico and Russia emerged at about the same time from their respective revolutions, both of which were directed in large measure against the existing world order, and thus it was natural that the two countries felt sympathy for each other. Moreover, Lenin saw in Mexico a potential counterweight to the expansion of the United States, the most powerful member of the imperialist bloc, while the Mexican government of President Carranza hoped that Russia's anti-imperialist policy would constrain future US interventions in Mexico.[1]

The apex of Soviet–Mexican relations was reached during the mid-1920s, when Alexandra Kollanti was appointed ambassador to Mexico. Relations deteriorated in 1930, when Mexico first alleged that the Soviet embassy had aided a Comintern-directed uprising in Veracruz province and then broke its diplomatic ties with the USSR. Relations remained poor during the Spanish civil war, despite the fact that Mexico and the USSR were the only countries to support the Republican side openly. This was due to Mexico's having granted refuge to Trotsky and its bitter criticism of the Molotov–Ribbentrop Pact of 1939.

Soviet–Mexican ties, renewed in 1942, remained minimal, even though Mexico and Argentina were the only Latin American countries to defy US pressure during the cold war and to refuse to sever ties with the USSR. Given Moscow's preoccupation with Asia and Africa, and its fear of challenging Washington in the United States' traditional backyard, Mexico was not included in the Soviet offensive toward the Third World in the mid-1950s. Between 1945 and 1958 the USSR's trade with Mexico amounted to less than $1 million.[2]

It was only after Khrushchev's visit to Camp David in 1959, and the subsequent relaxation of international tensions, that the USSR decided to activate its approach toward Mexico. Mexico, however, in spite of its tradition of independent foreign policy, was not willing to become the only country in Latin America with close ties to the USSR. As a result, Khrushchev's efforts to invite himself to the festivities marking 150 years of Mexican independence were rebuffed.[3] Instead, the USSR was invited to stage a trade exhibition in Mexico City in 1959, the practical results of which were meager, with the total volume of Soviet–Mexican trade in 1960 reaching a mere 4.4 million rubles.[4]

By the time Brezhnev came to power in 1964, the USSR enjoyed relatively good relations with Mexico, yet these were marked by several paradoxes. The USSR was very pleased with Mexico's positions on several key issues, such as its defiance of US pressure and refusal to join the OAS-imposed diplomatic and economic blockade of Cuba as well as its bitter criticism of the US-led intervention in the Dominican Republic in 1965.[5] However, the administration of President López Mateos resisted Moscow's overtures toward closer diplomatic relations,[6] and Moscow's efforts to expand trade relations with Mexico met with little success. Despite its offers to supply drilling equipment to Mexico's Penmex in 1964,[7] and despite the visit to the USSR by Mexico's trade official, Ricardo Zevada, Moscow's trade with Mexico actually fell to 2.2 million rubles in 1966.[8]

Although Mexico's Foreign Minister Flores visited Moscow in May 1968, a visit that resulted in the signing of a bilateral cultural accord, real improvement in Soviet–Mexican relations did not occur until the tenure of President Luis Echeverría (1970–76). Echeverría was anxious to reestablish his "leftist-revolutionary" credentials by following a sharply more anti-US and more radical foreign policy. His image had been tarnished under the previous administration when, as minister of the interior, he had presided over the suppression of the 1968 student demonstrations that resulted in hundreds of deaths.[9] Sharply increased diplomatic contacts with the USSR culminated in Echeverría's visit to Moscow in April 1973. The visit yielded a new trade agreement between Mexico and the USSR as well as the establishment of a mixed trade commission.[10]

The strongly anti-Western rhetoric of the Echeverría administration led the USSR to make policy moves aimed at consolidating the relationship between the two countries. Several parliamentary delegations were exchanged, and, according to one analyst, between 1973 and 1978 there were more contacts between the USSR and Mexico than in the entire postwar period.[11] In addition, Mexico was granted an associate membership in the CEMA and agreed to legitimize its communist party. Yet despite the dramatically improved climate, the establishment of the joint economic commission and Mexico's affiliation with CEMA did not result in a substantial increase in trade. In 1976 the USSR sold Mexico 6.9 million rubles' worth of goods and bought from it 11 million rubles' worth.[12]

Soviet–Mexican relations improved further during the tenure of President López Portillo, who, much as his predecessor had done, attempted to balance his rather conservative domestic policies with a radical foreign policy. In contrast to Echeverría, who was forced to spend the second half of his term dealing with a deepening economic crisis, López Portillo began his term on an optimistic note. The discoveries of oil in the area of the Yucatán Peninsula proved to be much larger than expected, making Mexico, by 1980, the world's fifth-largest oil producer.[13] The increased production of Mexican oil, which appeared to free Mexico from economic dependence on the United States, and López Portillo's strong desire to play a global role deepened the already close Soviet–Mexican relationship. In May 1978 López Portillo visited Moscow and was greeted by Brezhnev with the following words: "We find it is easy to find a common language [with Mexico] when dealing with questions of foreign policy, and our two countries take identical or similar positions when addressing major issues faced by the contemporary world."[14]

Improved relations prompted Moscow to declare that it would sign Protocol II of the Tlatelolco agreement banning nuclear weapons from Latin America. The Soviet announcement was significant, given that Cuba refused to adhere to the treaty. Soviet and Mexican approaches in the region further complemented each other, as shown by Moscow's warm applause for López Portillo's call for a regional effort to restore peace in Central America,[15] by Mexico's joint declaration with France, which called for a dialogue with the FMLN in El Salvador, and by López Portillo's visit to Managua in support of the Sandinista regime.[16]

It would be wrong, however, to assume that Soviet–Mexican relations were without tensions. Soviet analysts continued to complain that Soviet trade with Mexico had remained essentially nonexistent. As Zakharov noted, "Unfortunately relations between the USSR and Mexico have not developed fully . . . the trade between the two countries, in 1977, amounted to only 2.9 million rubles."[17] Furthermore, although Soviet commentators praised Mexico's increasing leadership among Third World countries, they rejected Mexico's support of the thesis that the world was divided between the rich "North," which included the USSR, and the poor "South." There is also speculation that the USSR did not appreciate López Portillo's offer of an oil swap, whereby Mexico would deliver oil to Cuba in exchange for equivalent Soviet deliveries of oil to Spain, thus saving both exporters the cost of transatlantic shipping. George Grayson, an authority on Mexican oil policies, claimed that the USSR effectively stopped the deal because it felt that by ending shipment of oil from the Black Sea to Cuba, it would be loosening the Kremlin's control over Castro.[18]

In conclusion, Soviet–Mexican relations during the Brezhnev era seem to have been marked by two consistent features. On the one hand, there was a continuing and deepening ideological affinity between the two countries, which appeared to agree on almost all political issues. Indeed, the political positions of both countries became increasingly close over the years. On the other hand, however, trade levels remained extremely low and, in fact, insignificant. Not only were the export profiles of the two countries incompatible, but the USSR was unable to penetrate the Mexican market, given Mexico's proximity to the United States and Mexico's traditionally easy access to US capital and technology markets. Indeed, Soviet analysts remained aware that Mexico's economy (revolutionary rhetoric notwithstanding) was drifting toward ever deeper dependence on the United States as a trade partner – which accounted for more than two-thirds of its foreign trade – and on the US corporations that increasingly dominated the most dynamic sectors of Mexico's economy.[19]

Furthermore, despite the emerging similarity in foreign policies and the praise of Soviet analysts for Mexico's independent foreign policy, the Soviets made no secret that they doubted the depth of commitment of Mexico's elites for genuine change in the existing international system. The prevailing perception among most Soviet analysts, as typified by Lapshev,[20] was that Mexico's foreign policy resulted from the clash between the elite and the emergent nationalist bourgeoisie: Whereas the elite affiliated with foreign capital sought a pro-US orientation, those affiliated with local capital sought a more flexible foreign policy that would enable Mexico to expand its export markets. Both elite groups, in order to retain the support of the growing working class, were following a "radical foreign policy" as a "balancing act" meant to placate nationalist and proletarian elements. Thus, it was concluded, the elites were using foreign policy as a tool to preserve the status quo at home.

Given this political skepticism and the absence of any meaningful economic relations with Mexico, the Soviet policy toward Mexico, despite its friendly rhetoric, was passive and reactive. Although Soviet officials continued to praise Mexico's foreign policy in the most lavish manner, the USSR did not attempt to create the kind of enduring institutional ties that it established at various times with Chile, Nicaragua, or Peru. Similarly, whereas other "progressive" Latin American regimes were depicted in the Soviet media as moving toward a noncapitalist model of development, the Mexican regime was never described in the Soviet media as anything more than a bourgeois regime. Although Soviet–Mexican relations are the oldest enjoyed by the USSR with any Latin American country, the absence of Soviet offers of credits and economic or technological support was conspicuous, even if one bears in mind the very modest overall level of Soviet aid to Latin America. It could be argued that, despite the strong similarity in Soviet and Mexican foreign policies, the relationship between the two countries had yet to emerge from its initial superficial phase.

12   Case study: Chile

Chile was always different from the rest of Latin America. Unlike much of the continent, Chile enjoyed a relatively enduring democracy and had a highly developed and politically active working class. In contrast with much of Latin America, where the communist parties rarely amounted to any more than political fringe groups, the communist party of Chile (PCCh) had been a significant factor in Chilean politics since the 1920s and had collaborated with the armed forces during the existence of the short-lived Chilean "socialist republic" in 1931. Aside from the Cuban communist party, which had joined the Batista government in 1942, the PCCh was the only other communist party in Latin America to have participated in a government during the "popular front" era. In addition, although most Latin American communist parties had lost their control over the labor movement by the early 1950s, the PCCh retained its control over the country's largest trade union until the 1973 coup.

Chile established diplomatic relations with the USSR in 1944. In 1946 Gabriel González Videla was elected to the presidency with the support of the communists, several of whom were awarded seats in the cabinet. The following year, as a result of the deepening cold war, Chile broke diplomatic relations with the USSR and outlawed the PCCh. Among the victims of this reversal were negotiations concerning the establishment of a regular ship link between Vladivostok and Valparaíso and barter agreements exchanging Chilean minerals for Soviet equipment.[1]

Progress toward renewed Soviet–Chilean relations was made in 1960, when Chile sent a commercial delegation to the USSR and the USSR airlifted emergency supplies to Chile after that country suffered an earthquake. In 1963 Chile's Julio Felipe visited Moscow, and the first bilateral economic treaty between the USSR and Chile was signed.[2] More indicative of the gradually improving relationship, however, were the 1964 elections that pitted the socialist–communist coalition of Salvador Allende against Eduardo Frei's Christian Democrats. The Soviet media had been very critical of candidate Frei, charging that he represented the interest of foreign capital and the Vatican. Yet although many Soviet analysts doubted Frei's sincerity about bringing genuine structural reforms to Chile,[3] the USSR was not unhappy to see Frei as Chile's president.[4] In fact, the PCCh, which was notorious for its subservience to Moscow, proclaimed strong support for Frei's domestic policies shortly after the election and probably would have done more had it not been restrained by its socialist partners.[5]

Soviet–Chilean ties then expanded greatly under the Brezhnev Politburo, with Politburo member Kirilenko traveling to Chile to take part in the 13th congress of the PCCh and meeting with President Frei. In 1967 the USSR granted Chile a substantial credit line of $57 million. Although Moscow remained skeptical about the depth and motives of Frei's agrarian reform and his efforts to "Chileanize" the copper industry, it pursued a greater relationship with Chile throughout Frei's tenure. In particular, Moscow praised the regime's opposition to US policies within the OAS and its bitter criticism of the US invasion of the Dominican Republic in 1965.

The election of Salvador Allende to the presidency of Chile in 1970 was a historic event without precedent. For the second time in history a Marxist regime had been voted into office in a freely contested election. The mere fact that a Marxist regime had come to power via the ballot box – with an explicit commitment to respect the pluralistic institutions of the country and simultaneously strive to attain the "dictatorship of the proletariat" by peaceful means – created a slew of ideological problems.

Since the mid-1960s some Soviet observers had supported the idea of a progressive coalition comprising various Latin American forces who had seized power, but it was generally understood that in such a coalition government the communists would play a minority role at best. Such a regime would follow a nationalist anti-US foreign and domestic policy; however, the coalition government would do no more than set the country on the long and arduous path toward noncapitalist development. Even the most optimistic of Soviet observers did not appear to share Corvolán's belief that the Marxists in any country could gain power without ultimately resorting to force. Allende's election challenged many of the standard assumptions. First, the communist party of Chile, by far the largest and the best organized in Latin America, strong and unwavering in its loyalty to Moscow, did not play a minor role (as had been the case in previous "popular front" governments of Chile and Cuba of the 1940s). Instead the communists formed a major component of the Unidad Popular bloc and controlled several powerful national institutions. Second, the classical gendarmes of the Latin American political order, such as the armed forces, the United States, and the existing political institutions of the old regime, appeared to accept the authority of the new president without any overt resistance.

This seemingly noneventful election of a Marxist president in Latin America forced even such a firm believer in armed struggle as Fidel Castro to concede that perhaps there might be such a thing as the "Chilean way." In the 1960s Castro had often chided the PCCh's insistence on a nonviolent path as cowardly and futile, but by 1970 he was attacking those in Chile who insisted on an armed path to revolution. By 1971 Castro was rebuking the ultra-leftist MIR for demanding violent revolution, stating that Allende was marching toward socialism, albeit in a manner different from the Cuban model: "The revolution in our country took place under specific conditions . . . every road was closed – a situation under which there was no alternative. It was under such conditions that a violent struggle, a bloody struggle was waged."[6]

Although the Soviet press superficially welcomed the election of Allende, from the very start there were doubts concerning the survivability of a Marxist regime that had attained power in such an "unorthodox" manner, especially given the volatile nature of Latin American politics and the enduring US interest in the region. Soviet analysts and policymakers, both those who were generally optimistic about the prospects of the Allende regime and those who remained pessimistic, were strongly affected by events in Chile. Allende's first year was a source of great encouragement, as his regime managed to survive the CIA-inspired assassination of General René Schneider without provoking a response from the armed forces, the Chilean economy expanded rapidly, and the inflation rate temporarily declined.

As examples, two statements by high-level Soviet leaders reveal the remarkable shift in the Soviet attitude toward the Allende regime. The first was made by Mikhail Suslov, member of the Politburo and the chief party ideologue, shortly after Allende's election. His characterization of events in Chile was cool: "The national struggle of people of Latin America is growing and intensifying. More than ten years ago, the Cuban revolution smashed the chain of imperialist oppression in

Latin America. New weak links in this chain have become apparent recently in Peru, Chile, and Bolivia."[7] The second was made a year later by Boris Ponomarev, the head of the international department of the CPSU responsible for dealing with the nonruling communist parties. He stated in *Kommunist* that Allende's election was "second only to the Cuban revolution . . . in its significance as a revolutionary blow to imperialism in Latin America."[8] Furthermore, Brezhnev, speaking at the 24th congress of the CPSU, described the victory of Unidad Popular as "a most important event."[9]

These statements reflected increasing Soviet confidence in Chile and the growing importance that the USSR was willing to bestow on it. Even the armed forces of Chile, which like other Latin American armies were the traditional gadfly of Soviet political literature, were referred to in the *World Marxist Review* as the defenders of the regime against "foreign or home reaction."[10] *Krasnaia Zvezda* commented that "the position taken by the armed forces of Chile shows that the political mood of the officers is expressing the will of the masses and allowing the political transformation."[11] There were also reports that the USSR was so impressed with the progressive nature of the Chilean armed forces, especially during the tenure of General Prats as chief of staff, that Moscow was willing to supply the Chilean military with weapons at discount prices.[12]

The euphoria emanating from Moscow in 1971 proved to be short-lived. The assaults on the Allende regime from the historically Castroite MIR raised concern among numerous Soviet observers and the Chilean communist party that MIR's violence might provoke a military reaction that would put an end to Allende's experiment. Furthermore, by 1972 the Chilean rate of inflation had reached 323 percent,[13] and the communist party predicted that "the strong inflationary pressures could make our situation acute."[14]

It was Allende's poor economic performance and his inability to control the ultra-left, rather than an imminent danger of direct US intervention, that was more troubling to the Soviets. Allende was criticized by the Soviets for not maintaining sufficiently close economic ties with such capitalist economic blocs as the EEC and the United States. The Chilean communist, Joaquim Cortes, writing in the Soviet publication *New Times* in February 1972, complained that Allende paid far more attention to distribution than to production, ignoring the needs of the politically vital middle class.

In light of the nagging doubts of many Soviet analysts about whether Allende was capable of surviving, it should be noted that although

Moscow was not willing to underwrite the Chilean economy on the same scale as Cuba's, the USSR granted Chile rather generous credits and significantly increased its purchase of Chilean exports. The exact amount of Soviet aid to Chile is uncertain but it was clearly higher than that given to any country in Latin America other than Cuba. According to the US Department of State, total Soviet aid in 1971–73 was $183 million; an additional $115 million was provided by CEMA.[15] Soviet and Chilean sources claimed that socialist-bloc aid to Chile amounted to $464 million in project aid and $156 million in short-term credits. Paul Sigmund estimated that Moscow's aid to Chile was $364 million.[16]

By late 1972 Moscow was convinced that Allende's days in power were probably numbered. Soviet aid to Chile was reduced sharply from $144 million in 1972 to $63 million in 1973.[17] When Allende made an emergency visit to Moscow in December 1972 to seek additional credits to purchase foodstuffs, the USSR did not offer any additional short-term grants, although it promised to supply Chile with additional aid to develop Chile's power stations, a fishing fleet, and agriculture.[18] Some have suggested that the reason the USSR continued to support the Allende regime at all was because of pressure from the Italian communist party, which considered the Unidad Popular regime to be a model for its drive toward power.[19]

Although there were some Soviet authors who typically blamed almost every problem that Chile confronted on the long arm of the CIA,[20] virtually the entire Soviet academic and political community, along with the Chilean communist party, saw the main challenge to the Allende regime in almost purely Chilean domestic terms. In fact, after the 1973 coup the Central Committee of the CPSU blamed "reactionary forces in Chile" and only once referred to "the support of foreign imperialist forces" – not even mentioning the United States by name. Two weeks after the coup, following extensive American media coverage of US involvement in the coup, *Pravda* referred to "allegations" concerning US involvement, without naming either Nixon or Kissinger.[21]

It is significant that the Soviet leadership, perhaps out of deference to the *détente* in which it had invested heavily, hardly blamed the United States for the misfortunes that beset the Allende regime. Instead the leadership chose to take the view that it was Allende's inept political and economic policies, not Nixon's "invisible blockade," that had led the regime to collapse. Boris Ponomarev, writing in June 1974, explained why the Russian revolution had survived an assault from foreign and domestic foes while Chile's experiment had not:

> Our revolution, too, came up against the fierce resistance of the reactionary bourgeoisie and world imperialism. That resistance suffered a crushing defeat due to a firm, farsighted, principled flexible Leninist policy accepting blocs with other parties, necessary compromises and temporary changes of policy, of which the New Economic Policy was a vivid example. That is why at crucial moments of the revolution, at its turning point, the working class had adequate support from the majority of the people, while the reactionary forces and their henchmen found themselves in isolation.[22]

Ponomarev cast Allende's failed revolution in terms of economic policy that failed to "consolidate" and "reinforce" the social basis of the revolution: "After decisive political success it is the economy that becomes the main field of battle for the revolution."[23]

Such views belonged to the "optimist" school of thought, which explained the fall of Allende's regime in terms of domestic problems caused by economic mismanagement or political inability to control the extreme left. The latter point was made forcefully by Mikhail Kudachkin, who declared: "The Chilean communist party repeatedly unmasked the traitorous and provocative role of the MIR, which by its irresponsible seizures of small private enterprises and lands pushed a significant part of the middle sectors into the camp of the reaction, facilitating the implementation of the fascist coup in the country."[24]

Although the general optimist view was the preferred interpretation – generally accepted as well by PCCh leaders[25] – a group of "pessimists" soon emerged in several circles and viewed the Chilean failure primarily through the traditional prism of US domination of the hemisphere.

After the Chilean coup in 1973 the Soviet-controlled *World Marxist Review* published two "pessimist" articles, in the same issue in which Ponomarev's article appeared – a fact that suggests there were those in positions of authority who believed the United States had almost mythical ability to control events south of the Rio Grande. The first article was by Cheddi Jaggan, general secretary of Guyana's communist party, who asserted that Allende's demise was due directly to US involvement, analogous to the US intervention that had prevented Jaggan's taking power despite an electoral victory.[26] In the second article Nina Tadeo, a Bolivian communist, openly accused the United States of engineering the coup: "Who nurtured the putschists and whom are they serving today? Diagrams, photostats of documents which expose international monopolies, the 'Centaur' plan hatched by the CIA to overthrow the Popular Unity government . . . *The Chilean tragedy is yet another vile crime of world imperialism"*[27] (emphasis in the original).

Pessimism that the United States would not allow a peaceful transition in Latin America was not limited to communist party leaders, such as Castro, who began again to argue that a revolution must take control of all levers of power if it was to withstand the assault of imperialist forces. Several Soviet scholars had cautioned all along that the United States, with numerous policy instruments, was capable of exerting enormous pressure on any Latin American regime. For example, Karen Khachaturov, noted especially as a commentator on ideological issues, asserted that the United States had penetrated all spheres of Latin America's economic, political, and cultural activities so deeply – and that it retained its grasp over Latin America so fundamentally – that, despite Nixon's "low profile" approach to Latin America, the United States had never abandoned the Monroe Doctrine. Given its enormous power it had been able to expand its investment in Latin America and easily topple the Torres and Allende regimes.[28]

Yet, despite several pessimistic voices after the collapse of the Allende regime, the general tone of Soviet analysts remained upbeat. Juan Cobo, the deputy editor of *Latinskaia Amerika*, wrote in 1975 that "given the present world balance of forces, it is possible in Latin America to throw off the imperialist yoke and select the road to development that the people of Latin America desire."[29]

A postmortem of the Allende regime, carried out by the Soviet Academy of Sciences with the participation of scholars from East European academies and Latin American communist parties, concluded that the Unidad Popular government and the PCCh had misread the Chilean domestic reality and thus had been unprepared to deal with the coup. Although the role of the United States was criticized, both Soviet academics and Chilean communists admitted that it was the mistakes of Allende's domestic policy that caused his demise.[30]

Teitelboim stated that the key mistake had been the regime's "inability to break the isolation of the working class and its failure to gain support of the majority of the population."[31] Kudachkin, in a lead article, enumerated the causes for Allende's demise in this way: (1) Allende's failure to resort to a plebiscite – despite a wave of popularity in 1971 – by which he could have altered the constitutional system that inhibited his programs; (2) ultra-leftist use of force, which lost Allende support among significant parts of the population; (3) the government's inability to forge a coherent program to combat Chile's deepening economic problems; and (4) Allende's policies, which polarized his supporters and led to the coalescence of wide segments of the population, which in the past had opposed imperialism, against the Unidad Popular government.[32] H. Neuberg, of the Latin American Institute in Rostock, stated that the coup had demonstrated that any successful struggle against a right-wing regime in Latin America must enlist the support of the progressive elements within the armed forces, or be doomed to fail.[33] E. Kosarev highlighted poor economic management and the inability to maintain high levels of industrial and agricultural output.[34] It is important to note that all authors stated that peaceful transformation in Chile would have been possible if Allende had not committed crucial mistakes at crucial moments.

It is also significant that all these Soviet analysts maintained that the United States played a very minor role in the fall of Allende. This was despite the fact that hearings by the Church Committee of the US Senate had made public the extent of CIA covert activities in Chile. Grigulevich responded to this investigation with the tepid observation that all revolutions encounter foreign intervention. Such had been the case in the French revolution, Mexico's revolution of 1910, and the Russian revolution of 1917, yet all these revolutions had survived. Although he documented and denounced American pressure on the Allende regime, he laid the ultimate blame for the debacle of Allende on Chile's domestic scene.[35]

Thus, a significant change in Soviet perceptions of US ability to influence events in Latin America was apparent, especially if one compares how the Soviets explained the causes of the Chilean coup with how they billed Goulart's fall in Brazil in 1964. Despite numerous domestic causes that could easily have accounted for the coup against Goulart, Soviet commentators almost unanimously saw his collapse as yet another manifestation of US omnipotence. Yet despite documented US efforts to provoke a coup against Allende, most Soviet analysts viewed these efforts as a minor factor at most.

It is probably because of the above conviction that both the Soviet media and the Chilean communist party continued to insist that the "peaceful way" to power was the correct method, given Chile's conditions. Only after the victory of the FSLN in Nicaragua did the Chilean communist party establish the Manuel Rodríguez front, aimed at the violent overthrow of the Pinochet dictatorship. Nevertheless, the final nine years of the Brezhnev era were marked by a relentless insistence that the peaceful way toward social transformation remained viable for Latin America.

13   Case study: Brazil and Argentina

Whereas in Chile a strong and a well-organized communist party had provided a link with the USSR since the 1920s, and in Mexico a shared revolutionary ideology and mutual fear of the United States had fostered a close relationship with Soviet Russia, there were no significant political or ideological links between the two South American giants and the Soviet Union. Neither Brazil nor Argentina had developed massive communist parties, and in both countries homegrown populism, led by Vargas and Perón, respectively, dominated the political left. Similarly, neither Argentina nor Brazil had ever experienced a major revolution, and therefore anticapitalist and anti-imperialist rhetoric had never become the political staple it had in Mexico. The case of Brazil and Argentina is particularly intriguing, because this was a situation in which almost the entire attraction between the USSR and those two countries was economic.

Brazil

Although Brazil was the only Latin American country to dispatch an expeditionary force to Europe during World War II, it did not establish diplomatic relations with the USSR until April 1945 – and then, reluctantly. Brazil's military leadership, which had faced a communist-led uprising in 1935, remained suspicious of and hostile toward the USSR. In 1947 Brazil, responding to the pressures of the cold war, broke off diplomatic relations.

The two countries resumed contact in 1959, when the populist President Kubitschek arranged a barter deal with the USSR in which Soviet oil was traded for Brazilian coffee and hides. In 1962 President Goulart reestablished diplomatic ties, and this was followed by a Soviet trade exhibit and major trade accord. In 1963 a Soviet geological survey concluded that Brazil's north had significant oil reserves, a finding that implied the previous oil surveys carried out by Standard Oil had deliberately misled Brazil in order to perpetuate its dependence on the United States. Because of the very low baseline, Soviet–Brazilian trade rapidly expanded from .8 million rubles in 1959 to 38 million rubles by 1961.[1]

Despite its strong interest in developing economic ties with Brazil, Moscow remained cool to the idea of closer alignment with the leftist regime of President Goulart. Whereas the USSR welcomed the leftward tilt of Nasser, Sukarno, and Castro, it remained suspicious of Goulart's overtures. As noted earlier, Moscow even suspected Goulart's attempt to win the Brazilian communists' support, questioning whether this was an effort to gain leverage with Washington.[2] In fact, the initial sharp response of the Soviet media to the 1964 military coup against Goulart, which accused the Brazilian military of carrying out orders from US multinationals,[3] quickly gave way to a different attitude. *Izvestiia* published an article congratulating Brazil on its national holiday and stressing that countries with different political systems could cooperate.[4]

Moscow continued to cultivate economic ties with Brazil, despite the fact that the military regimes of presidents Branco, Costa e Silva, and Medici waged a bloody, repressive campaign against Brazil's leftists and froze all cultural exchange between Brazil and the Soviet Union.[5] As noted by a Brazilian diplomat, Moscow appeared to prefer dealing with this stable and pragmatic, albeit military, government, rather than with the weak, erratic, "leftist" government of Goulart.[6] Similarly, the Brazilian communist party, which in the past had flirted with Goulart, now stated that he was not a leftist, as he had claimed, but "a result of a compromise between the national bourgeoisie and the forces of reaction"[7] – and thus not worthy of communist support.

Economic ties expanded under the Goulart regime subsequently grew under the military regime of Castelo Branco. It was at this time, in 1965, that the USSR extended Brazil the credit line of $100 million (of which Brazil used less than $6 million by 1971); the following month Brazil's minister of planning, Roberto Campos, visited Moscow.[8] A year later Soviet Trade Minister Potalichev visited Brazil and signed a trade protocol whereby the USSR would provide Brazil with oil and some manufactured goods in exchange for a basket of goods, at least 25 percent of which were to include Brazilian industrial products. By 1966 the turnover in Soviet–Brazilian trade bounced to 52 million rubles (about $68 million),[9] making Brazil one of the largest trade partners of the USSR in the developing world.[10]

For its part, Moscow desired the expansion of commercial ties but had no interest in major projects that would not yield an immediate benefit to the Soviet economy. Thus, it refused to furnish Brazil with credits to purchase Soviet equipment for the huge Urupunga hydro-electric project.[11] Brazil's willingness to expand trade with the USSR during the 1970s primarily reflected domestic changes, such as President Geisel's endorsement of "political pluralism" among countries, which signaled a less ideological orientation in Brazil's foreign policy. In addition, the economic recession that hit the Western world after the 1973 increase in oil prices, along with a burgeoning foreign debt, forced Brazil to seek new trade partners.

In 1972 Brazil and the USSR signed a new trade agreement, which resulted in the expansion of trade and shipping links; in 1973 they exchanged industrial exhibitions. When the traditional Soviet deficit in its trade with Brazil was further aggravated by the USSR's inability to continue to supply Brazil with oil after the 1973 price hike, Brazil responded and agreed to purchase Soviet-made rolling stock and earth-moving equipment. In 1975 Elektromashineksport signed a contract to supply Brazil with several turbines for a large hydroelectric project in Pernambuco[12] – a collaboration that seems to have led to the Soviet–Brazilian hydroelectric project on the Cuanza River in Angola and to similar projects in Peru and Ethiopia. The two countries also entered negotiations to launch a project in which both countries would combine their titanium and vacuum technologies.[13] In 1976 cultural exchanges were resumed.[14]

Soviet–Brazilian political relations began to warm in 1980 when Brazil refused to go along with the US-led boycott of the Moscow Olympics and the grain embargo against the USSR after the Soviet invasion of Afghanistan. Brazil's willingness to supply the USSR with feedstock, which in the past had been purchased from the United States, resulted in an increase in the trade turnover between the two countries from 179.9 million rubles in 1979 to 275 million rubles in 1980.[15] Then a new four-year trade agreement (1982–86) was signed by Brazil's planning minister Neto during his visit to Moscow. For the first time in history a Soviet parliamentary delegation, led by Eduard Shevardnadze, visited Brazil in 1980 and was received by President Figueiredo.

Yet despite the growing Soviet–Brazilian trade, despite Brazil's active role within the Non-Aligned Movement (whereby the Brazilian voting pattern at the UN became much closer to Moscow's than Washington's), and despite the political relaxation occurring under presidents Geisel and Figueiredo, Soviet policy toward Brazil remained one of pragmatic utilization of mutually beneficial economic exchanges. As Brezhnev noted, "Soviet–Brazilian relations are based on purely mutually beneficial collaboration between the two states, upholding the principle of respect for each other's sovereignty and non-interference in internal affairs."[16]

Argentina

Argentina never developed close ties with the USSR, although it has always been the maverick of the Western hemisphere and since the late nineteenth century conducted a foreign policy aimed at reducing US influence in Latin America (either by expanding Argentine influence or that of extra-hemispheral powers, such as Britain early in this century and later the Axis powers). Soviet–Argentine ties, much like the USSR's ties with Brazil, were primarily economic. Yet, despite far greater complementarity between the Soviet and Argentine economies, these ties were constantly disrupted by Argentina's political instability.

Although Argentina was the first Soviet trade outpost in Latin America (Iuzhamtorg was established in the late 1920s), and although the two countries had maintained uninterrupted diplomatic relations since 1946, bilateral relations were shallow and erratic. As early as 1953 the USSR and Argentina signed a trade agreement that resulted in a rapid increase in trade, from nil in 1953 to more than $60 million in 1954.[17] However, the military coup of 1955 that ousted Perón and brought to power right-wing military officers chilled relations, and by 1957 Soviet–Argentine trade fell to less than $20 million.[18]

The 1955 coup was followed by the civilian presidency of Frondizi (1958–62) during which the USSR, despite several attacks on the Soviet embassy and expulsions of Soviet diplomats, persevered in its efforts to expand economic ties with Argentina. In 1958 the USSR granted Argentina a $100 million credit to purchase Soviet-made oil-drilling and oil-processing equipment,[19] and in 1960 Deputy Prime Minister Kosygin visited Argentina and granted that country an additional credit line of $56 million to purchase Soviet road-building equipment.[20] Moscow's efforts to expand its economic ties with Argentina were less than totally successful, however. In fact, when Frondizi was overthrown in 1962, only 30 percent of the Soviet credits had been drawn upon.[21] The military coup of 1962, led by rightist officers, resulted in the annulment of the 1960 trade agreement, as well as in an almost total freeze in contacts between the two countries.

In contrast, the Brezhnev era began at an auspicious moment in Soviet–Argentine relations. President Illia, who was elected in 1964, preferred a neutralist foreign policy and refused to go along with the rest of Latin America, which generally supported the US-initiated political and economic blockade of Cuba. Nor did he allow any Argentine participation in the occupation of the Dominican Republic. As a reflection of this more positive Argentine attitude toward the USSR, trade between the two countries rose from only $19 million in 1962 to $113 million by 1966.[22]

Nevertheless, Soviet–Argentine relations continued to be bedeviled by Argentina's political instability and the extreme anticommunist mind-set of the country's military establishment. After General Onganía took power in a coup in July 1966, he immediately declared that his foreign policy would reflect the doctrine of "ideological frontiers," with Marxism being Argentina's prime enemy.[23] Between 1967 and 1970 Soviet–Argentine relations continued to deteriorate, to the point that a branch of the Argentine police attempted to abduct a Soviet diplomat. As a reflection, Soviet–Argentine trade fell to its lowest level since 1962.

In 1971 Argentina, under General Lanusse, abandoned the doctrine of "ideological frontiers" in favor of "ideological pluralism." Despite US opposition, Lanusse extended credits to the leftist regimes of Bolivia, Chile, and Peru, simultaneously distancing Argentina from Brazil and other right-wing military regimes. In 1972 the USSR and Argentina agreed to implement the 1966 trade agreement originally negotiated by President Illia.

Returning to power in 1973, Perón insisted on a "third position" between the superpowers, encouraging Argentina to improve its ties with Moscow. The USSR responded warmly, receiving one of Perón's economic ministers, Gelbard, in Moscow and inviting Perón to visit in September 1974. The USSR was pleased with the expansion of ties between Argentina and Allende's Chile and with Perón's moves toward Cuba, which included not only the restoration of diplomatic ties but also a credit line of $1.2 billion to Cuba. The Soviet media, which had made much of Perón's pro-Axis sympathies during World War II and had attempted to bar Peronist Argentina from the UN, now praised Perón's anti-imperialism and noted that he had the support of the communist party.[24]

Improved ties between the USSR and Argentina had been stimulated, on Moscow's side, by Argentina's refusal to observe the OAS trade embargo against Cuba. This lightened the burden that Cuba's need for economic support was imposing on the USSR. On the Argentine side, growing barriers to Argentine exports imposed by the EEC, along with the traditional Peronist desire to foster industrial growth in Argentina, made it imperative that Argentina find trade partners who would be willing to barter agricultural goods for capital goods.

In 1973 Gelbard imposed on Argentina an essentially traditional "import substitution" economic policy and traveled to the USSR, where he was received by Brezhnev, Kosygin, and Potgorny. As a result of Gelbard's mission, Soviet–Argentine trade rapidly expanded, with the USSR's Energomashexport obtaining several major contracts to supply generators to Argentina's hydroelectric stations. By 1975 the trade turnover passed the $310 million mark.[25]

Nevertheless, when General Videla led a military coup against the Perón regime in 1976, the Soviet media responded with some enthusiasm. This reflected, in part, the Soviets' increasing irritation with the anticommunist and anti-Soviet outbursts of Mrs. Perón's closest confidant, López Rega. As noted previously, some Soviet analysts believed that the coup might result in a military regime with an orientation similar to that of Peru.[26] Although the military regime had banned most political parties, the communist party of Argentina went unmolested. Led by the old Comintern operative, Rodolfo Ghioldi, it launched a campaign stressing the positive aspects of the coup.[27] That both the USSR and Cuba recognized the new regime less than two weeks after the coup illustrates the Soviets' deep desire to retain links with Argentina. Cuba's recognition of the Videla regime is particularly interesting, since it represented a shift in the traditional Cuban policy of not recognizing right-wing military regimes in Latin America.

Although Soviet hopes that the 1976 Argentine coup would turn into a leftist, anti-imperialist swing did not materialize, the Videla–Viola–Galtieri era proved to be a period of rapid expansion in bilateral trade between the USSR and Argentina and witnessed increasing Soviet support for Argentina in international forums. Moscow consistently blocked UN attempts to investigate the state of human rights in Argentina and refrained from condemning violations of such rights, even as the Argentine generals launched their "dirty war" against "subversives" in which about 10,000 people have "disappeared."[28] Argentina reciprocated this diplomatic support by voting with Cuba at the 1979 NAM meeting in Havana to support the Nicaraguan Sandinistas, by calling for the independence of Puerto Rico, and by refusing a US request to send troops to Sinai to police the Camp David accords. No doubt, Argentina's closer alignment with Cuba and the USSR, and its support for Puerto Rican independence in particular, reflected irritation with President Carter's "human rights" policy, which was often critical of Argentina.

Trade, always a key factor in Soviet–Argentine relations, had by 1978 reached a new high. The USSR, purchasing almost $380 million in Argentine commodities, became one of Argentina's largest trade partners.[29] After the Soviet invasion of Afghanistan prompted the United States to impose a grain embargo on the Soviet Union on 5 January 1980 (an embargo partially supported by other major grain exporters, such as Canada and Australia), Soviet grain purchases from Argentina rapidly increased. Despite urgings from US General Andrew Goodpaster to defend "Western values," Argentina declined to follow the US lead and agreed to sell more than 60 percent of its grain exports to the USSR, thereby enabling Argentina to earn more than $1 billion over regular market prices.[30] As its contribution to the defense of "Western values," Argentina (unlike Brazil) refused to send its team to the Moscow Olympics.

Although President Reagan lifted the US grain embargo in April 1981, the USSR continued to direct most of its purchases toward Argentina. In addition, it agreed both to supply Argentina with heavy water for its atomic power station at Arroyito and to enter negotiations concerning Soviet sales of nuclear reactors to Argentina. By 1982 the USSR was buying between 30 and 90 percent of Argentina's total commodities export, depending on the commodity, and at the same time was accepting Argentine uranium for enrichment.[31] Moscow made strenuous efforts to increase its exports to Argentina. However, while the USSR bought more than $1.6 billion of Argentine products in 1982, its sales to Argentina totaled a mere $44 million.[32]

Notwithstanding this immense expansion in Soviet–Argentine trade between 1980 and 1982, bilateral relations cooled considerably after General Galtieri took power in late 1981. This cooling occurred, in part, because the Reagan administration was willing to resume military and economic aid to Argentina without insisting on changes in Argentina's human rights record and, in part, because of Galtieri's support for the doctrine of ideological frontiers. Political relations between Argentina and the USSR were further strained when the Argentine foreign minister threatened economic sanctions if the USSR invaded Poland,[33] when Argentina decided to provide military aid to El Salvador, and when it agreed in principle to cooperate with the United States in the creation of a South Atlantic military bloc. Despite these tensions, Soviet–Argentine trade continued to grow, and the immense expansion of ties between 1973 and 1982 showed that the relationship between the two countries remained, as Ambassador Luers described it, "increasingly pragmatic, close, but not intimate."[34]

The shallowness of the Soviet political commitment to Argentina was illustrated by the Soviet posture during the Falkland Islands crisis of 1982. Whereas the USSR had supported India's invasion of Portuguese-held Goa in 1960 and supported President Nasser's seizure of the Suez Canal Zone in 1956 (and continued to support Nasser's policies even after Egypt closed the straits of Tiran to Israeli shipping in May 1967), the Soviet response to the Argentine invasion of the British-held islands was cool and noncommittal. The initial Soviet reaction to the Argentine invasion of the Falklands was one of utter confusion, and it is significant that the Soviet media did not refer to it as a justifiable war of liberation against a remnant of colonialism. On 3 April 1982 the USSR failed to veto, and thus allowed the passage of, a UN Security Council resolution calling upon Argentina to withdraw its troops from the islands. Moscow's attitude toward the Argentine adventure could be glimpsed from an interview on Soviet television with *Izvestiia*'s commentator, Bovin, who was sympathetic to Argentina but felt that it had violated international law by resorting to force and by denying the islanders their right to self-determination by annexing them to Argentina against their will.[35]

Although the USSR did launch several satellites to follow the British fleet in its voyage across the Atlantic, the posture of the Argentine navy did not indicate that it received any information gathered by these satellites. Assistance from Cuba came in the form of a $100 million trade accord and a vague promise of military aid; however, aside from criticizing British and US colonialism, the USSR did very little to help Argentina in its war effort. As if to underscore that Soviet–Argentine relations were strictly economic, the Soviet deputy foreign minister traveled to Argentina during the crisis and signed a series of trade agreements, which included increased Soviet grain purchases from Argentina (up to 77 percent of Argentina's total export) and cooperation in the fishing and nuclear industries.[36] Despite persistent rumors (spread mainly by Argentina) that the USSR was willing to provide military aid to Argentina, there is no evidence of such Soviet aid. On 5 May Brezhnev made a veiled criticism of Argentina when he stressed that although some forces might attempt to "preserve or restore" colonialism in Latin America, he urged the Latin Americans not to resort to force.[37] Thus, Soviet propaganda during the Falklands War matched Mastny's observation that "the Soviet line was more anti-British and anti-American than pro-Argentine."[38]

There are three plausible explanations for the USSR's rather passive posture during the Falklands War. First, it is conceivable that, given the declining health and vigor of Brezhnev during 1982, there was a vacuum in the center of the Soviet decision-making apparatus that made Moscow unable to respond assertively to a rapidly developing crisis situation. Those who accept this explanation often cite the mild and incoherent Soviet response to the Israeli invasion of Lebanon in June 1982, despite the humiliation of two of Moscow's close allies, Syria and the Palestine Liberation Organization.

Second, hostile relations between the USSR and the Argentine navy may have been a factor. Although the USSR had managed to develop good working relations with Argentina's army and air force, relations with the Argentine navy, historically the most conservative among the Argentine military services, remained very poor. In late 1977 the Argentine navy had forced seven Soviet fishing ships to sail to Argentine ports, where the navy confiscated the ships' cargo and forced them to pay high fines for violating Argentina's sovereignty. Soon after that incident the navy announced that Argentina would hold talks with South Africa concerning the defense of the South Atlantic (presumably against the USSR). The Soviet media reacted to these incidents by accusing the Argentine navy of being an instrument of reactionary factions determined to undermine Soviet–Argentine relations.[39] Thus, it is conceivable that the USSR did not want to see Argentina prevail in the Falklands undertaking, because this would strengthen the political weight of the navy (which had initiated the invasion) and further encourage Argentina's ambition to press its territorial claims in Antarctica, a position Moscow consistently opposed.

Third is the most plausible explanation that Moscow decided there was little it could do (short of direct military involvement) to alter significantly the course of events in the South Atlantic, given the location of the crisis and the Thatcher government's determination to reclaim the islands. Furthermore, given the immense trade surplus that Argentina enjoyed with the USSR, it was unthinkable that Argentina under any government would curtail grain sales to the USSR. Thus, there was no compelling reason for Moscow to endear itself to the Galtieri junta, and Moscow recognized that overt Soviet identification with Argentina would push the British Labour party toward the United States. Further, since it appeared that Argentina received virtually no support from much of Latin America and the Third World – and given the high probability that Britain, led by Thatcher and supported by both the United States and Western Europe, would prevail – Moscow may have decided not to ally itself with an undertaking that was bound to fail and adversely affect Soviet prestige.

Thus, throughout Brezhnev's tenure, Soviet–Argentine relations remained what they had been since the 1920s, when Iuzhamtorg opened its offices in Buenos Aires: almost exclusively economic.

Part IV

Conclusion: the emerging Soviet perception of Latin America and the future of Soviet policy toward the hemisphere

Conclusions

There are several pertinent conclusions to be drawn from the evolution of Soviet perceptions of Latin America during the Brezhnev era. Perhaps the most striking aspect of this evolution was the dramatic improvement in the quality and sophistication of Soviet analysis of the continent. Between 1917 and 1969 (the year *Latinskaia Amerika* was launched) most Soviet analysis resembled the caricature by the Colombian primitivist master, Botero, that depicted Latin America as a hemisphere made up of poor campesinos dominated by the obese church and military and *comprador* elites, which in turn acted as marionettes for US interests. This rather simplistic Soviet perception was further trivialized by the almost universal tendency to view all of Latin America as an essentially undifferentiated block of countries, from the Rio Grande to Patagonia. Only occasional attention was paid to the fact that, despite some cultural and linguistic commonalities, Latin America comprised a set of distinct countries with very different social, political, and economic structures.

By the mid-1970s, and particularly after the victory of the FSLN in Nicaragua, Soviet analysis of Latin America ceased to treat the hemisphere as a unitary body. Instead, the scholarly community in the USSR began to divide the hemisphere into various subgroupings, such as the Southern Cone, the Andean countries, Central America, and the Caribbean and Mexico. This new, non-monolithic view of the area led to far more sophisticated expectations and policies *vis-à-vis* Latin America. The Soviets began to perceive political change in South America much more in terms of the area's domestic politics than in terms of US influence, given South America's relatively developed economies, a large politicized middle class, and other active social groups. Still, the Soviets continued to view much of Central America in the traditional light as "banana republics," dominated by US capital and governed by a subservient clique of local oligarchs, reactionary generals, and the *comprador* class.

Thus, by the early 1970s the Soviets had come to recognize that in the more developed countries of the hemisphere, military coups would occur only when the governments in power lost the support of the politically relevant middle and lower middle classes. Even after the fall of Allende, Soviet analysts did not resort to their classic model of the "invisible hand" of US imperialism dominating political events in Latin America. Rather, they attributed events to misguided policies that led to the loss of support from vital elements of Chilean society.

Changing Soviet perceptions also brought a new awareness of the great variety of political opinion within Latin America (again especially in the more developed countries of the hemisphere). The traditional pre-Brezhnev perception was that the institutional pillars of Latin America (the "dependent" bourgeoisie, the armed forces, the church, the various political parties, and the rural oligarchs) were uniformly committed to preserving the existing order. Given these perceptions, the Soviet Union, even in the rare cases where it maintained a diplomatic presence, did very little to develop an institutional dialogue with the various political players. Only in the late 1960s did the Soviets discover that there were elements within the ranks of the Latin American military who saw their task as the promotion of independent economic development for their countries, rather than simply the support of US interests. The Soviets learned that the Latin American church, despite its traditionally reactionary character, contained segments that were far more concerned with restructuring the social order in the hemisphere than with defending it. Soviet analysts, who until the 1960s had viewed most Latin American political parties as mere extensions of the nineteenth-century criollo "liberal" and "conservative" parties, by the late 1960s realized that many of the region's parties were closely linked to Europe's Social and Christian Democrats and indeed enjoyed a considerable degree of legitimacy with the Latin American public.

The realization that Latin American political institutions were far more diverse than the Soviets had ever imagined, and that some of these institutions actually possessed broad political backing and did not derive their political influence from links to US capital, prompted major changes in Moscow's policy toward the hemisphere. In recognizing the political credibility of the major political institutions in much of Latin America, the Soviets also understood that most South American regimes had sufficiently broad popular backing and legitimacy to endure even a very long and difficult guerrilla insurrection (unlike the narrowly based Somoza and Batista regimes, which had been over-thrown with relative ease). Venezuela's experience during the mid-1960s, and Colombia's experience during the past thirty years, convinced Soviet analysts that although Guevara's "foco" theory may have worked in Cuba and Nicaragua, and might work in El Salvador, the prospects for a successful insurrection outside Central America were very remote. In fact, it can be argued that these "Brezhnev era" perceptions of South American regimes generated the Soviet refusal to support guerrillas in any South American country, including Chile, whereas the USSR did provide some help to the "final offensive" in El Salvador.

Another important result of the changed Soviet perception of Latin America's domestic political institutions was a greater Soviet persever-ance in attempting to enter a dialogue with the major political players in South America. Thus, since the USSR no longer viewed the armies, the church, and the political parties as reactionary monoliths, it in-creasingly tried to influence the course of Latin American politics by strengthening its links with segments of those institutions that might be sympathetic to the USSR. In that sense, Brezhnev's policy toward South America was similar to the USSR's policy toward India or West-ern Europe, where Moscow was no longer attempting to overthrow the bourgeois regimes in power but to influence political decisions by cultivating elements of the existing political establishment.

Another evolution in the Soviet perception of Latin America was a changed understanding of US–Latin American relations. By the mid-1970s the Soviets understood that the "technological revolution," despite the nationalization of US-owned extractive industries, had made Latin America far more dependent on the United States. In the past Latin America's fungible primary commodities had been traded throughout the "capitalist center." The new age of technology, how-ever, meant dependence on the multinationals for technology, capital, components, and a global distribution network – making national-ization of the dynamic manufacturing sector difficult if not impossible. In addition, the decline in the relative global demand for primary commodities, combined with Europe's granting of trade preference to its former colonies and the decline in Latin America's share of overall global trade, led the Soviets to conclude that the hemisphere's eco-nomic dependence on the United States was constantly deepening. Furthermore, in the pre-Brezhnev era the Soviets had tied economic dependence to political dependence. Yet during Brezhnev's tenure, most Soviet analysts realized that Latin America's foreign policy was far more a product of deep-seated nationalism and a historical resentment of the United States and that, despite the region's growing economic dependence on North America, Latin America would increasingly strive toward an independent and "nonaligned" foreign policy.

In Central America, which the Soviets historically perceived as being the least developed and most dependent region on the United States, the Soviets did not expect the fall of the Somoza regime. However, the USSR did benefit from the turmoil in Central America, especially in view of the tension that this crisis engendered in the US domestic political scene, US–Latin American relations, and US–European ties. Naturally, the most important outcome of the successful Nicaraguan revolution was the destruction of the prevailing Soviet belief in "geographic fatalism," the belief that the United States would never allow a "second Cuba."

Finally, the Brezhnev era was a period of minimal change for the perceived importance of Latin America to the USSR. Despite twenty years of effort by both sides to expand Soviet–Latin American ties, and despite the fact that two out of three authentic postwar Marxist-Leninist revolutions took place in Latin America, the region remained the USSR's lowest global priority, trailing behind Europe, Asia, and Africa. Several explanations may be given.

In geostrategic terms, the Cuban missile crisis had convinced the Soviets that the risk of stationing nuclear weapons in Latin America, to offset the US nuclear presence along the periphery of the USSR, was far greater than any possible advantage. Further, with the advent of both land- and sea-launched intercontinental ballistic missiles, the geographic proximity of Latin America to the United States ceased to be a major strategic asset. Indeed, the Cienfuegos crisis proved that although an overt military presence in the Caribbean might be a convenience for the USSR, it was not a must.

Although Latin America may have ceased to be a potentially important military asset for the USSR so far as nuclear weapons were concerned, it would be a mistake to disregard totally the military importance of Latin America, as perceived by the Soviets. Throughout the Brezhnev era Soviet military analysts continued to consider Latin America the United States' strategic rear (*stratygecheskii tyl*). Soviet analysts continued, as during the pre-Brezhnev era, to catalogue the US dependence on Latin America's mineral wealth and the geostrategic importance to the United States of the Caribbean sea-lanes.

In economic terms, despite substantial growth in the volume of Soviet–Latin American trade, especially in 1979–82, the turnover never amounted to more than a tiny fraction of either partner's overall trade. In 1975–78, for example, Latin America supplied 1 percent of the USSR's imports and took less than .0025 percent of the USSR's exports.[1] This very low trade turnover has numerous explanations. Geographic distance made trade between the USSR and Latin America too expensive and, in many cases, totally uneconomical. The fact that both Latin America and the USSR were primarily commodity exporters made the two economies rather noncomplementary. Latin America's long history of reliance on Western machinery and technology made a switch to Soviet capital goods, which were generally of lower quality, unlikely. Finally, the serious shortage of hard currency in both the USSR and Latin America inhibited trade between the partners.

The strongest basis for economic links between the USSR and Latin America was the fact that the Soviets, despite massive investments in agriculture during the previous two decades, remained heavily dependent on the importation of cereals. The USSR began to import large quantities of grain from the United States in 1963, but it was only in 1973 that Soviet buyers, responding to US public opposition to the grain deal of 1972, started to perceive Argentina as a potential alternative source of grain. Between 1973 and 1979 the USSR bought Argentine grain, then massively increased purchases from Argentina after the US grain embargo in 1980. Yet the USSR did not allow Argentina to become a permanent substitute for the United States as a source of grain and, in fact, in 1983 resumed its purchase of US cereals. Among the reasons for preferring the United States as the main source of grain were: (1) the poor quality of the Argentine product; (2) the very high transport costs from Argentina to the USSR; and (3) the poor reliability of Argentine deliveries, caused, in part, by that country's chaotic ports.[2] Thus, even in the sphere of grain trade, where the Soviet and Latin American economies appeared to be complementary, trade between the USSR and Latin America did not attain the maximal level.

Outlook

It is clear that, despite the very significant changes that have taken place in the Soviet perception of Latin America, Latin America will remain the region of lowest priority for Soviet policymakers. Unlike in Asia and the Middle East, where the US presence is perceived by the Soviets as a threat to the USSR, an increased US presence in Latin America will not have any impact on the security of the Soviet Union. Unlike southern Africa, where it appears likely – if not imminent – that realignment could occur that might be beneficial to Moscow, the situation in the major countries of Latin America is rather stable and not open to direct Soviet influence. Furthermore, the close integration of Latin America into the economy of the United States, along with the 10,000 miles of ocean between Latin America and the USSR, makes the prospect for a substantial increase in Soviet–Latin American trade unlikely.

Yet, despite these inherent limitations on Soviet–Latin American relations, the USSR, now cognizant of its ability to influence many segments of the Latin American political scene, will continue efforts to expand this influence. The USSR no longer feels that the region's communist parties alone are sympathetic to it, and so it intends to expand its links throughout Latin American society.[3] Although closer ties with Latin America may be of lesser significance to the USSR than ties with other parts of the world, such ties are bound to expand the USSR's diplomatic leverage both within the Third World and in the international arena as a whole. Furthermore, just as the United States welcomes the increased assertiveness of Eastern Europe *vis-à-vis* the USSR and believes that such behavior may moderate Moscow's global policies, Soviet analysts seem to feel that an assertive Latin America with closer links to the USSR will moderate the United States' global posture. Rumors about a forthcoming tour of Latin America by Mikhail Gorbachev (the first ever by a Soviet leader) appear to be an attempt to expand Latin American acceptance of the Soviet Union as a potential friend and partner, as well as to expand the USSR's global presence (similar to President Nixon's attempt to enhance the United States' global presence during his visit to Eastern Europe in 1969).

So far as Central America is concerned, it appears that the Soviets are convinced that the era when the United States could prevent the emergence of "second Cubas" has passed and that Nicaragua has already managed to weather the worst of the US opposition to the FSLN regime. Increasingly, the Soviet media refer to the Nicaraguan revolution as a "revolution that knows how to defend itself," treating the survival of the Sandinistas as essentially a foregone conclusion. It is perhaps as a result of this confidence in the ability of the Sandinistas to retain power that the Soviet media has ceased to call upon the FSLN to make "tactical concessions" to the regime's domestic opponents.

An interesting debate over the future of the rest of Central America, which started during the twilight of the Brezhnev era, continues. Some analysts still feel that there is a high probability that the Nicaraguan revolution can be repeated in El Salvador and, perhaps, in other countries of Central America and that the final offensive in El Salvador failed simply because of massive US support to the incumbent regimes. However, regarding El Salvador, a new consensus appears to be emerging in the Soviet academic community: The final offensive failed because, unlike the Somoza regime, which had lost all support within Nicaragua, the Salvadoran regime retained the support of much of the urban population. This support, the argument continues, prevented a general insurrection similar to the one in Managua in the summer of 1979. Furthermore, the prevailing perception in Moscow seems to be that the new pluralistic regimes in Central America, despite their shortcomings, enjoy sufficient popular support to preclude successful revolutions. One can note, as a result of this altered perception, increased calls in the Soviet media for the Salvadoran guerrillas to explore any potential political opening that the Duarte regime may allow.

Therefore, it appears that the USSR will continue to expand its level of support for Nicaragua, but it has no expectation of any radical transformation anywhere else in Central America. In fact, one could argue that, should these new, democratically elected regimes in Central America take hold and broaden their bases of domestic legitimacy, Moscow would adopt a posture *vis-à-vis* Central America similar to the one it has already adopted toward the major states of the hemisphere.

Epilogue
Latin America: the Long March

Mikhail Gorbachev's election as General Secretary signaled a major shift in Soviet perceptions of the Third World. Unlike his predecessors, Gorbachev did not attempt to use ideological success in the Third World as a substitute for economic performance within the USSR.

From the start, Gorbachev argued that the key determining factor in the global "correlation of forces" lay in the strength of the Soviet economy and its ability to adapt to high technology.

The new emphasis on the USSR's own economic performance has had several profound effects on Soviet policy in the Third World. Karen Brutents, for example – one of the Central Committee's key authorities on the area – has noted that the USSR stands to gain far more from closer ties with non-Marxist Third World countries such as Brazil and Mexico than from economically insignificant countries that might profess a "socialist orientation."[1] Thus, while Soviet aid to Ethiopia, Angola, Cuba, Nicaragua, and Vietnam has continued at high levels, the USSR has appeared to be reluctant to seek new Third World allies that might well become burdens.

Gorbachev's *perestroika*, with its emphasis on ever-greater Soviet participation in the international division of labor, led Moscow to seek improved political and economic links with those Third World countries that might buy Soviet industrial goods and commodities or sell needed technology to the USSR. This "new thinking" resulted in Soviet overtures toward the ASEAN bloc, Saudi Arabia and the Gulf states, and most dramatically toward Latin America.

Gorbachev's policy toward the major states of Latin America is based on four perceptions. One is that they have reached a level of socio-economic development similar to that of the less-developed capitalist states such as Spain, Ireland, and Portugal. The prospects for radical transformation of such states are, in Moscow's view, neither likely nor particularly desirable.. Second, although all the major states of Latin

188

America are dominated by middle-class elites, these are essentially "national bourgeoisies" which are inherently anti-American. This limits the region's diplomatic cooperation with the United States, and affords the USSR a political opening. Third, the larger states of the region possess a level of technological "know-how" which can be useful for Gorbachev's *perestroika*. Given the substantial Western investment in Latin America and the region's nationalist mood, Latin America might well become a back channel for Western technology which the USSR cannot purchase directly from the West. Finally, though there is little hope for a rapid increase in trade between Latin America and the USSR, some Soviet observers nevertheless believe that given the magnitude of Latin America's debt crisis and the resulting hard currency shortages, the region is bound to resort to countertrade, something at which the USSR is far more adept than the West. Each of these points deserves further analysis.

The recognition that much of Latin America has reached the level of developed or at least semi-developed capitalism dates back to the Brezhnev era. However, this notion gained even greater currency in Moscow in the mid-1980s, as right-wing military regimes were widely replaced by relatively robust bourgeois democracies. The resilience and relative friendliness of these regimes led one prominent Soviet analyst to conclude that they are the best that the Latin American "toiling masses" can hope for: "In a whole group of (Latin American) countries the toilers, in practice, have to select not between capitalism and socialism, but between bourgeois democracy and fascism."[2]

Ironic as it seems, therefore, the USSR and its closely allied communist parties are doing their best to bolster the power of Latin America's bourgeois regimes. In the 1960s, local communists were often the prime force behind the labor unrest that helped bring down several bourgeois democracies; in the 1980s the communist parties of both Brazil and Argentina made major efforts to support the elected governments. Even in violence-prone Colombia, the communists tried seriously to enter the political system as a bona fide party. It should be noted, moreover, that most Latin American regimes view good relations with the USSR as a source of political stability at home. In several countries the local communist parties were willing to exchange their support for some degree of labor and social peace for good diplomatic relations with the USSR.

In fact, the level of Soviet support for the bourgeois regimes in Latin America probably reached the absurd stage when the Soviet ambassador to Mexico, Sergeev, to the dismay of Mexico's communist party, expressed his "endorsement" of the ruling party's candidate, Salinas – against whom the communists were campaigning.[3]

The USSR's courting of middle-class opinion in Latin America was perhaps best illustrated during Shevardnadze's visit to South America last November. Shevardnadze expressed strong support for Argentine president Alfonsín's economic policy – a point that drew strong protests from that country's socialist party.[4] Similarly, in order to curry favor with the influential Jewish community of South America, Shevardnadze met with Uruguay's Jewish leaders, promising them accelerated Jewish immigration from the USSR and better Soviet attitudes toward Israel. In addition, he invited their leaders to visit the Soviet Union.[5]

The USSR also changed its academic scholarships policy toward Latin America. The number of scholarships granted to Latin American students jumped from 2,900 students in 1980 to nearly 10,000 in 1987, and Soviet recruitment policies have changed as well.[6] If most of the Latin American students who went to study in Moscow in the past had good "leftist" credentials, today most are of middle-class origin. In order to sustain the level of student recruitment and to broaden the base of pro-Soviet sentiment among the middle class, the USSR expended considerable effort in negotiating accords with Costa Rica, Ecuador, Venezuela, and other countries, to ensure that the academic credentials earned in the USSR would make these graduates eligible for local licensing and employment in state bureaucracies.

Furthermore, in order to reassure the Latin American bourgeoisie, which has many trade and investment ties to the United States, Gorbachev has stated openly in *Pravda* (4 April 1987) that while the USSR might seek to improve its relations with Latin America, it has no wish to disturb Latin America's vital links with the United States.

A second perception shaping Soviet policy has to do with bourgeois anti-American sentiment in Latin America, which the Soviets are seeking to harness to their own political advantage.

Gorbachev's campaign in Latin America is similar to Soviet efforts to exploit neutralist tendencies in Western Europe. For example, the USSR heaps lavish support on the so-called "Group of Six" (Mexico, Argentina, India, Sweden, Greece, and Tanzania), which has led a crusade for nuclear disarmament, with strong opposition to the US Strategic Defense Initiative. Shevardnadze stated that it was the initiatives of Argentina and the rest of the Group of Six that had made the

INF accord possible.[7] Similarly, Shevardnadze invited Brazil to become an observer in the Soviet–American disarmament talks.[8] In order to sustain Latin American support in its propaganda war against the United States, the Soviet Union sent delegations to most of Latin America after both the Geneva and the Reykjavik summits. Statements of the eight Latin American presidents who met in Acapulco last November noted that the USSR had informed them about the progress in disarmament talks, and complained that the US continues to ignore Latin America's interests in that area.

In the international arena, Moscow's diplomatic activism has paid off nicely. In order to coordinate Soviet–Latin American positions at the UN, the USSR has established a permanent consultation mechanism with Brazil and Mexico. And – in a move whose long-term consequences are even more serious – Uruguay's President Sanguinetti agreed in March to lead an effort to secure Soviet membership in GATT[9] despite the United States' current opposition to Soviet membership.

The Soviet Union's ardent defense of Panama's strongman Noriega is perhaps the most blatant attempt to fortify anti-American tendencies in the hemisphere. Despite Gorbachev's repeated statements that drug abuse is a global problem that does not respect international borders, the Soviet media continues to defend Noriega as a national patriot who faces a challenge from the United States and "reactionary forces under Washington's control." The Soviets claim that the sole reason the US is attempting to oust Noriega is because of his insistence that the US honor its 1977 undertaking to transfer ownership of the Panama Canal.[10] Nor has Radio Moscow hidden its satisfaction with the fact that the Panamanian crisis has led to the consolidation of Latin America's opposition to the United States.[11] The murder and drug smuggling charges levied by the United States against Noriega have yet to be mentioned in the Soviet media.

Other Soviet attempts to exacerbate anti-Americanism were revealed in the USSR's coverage of the British naval exercises off the Falkland Islands in February 1988. According to the Soviet media, these exercises were part of a direct US–NATO plan to militarize and dominate the South Atlantic. The Soviets are also alert to the political explosiveness of the debt problem. Although the USSR has never adopted Castro's calls for a unilateral disavowal of debts, Soviet spokesmen increasingly blame the West for the debt crisis because of its alleged unwillingness to be paid in Latin American products.

Finally, Shevardnadze's visit to Mexico, Argentina, Brazil, and Uruguay, along with Soviet hints that Gorbachev himself might visit these countries, signals Soviet willingness to engage the highest circles of diplomacy in the effort to affect Latin America's global orientation.

A third perception behind Gorbachev's initiative toward the region – and perhaps the most important one – is the belief that Latin America could become an important source of technology for the USSR. The success of *perestroika* depends on an "intensive" economic model, relying on a more efficient application of technology, which the USSR has to purchase abroad – perhaps from Latin America. Brazil and Argentina, for example, possess some applied technologies in which the USSR lags behind. The deepening debt crisis and the chronic shortages of foreign currency that come with it make Latin America a most willing supplier of almost any export item for which a buyer can be found. The examples of the OECD and ASEAN – groups with political constituencies which fear the USSR and thus oppose transfers of technology to Moscow – have no analogue in Latin America. Sales to the USSR are therefore far less controversial politically than they would be elsewhere outside the Soviet orbit. Indeed, Panama (with its remarkably uncontrolled banking and incorporation laws) gives the USSR a local base of operations from which it can carry out sensitive purchases without attracting much attention. In Brazil, poor administrative controls and very lax patent and copyright laws make that country a haven for producers of pirated Western drugs and computer software. The Soviets are already purchasing Peruvian microchips (produced by multinational corporations) and Brazilian computers,[12] and Brazil has offered to export software to the USSR.[13] Such arrangements may become models for the transfer of Western technology to the USSR. The Soviet launching of a Brazilian-made communication satellite, meanwhile, may give the USSR a glance at Western technology.[14]

The Soviets are also interested in participating in the *maquiladora* system, where hundreds of US, Japanese, and European firms assemble goods for the US market along the US–Mexican border.[15] Since this region is the world's largest industrial park, participation may also allow the USSR to gain access to needed technology. While Latin America may not be able to supply state-of-the-art technology in all the fields that the Soviet Union may need in order to become a first-rate technological power, the existence of major assembly plants in Latin America for virtually every significant Western company means that the Soviets can gain access to sophisticated technology.

Thus, although there is little hard evidence to substantiate the claim that large amounts of modern technology have flowed from Latin America to the USSR, the circumstantial evidence is convincing.

The final factor shaping Gorbachev's initiatives is trade. The successful promotion of growth in trade between the USSR and Latin America so far appears to have eluded Gorbachev, as it did all his predecessors. In fact, according to Soviet officials Soviet–Latin American trade has declined from 3.2 billion rubles in 1985 to 920 million rubles in 1986.[16] Despite this decline, however, the violent fluctuations of Soviet–Latin American trade caused by sudden Soviet purchases of Latin American grain and by jumps in Latin America's purchases of Soviet oil may be coming to an end. Both sides realize that each will always be a marginal trade partner for the other; both are primary commodity exporters. The great geographic distance makes some trade uneconomic, and Soviet machinery is incompatible with much of Latin America's industry. However, a new pattern of Soviet–Latin American trade appears to be emerging: the exchange of Soviet services for Latin American products; Soviet direct investment in Latin American extractive projects in which the USSR is repaid in kind; and counter-trade, in which the USSR typically improves the infrastructure in exchange for Latin American goods.

The Soviet counter-trade offensive has been most successful in Brazil, where the USSR invested $60 million in a ferro-manganese plant, signed an accord to swap its turbines for Brazilian coffee, and signed cooperation accords under which the USSR and Brazil will jointly build dams and explore for oil in third countries.[17] Isakov, the Soviet ambassador to Brazil who spearheaded his country's effort to expand commercial ties there, said: "I know more businessmen than communists in Brazil."[18]

Soviet efforts to expand trade with Latin America are certainly not limited to Brazil. The USSR has agreed to trade Soviet shipping services for Mexican pipes, and to provide Bolivia with $200 million worth of equipment for hydroelectric projects in exchange for that country's minerals.[19] Similar deals have been arranged with Argentina, trading Soviet work in infrastructure for commodities. And while the counter-trade turnover between the USSR and Latin America remains low, its growth since Gorbachev came to power has been quite impressive, and more such trade is likely in the future. A particularly interesting phenomenon is that Soviet officials from Gorbachev on down rarely fail to stress that *perestroika* will lead to an expansion in Soviet–Latin American trade.

On the whole, Gorbachev's trade offensive has been successful inasmuch as it has diverted potential future growth away from the classic pattern. On that pattern, the USSR used Latin America as a grain supplier of last resort, while Latin America used the USSR as a source of oil when markets were tight. The long-term potential for counter-trade appears to be very good given the chronic hard currency shortages in both Latin America and the USSR. And when the United States cut the sugar quotas of Costa Rica and the Dominican Republic, in both cases the USSR agreed to purchase some of their sugar at prices well above those prevailing on the world market.[20]

By the time Gorbachev came to power in 1985 the USSR faced several challenges in its Central American policy. The Salvadoran final offensive had failed; the US-supported candidate for El Salvador's presidency – José Napoleón Duarte – was elected; Guatemala ended its long stint of direct military rule and elected a nominally democratic regime; and both Mexico and Venezuela, which in the past had supported the Sandinistas, became far less supportive.

In the United States, despite a continuous and divisive debate, President Reagan managed to secure modest yet significant aid for the *contras*. Finally, in Nicaragua itself, a country on which the Soviets pinned so many hopes in the early 1980s, the situation has continued to deteriorate. The *contras*, which started out as a rag-tag outfit consisting mainly of former Somozista officers, grew into a significant force drawn mainly from peasants resentful of the Sandinistas' policies. Despite large amounts of aid from Western Europe and Latin America, the Nicaraguan economy continued to falter, experiencing hyper-inflation and ever-growing dependence on the USSR. Diplomatically, the Sandinistas were becoming increasingly isolated, losing the support of Costa Rica, Venezuela, Panama, Ecuador, and to a lesser degree even that of Mexico. The successful US intervention in Grenada impressed on the Soviets that the US may well be overcoming the "Vietnam syndrome" and that it indeed was ready to reassert itself forcefully in its traditional sphere of influence. Nicaragua, and with it the USSR, faced either a potential US military intervention or a prospect of a long "low intensity" civil war with the same debilitating results that Angola and Mozambique are experiencing.

Mindful of this gloomy prospect, Gorbachev's policy in Central America is based not on the euphoric expectations of his predecessors, but rather on an effort to find a diplomatic solution which will enable the Marxist regime to survive. Moscow seeks to stabilize the region so that Central America will not become destructive of Gorbachev's efforts to improve relations with the United States, concerns which are central to his foreign policy. Simultaneously, while Gorbachev appears to be very interested in stabilizing the situation in Central America, he is cognizant of the fact that an abrupt change in Soviet policy toward that region will lead to a revival of an acrimonious debate with Fidel Castro over the ideological content of Soviet foreign policy. Although few would argue that Gorbachev's political position at home depends on the good graces of the Cuban leader, it is simplistic to assume that Gorbachev would want to forfeit his ideological credentials.

The USSR under Gorbachev has launched a three-pronged initiative toward Central America. To discourage the United States in Nicaragua, Gorbachev has dramatically increased the level of arms transfers to that country, insuring that any US intervention would be a long and bloody affair rather than a repeat of Grenada. To facilitate a diplomatic solution which would enable the Sandinistas to remain in power, he has launched a diplomatic offensive in Central America, creating closer ties with Costa Rica, Panama, Guatemala, and Honduras. Finally, in order to avoid a schism with Cuba and to protect Gorbachev's ideological credentials at home, the USSR has continued to shun the Duarte regime in El Salvador and maintained its rhetorical support for the El Salvadoran guerrillas.

Gorbachev's policy toward Nicaragua appears to be built around several premises and assumptions. The USSR is clearly pleased that a "socialist-oriented" state has emerged on the American mainland. The Sandinista regime fulfilled four tasks for the Soviet Union: it proved again the ideological vitality of the USSR; it drew US attention to an arena of secondary importance to the Soviet Union; it strained relations between the US and its European and Latin American allies; and it put pressure on the foreign policy consensus in the United States that had finally begun to heal from Vietnam. Despite all these gains, the cost to the Soviet Union has been relatively small. Aside from oil and grain, almost all Soviet aid to Nicaragua consists of either obsolete weapons or infrastructure projects which do not require hard currency expenditure.

While there was a time, especially after the invasion of Grenada in 1983, that Soviet analysts feared US intervention, it seems that Moscow now feels confident that the Sandinistas will survive in power. Soviet analysts note that even at the height of his power President Reagan was not able to mobilize the US public in support of his policy toward Nicaragua. Gravely weakened by the Iran–*contra* scandal and enjoying no public support, the United States is most unlikely to involve itself directly in Central America. Increasingly, the Soviet media refer to the Nicaraguan revolution as one that "knows how to defend itself." Although few in Moscow now fear direct US intervention, there is a growing recognition that the *contras* are more than a rag-tag group of Somozista officers financed by Washington. In private conversations, Soviet Latin Americanologists appear to realize that the *contras* are a credible fighting force with a base of support within Nicaragua.

There is growing concern in Moscow that Nicaragua, much like Angola, Afghanistan, and Mozambique, may become the scene of a protracted low-intensity conflict which will continue to be a drain on the anemic Soviet economy. Moscow has thus pushed Managua to retain its economic links with the capitalist world, and has actively campaigned throughout Latin America for the inclusion of the Sandinistas in regional arrangements. Soviet support for the Guatemala Accord reflected Gorbachev's recognition that the Sandinistas would have to seek some political accommodation with their opponents. Gorbachev has been most impressed in Poland by Jaruzelski's ability to concede judiciously to the opposition without actually giving up political power. The fact that Daniel Ortega was seated next to Jaruzelski during his visit to Moscow in November 1987 may not have been mere coincidence. It should be noted that today's Poland represents the most successful example of a Marxist-Leninist regime's ability to come to terms with hostile political forces without a basic abdication of power. The Soviets may well feel that the Polish model has some utility in Nicaragua.

It is worth remembering that when the USSR sought to modify Castro's "ultra-leftist" policies in the 1960s, it resorted to the "oil weapon," or slowing oil deliveries to Cuba to the point where the Cuban economy was close to a complete collapse. One reason for the USSR's reluctance to continue to meet all of Nicaragua's oil needs was its desire to impress on the Stalinists in the Nicaraguan government, such as Tomás Borge and Bayardo Arce, that Soviet willingness to underwrite the civil war is limited.

Gorbachev's current policy toward Nicaragua has drawn mixed reviews from the region. Daniel Ortega, who leads the *tercerista* faction within the FSLN, has always advocated broad cooperation with non-Marxist groups and enthusiastically endorsed Gorbachev's *perestroika* and *glasnost*:

> We cannot help but rejoice at the inspiring atmosphere of change in the land of the Soviets. We welcome Soviet reconstruction in every way.

The response from Cuba was very different. Fidel Castro lashed out at the Gorbachev idea of *perestroika*, ordering the closure of the open farmers' market in Havana, and he increasingly stressed traditional communist purity, moral values, and revolutionary fervor to revitalize the sagging Cuban economy. Prior to the last CEMA meeting where Gorbachev's *perestroika* was on the agenda, Castro allegedly said that "if Che Guevara heard that money would become people's main motive, he would be astounded."

On the issue of Central America, the USSR and Cuba again appear to be parting ways. While the USSR praised Nicaragua's efforts to comply with the Arias plan, the Cuban media was actually hostile. When Ortega allowed *La Prensa* to resume publication, Radio Havana retorted that *La Prensa* was a propaganda organ of the US embassy in Managua which would play the same role that the newspaper *El Mercurio* played in Allende's Chile. (Since communist analysts hold that *El Mercurio* was one of the key orchestrators of Allende's downfall, Cuba is clearly less than ecstatic about the current situation in Nicaragua.)

It is interesting to note that while the Cubans continue to refer to the *contras* as "Somozista bandits" with whom the Sandinistas should not negotiate, the Soviet media have started to use the more neutral term for the Nicaraguan guerrillas, referring to them as the *contras*. Furthermore, although President Daniel Ortega vowed never to negotiate with the US-supported guerrillas in Nicaragua, it was during Ortega's visit to Moscow in November of 1987 that he abruptly changed his position and agreed to enter negotiations with the *contras* through the mediation of Cardinal Obando y Bravo. From the beginning of these talks the Soviet Union continued to exert its influence to encourage their continuation. Bayardo Arce, perhaps the most militant member of the Sandinista directorate, visited Moscow on the eve of the start of the talks between the *contras* and the Sandinistas in Sapoa, Nicaragua, and held a meeting with Karen Brutents and Anatoly Dobrynin. In the press release describing the meetings, characterized as being held in "friendship and confidence" (a designation which in Soviet political parlance indicates disagreement), Arce stressed the "struggle of the Nicaraguan people" while Dobrynin stressed the USSR's "support for regional peace efforts."[21] While Soviet leaders were making no effort to conceal their disagreement with Arce, the *contra* leader Adolfo Calero was praised in the pages of *Izvestiia* (2 April 1988) for defying the Reagan administration and signing the Sapoa accords.

On the whole, the Soviet Union appears to continue to press for Nicaraguan compliance with the Arias plan while at the same time predicting that the peace process will lead to greater divisions within the *contra* movement, which will ultimately result in its weakening and disintegration.[22]

Perhaps the greatest innovation of Gorbachev's Central American policy is his effort to improve ties with Honduras, Guatemala, Panama, and Costa Rica. Honduras, Guatemala, and Panama spent most of the last forty years under right-wing military regimes, and their current governments, although democratically elected, remain under strong military influence. Traditionally, the Soviets have viewed these countries with contempt, and the USSR still does not have diplomatic relations with most of them. For decades, the Soviet media have depicted these states as fascist puppets of the United States. It was therefore most surprising when the Soviet ambassador to Costa Rica made a "private visit" to Guatemala (the first contact between the two countries since 1954) and met President Cerezo. Since then the USSR has agreed to purchase Guatemalan cotton and coffee, and has even offered to establish diplomatic relations (an offer that was rebuffed by Guatemala). The USSR nevertheless hosted a Guatemalan parliamentary delegation in August 1987, and the Soviet media continued to praise President Cerezo.

A similar change has occurred in Moscow's attitude toward Honduras. Until very recently, Honduras was treated by the Soviet media as the prototype of a US pseudo-colony, playing "host" to the *contras* and thousands of US troops sent to Central America to intimidate Nicaragua. Although an elected government was installed in Honduras in 1981, the Soviet attitude toward that country did not change until 1987. While President Azcona of Honduras does not receive the same billing as Guatemala's Cerezo, the USSR established trade links with Honduras in May 1987, and in September the Honduran trade minister Panting visited Moscow at the invitation of the USSR.

In the case of Panama, as noted, the USSR has extended strong diplomatic and moral support to General Manuel Noriega. The Soviets continue to insist that Noriega's sole crime was his refusal to turn Panama into a base of operations against Nicaragua and his insistence that the US honor its promise to relinquish the control of the Panama Canal in the year 2000. The USSR's overtures have paid off, with Panama increasingly aligning its foreign policy with that of the USSR, although the two countries still do not have diplomatic relations. Last year Panama finally agreed to meet a long-standing request of the USSR by granting the Soviet national carrier Aeroflot landing rights in Panama City.

Although the USSR has maintained diplomatic relations with Costa Rica since 1970, relations between the two countries have remained cool. Traditionally, Costa Rica has been one of the most pro-American countries in Central America, and indeed Costa Rica's President Monge was one of the most eloquent critics of the Sandinista regime in Nicaragua. The ascent of Gorbachev to power in the USSR and the election of Oscar Arias led to a rapid improvement in Soviet–Costa Rican relations. The USSR appreciated President Arias' opposition to President Reagan's Central American policy. Thus, even before the launching of the Arias plan for peace in Central America, Soviet–Costa Rican relations showed signs of improvement. The USSR generally expanded its purchases of Costa Rican exports, and since 1987 the Soviet Union agreed to purchase all the sugar that Costa Rica could not sell to the US due to the cuts in US sugar import quotas.

There are several possible motives for these overtures. First, the improvement in Moscow's attitude toward Honduras, Guatemala, Costa Rica, and Panama is consistent with Gorbachev's general pattern of attempting to improve relations with states that the USSR eschewed in the past (for example, Israel and Indonesia). Second, since there was never a serious guerrilla challenge in Honduras, and since the Guatemalan guerrillas were effectively defeated in the late 1970s, Soviet efforts to alienate these countries were gratuitous and yielded no benefits to the Soviet Union. Third, Soviet hostility toward Guatemala and Honduras merely pushed these countries even more into the orbit of the United States, thus enabling Washington to frustrate Nicaragua's effort to attain political accommodation through the Contadora process. Finally, Gorbachev appears to realize that the recognition of the Sandinistas by the rest of Central America as a legitimate entity is critical for the survival of the Sandinistas in power.

Numerous Soviet analysts have pointed out that the US was able to oust the Arbenz regime in Guatemala and the Bosch regime in the Dominican Republic only after those regimes were isolated from the rest of Latin America. To avoid the isolation of Nicaragua, Gorbachev has reversed the traditional Soviet policy of opposing Central American integration. Hence the USSR is enthusiastically supporting the establishment of a Central American parliament, a Central American common market, and any other regional organization which would include the current regime in Nicaragua. The USSR was the first outside power to endorse the Guatemala Accord signed in August 1987. The isolation of the Reagan administration after the signature of the accord appears to vindicate Moscow's new policy toward the region. It is doubtful that the Arias plan, which had isolated the US in its policy toward Nicaragua and Central America, would have gained the essential support of Guatemala and Honduras had these regimes continued to feel threatened by the USSR. Furthermore, the Arias plan was facilitated in part by the Soviet diplomatic initiative and Moscow's pressure on Ortega to negotiate with the *contras*. It is doubtful that the US Congress would have defied the Reagan administration and cut off funding to the *contras* had Ortega continued to refuse to negotiate with the rebels.

If Soviet policy toward most of Latin America is a reflection of the "new thinking" in the USSR, the case of El Salvador seems to illustrate the French saying that the more things change the more they remain the same. There, the Soviet position has not changed very much since the death of Brezhnev.

Although there is no indication that the USSR is currently involved in any significant weapons transfers to the Salvadoran guerrillas, Soviet hostility toward the Duarte regime is implacable. Several prominent Soviet analysts appear to believe that an armed struggle in El Salvador is bound to succeed.

Despite the efforts of President Duarte to bring about a democratic change along the lines of recent developments in Guatemala and Honduras, and despite his efforts to comply with the Arias plan, the Soviet media have remained adamant in their hostility to the regime. A recent article in *Sovietskaya Rossiya* described El Salvador as a "vast concentration camp" which was governed by the "anti-popular" regime of the "puppet" Duarte. Given Soviet efforts to improve its links with almost all regimes in Latin America, it is interesting that the USSR has remained so hostile to Duarte. There are several possible explanations for Moscow's policy.

First, the war in El Salvador is indeed a major financial and political drain on the United States, while costing Moscow little more than rhetoric. Second, accommodation with the Duarte regime would inevitably provoke an acrimonious exchange with Cuba at a time when Soviet–Cuban relations are already tense over economic and ideological issues.

Third, given the role of the armed forces in El Salvador's history, Soviet analysts must be aware that if the leftist guerrillas were to abandon their struggle and join the existing political system, their politics would not be like that of the Venezuelan communists, who ceased being guerrillas and became part of the legal opposition. In El Salvador, a repetition of the 1927 Kuomintang massacre of the Chinese communists or of El Salvador's own 1932 *matanza* is far more likely. Although Soviet leaders in the past have not hesitated to sacrifice local communists when they felt that it served their interests, a massacre of Salvadoran communists might provide Gorbachev's right-wing opponents with more ammunition to discredit his policies.

Finally, the success of the ultra-rightist Arena party in the recent parliamentary elections convinced Moscow that El Salvador's drift back to an ultra-right military dictatorship is inevitable. For all these reasons, as well as the continuing Soviet insistence that Marxism-Leninism is the tide of history, the USSR continues to pursue its radical policies in El Salvador.

Gorbachev's policy toward Latin America has been largely viewed as successful. Latin American leaders now see the USSR as a great power with legitimate interests in the region, which are actually complementary to theirs *vis-à-vis* the United States. Unlike the recent past, when most Latin American leaders ignored the USSR, today Latin American politicians travel to Moscow in order to bolster their political standing at home.

President Arias' public call for a US–Soviet dialogue on Nicaragua is indicative of a widespread acceptance of the USSR as a legitimate power in Latin American affairs. Furthermore, the USSR perceives itself as a power with major interests and responsibilities in the region. Thus, for example, when Costa Rica's President Arias asked the USSR to terminate military aid to Nicaragua following the US Congress' termination of military aid to the *contras*, Gorbachev in his reply note to Arias stated that the USSR was willing to consider an arms embargo to Nicaragua only in exchange for a US embargo – an embargo not only to the *contras*, but to the governments of Honduras and El Salvador as well.[23] The notion that the USSR would attempt to regulate the flow of US military aid to the regimes of Latin America is indeed a new development.

Despite heightened Soviet ambitions in Latin America, the relations between the two continue to improve. In most international forums Latin Americans have more in common with the USSR than with the United States. Although the volume of trade between the USSR and Latin America remains small, it appears to be entering a more stable phase in which mutual dependence will grow. The Soviet cultural presence in Latin America is expanding rapidly. Unlike past Soviet "diplomatic offensives" in other parts of the world (such as the Middle East, black Africa, or the Indian subcontinent), where the USSR was able to expand its political presence only after spending billions of rubles, in the case of Central America such an undertaking has been almost cost free.

The extent of Soviet penetration in Central America should not be overemphasized. The region will remain for the USSR the region of least importance in economic, political, and geostrategic terms. For Central America, the crucial economic and political arena will remain Washington, with the USSR playing a very marginal role. However, the era in which the USSR was perceived by most Latin Americans as either menacing or irrelevant is over.

Notes

PART I

Introduction

1 For a good discussion of the origins of the Monroe Doctrine, see Ernest R. May, *The Making of the Monroe Doctrine* (Cambridge, MA: Harvard University Press, 1975).
2 Stephen Clissold, *Soviet Relations with Latin America 1918–1968: A Documentary Survey* (New York: Oxford University Press, 1970).

1 Soviet perceptions of US–Latin American relations

1 See D. Bruce Jackson, *Castro, Kremlin, and Communism in Latin America* (Baltimore, MD: Johns Hopkins University Press, 1969).
2 For the Soviet perception of Johnson, see Arkady Shevchenko, *Breaking With Moscow* (New York: Knopf, 1985), 124.
3 Anna Matlina, *Kritika Kontseptsii "Mirnoi Reguliruemoi" Revoliutsii* (Moscow: ILA, 1968), 191.
4 V. Matveev, "Agressivnye deistviia amerikanskogo imperializma," *Kommunist* 9 (1965): 98–99.
5 V. Korionov, "Mechtaniia Obrechionykh," *Kommunist* 15 (1965): 109.
6 G. Veshnevskii, "Uzakonivatom Bezzakonie," *Pravda*, 22 September 1965, 4.
7 V. Korionov, "The Mask Is Torn Off," *Pravda*, 29 September 1965, 5.
8 For the text of Rashidov's speech, see Clissold, *Soviet Relations with Latin America 1918–1968*, 161.
9 Jackson, *Castro, Kremlin, and Communism in Latin America*, 93.
10 Boris Gvozderov, "Latin America: Wall Street's New Tactics," *New Times* 36 (1967): 19–21.
11 A. Mashbitz, "Latinskaia Amerika v Mezhdunardnom Kapitalisticheskom Razdele Truda," *MEMO* 11 (1964): 29–39.
12 Oleg Ignat'ev, "Dlinnye Ruki Monopolii," *Pravda*, 9 January 1967, 4.
13 For example, see V. Levin, "OAG Orudie Imperializma SShA," *Kommunist Vooruzhionnykh Sil* 2 (1965): 83.
14 Vitalii Levin, "The Big Stick's Modern Version," *New Times* 39 (1967): 13.

15 Viktor Bobovskii, "V Tupike," *Pravda*, 27 May 1966.
16 Zoia Romanova, *Problemy Ekonomicheskoi Integratsii v Latinskoi Amerike* (Moscow: Nauka, 1965), 243–50.
17 M. Gerechev, "Porochnyi Krug Politiki SShA v Latinskoi Amerike," *MEMO* 4 (1967): 63.
18 The Soviet press started to view the Andean Pact in that light after the Declaration of Lima (October 1969), whereby the group members vowed to take a joint position in limiting the penetration of foreign capital.
19 Wolfgang W. Brener, "The Place of Cuba in Soviet Latin American Strategy," *Studies on the Soviet Union* 2 (1968): 91.
20 B. Leibzon, "The Leninist Criteria for Revolutionaries: The Forms of Armed Struggle," *Kommunist* 8 (1968): 38–51.
21 K. S. Karol, *Guerrillas in Power: The Course of the Cuban Revolution* (New York: Hill & Wang, 1970), 408–9.
22 For example, see Karol, *Guerrillas in Power*, or Maurice Halperin, *The Rise and Decline of Fidel Castro* (Berkeley, CA: University of California Press, 1972), or Cole Blasier, *The Giant's Rival* (Pittsburgh, PA: University of Pittsburgh Press, 1983).
23 See Herbert S. Dinerstein, "Soviet Policy in Latin America," *The American Political Science Review* 1 (1967): 80–90.
24 *Pravda*, 9 April 1966, as quoted in Brener, "The Place of Cuba," 94.
25 Stanley Karnow, *Vietnam: A History* (New York: Viking Press, 1983), 494–95.
26 Matlina, *Kritika Kontseptsii "Mirnoi Reguliruemoi" Revoliutsii*.
27 See Kiva Maidonik, "Imperializm i razvivaiushchiesia Strany," *Latinskaia Amerika* 2, conference notes (1973): 3.
28 V. G. Bushuyev, "Latinskaia Amerika v Pervom Godu Novogo desintiletiia," *Mezhdunarodnaia Zhizn'* 2 (1972): 64–72.
29 Rubén Souza, "Revoliutsiia i Kontra Revoliutsiia v Latinskoi Amerike," *Kommunist* 1 (1975): 84.
30 V. G. Bushuyev, "Latinskaia Amerika v peredi Eshchio Trudnaia Bor'ba," *Kommunist Vooruzhionnykh Sil* 21 (1973): 80.
31 See Anatolii Shul'govskii, *Latinskaia Amerika: Armiia i Osvoboditel'noe Dvizhenie* (Moscow: Znanie, 1972), 32.
32 Iu. Antonov and V. Karpov, "Pentagon v Latinskoi Amerike," *Mezhdunarodnaia Zhizn'* 12 (1970): 82–86.
33 Shul'govskii, *Latinskaia Amerika*, 46.
34 Ibid., 49.
35 M. Bareshev, "Latinskaia Amerika v OON," *Latinskaia Amerika* 5 (1971): 15–25.
36 Ibid., 22.
37 E. Rusakov, "Protivorechiia Ostaiutsia," *Pravda*, 21 April 1975, 5.
38 V. G. Bushuyev, *Veter' Peremen nad Andami* (Moscow: Politizdat, 1972), 5.
39 G. F. Vishnia, *SShA-Latinskaia Amerika: Vnshnepolitichiskie Otnosheniia V Sovremenykh Usloviakh* (Moscow: Nauka, 1978), 65.
40 V. G. Bushuyev, "Latinskaia Amerika Na Novykh Rubezhakh," *Mezhdunarodnaia Zhizn'* 4 (1973): 53.

41 N. D. Turkatenko, "Korporatsii SShA i Politika Vashingtona v Latinskoi Amerike," *Latinskaia Amerika* 5 (1974): 29. (Note: Turkatenko wrote several articles on Latin America in *Kommunist* during the 1960s.)

42 For an example of such a view, see Iu. Sumbatian, "Latinskaia Amerika na Novykh Rubezhakh," *Kommunist Vooruzhionnykh Sil* 3 (1975): 79–83.

43 See Richard M. Nixon, *The Memoirs of Richard Nixon* (New York: Grosset & Dunlap, 1978), 394–95.

44 In 1970 Israel, in direct collaboration with the United States, used its military weight to thwart the PLO–Syrian effort to topple King Hussein's regime in Jordan; in the early 1970s Iran and Pakistan, in a joint effort, defeated a Marxist uprising in the Dhofar region of Oman.

45 Viktor Vol'skii *et al.*, eds., *Braziliia: Tendentsii Ekonomicheskogo i Sotsial'no-Politicheskogo Razvitiia* (Moscow: Nauka, 1983), 252–53.

46 For example, see B. Antonov, "Latinskaia Amerika Protiv Zasiliia SShA," *Mezhdunarodnaia Zhizn'* 7 (1971): 66–73.

47 Zoia I. Romanova, "Neokolonializm SShA v Latinskoi Amerike," *Novaia i Noveishaia Istoriia* 4 (1968): 22–38.

48 S. Onskii, "SShA-Latinskaia Amerika: Trudnyi Dialog," *Mezhdunarodnaia Zhizn'* 6 (1974): 75–78.

49 Ia. Kalinin, "Imperializm i Razvivaiushchiesia Strany," *Latinskaia Amerika* 2, conference notes: (1973) 210.

50 V. N. Selivanov, *Ekspansiia SShA v Latinskoi Amerike* (Moscow: Voenizdat, 1975), 10.

51 Vasilii Kuzentsov, "Obostrenie Ekonomicheskikh Protivorechii," *Latinskaia Amerika* 2 (1976): 5–88.

52 Lev L. Klochkovskii, "Novyi Mezhdunarodnyi Ekonomicheskii Poriadok i Latinskaia Amerika," *Latinskaia Amerika* 2 (1976): 55–70.

53 Ibid., 61–62.

54 Viktor Vol'skii, "Latinskaia Amerika v Sisteme Sovremennogo Kapitalizma," *Latinskaia Amerika* 3 (1979): 6–31.

55 Lev L. Klochkovskii, "Ekonomicheskaia Strategiia Monopolii SShA v Latinoamerikanskom Raione," *Latinskaia Amerika* 1 (1979): 38–39.

56 Zoia I. Romanova, "Ekonomicheskoe Osnovanie Gospodtsva SShA v Latinskoi Amerike," *Latinskoi Amerike* 2 (1970): 113.

57 Karen Brutents, as quoted in Erik Hoffmann and Frederik Ferlon, *The Soviet Conduct of Foreign Policy* (New York: Aledine Publishing Co., 1980), 482.

58 For example, see Anna Matlina, "Vneshniaia Politika: Samostoiatel'nosti v Usloviiakh Ekonomicheskoi Zavisimosti," *Latinskaia Amerika* 7 (1981): 78.

59 K. S. Sergeev and V. G. Tkatchenko, *Latinskaia Amerika: Bor'ba Za Nezavisimost'* (Moscow: IMO, 1975), 184.

60 L. Klochkovskii and I. Shermet'ev, "Latinskaia Amerika Krizis Zavisimogo Kapitalizma," *MEMO* 4 (1978): 53–66.

61 V. N. Selivanov, "Latinskaia Amerika v Planakh Imperializma SShA," *Kommunist Vooruzhionnykh Sil* 21 (1978): 80–85.

62 Leonid Brezhnev, *On Relations Between Socialist and Developing Countries* (Moscow: Progress Publishers, 1984), 69.

63 P. N. Fedoseev and I. R. Grigulevich, eds., *Pan-Americanism: Its Essence and Evolution* (Moscow: Academy of Sciences Press, 1982), 126.

64 Ibid., 127.
65 Viktor Lukin, "Kontseptsiia Tsentrov sily' i Latinskaia Amerika," *Latinskaia Amerika* 8 (1980): 5–19.
66 Y. Yelutin, "U.S.–Latin America Equal Partnership?" *International Affairs* 8 (1970): 65.
67 N. V. Mostovets, ed., *SShA i Latinskaia Amerika* (Moscow: Nauka, 1978), 6.
68 G. Vishnia, "SShA i Latinskaia Amerika Vzaimootnosheniia v Usloviiakh Razriadki," *MEMO* 8 (1975): 83–89.
69 Sergeev and Tkatchenko, *Latinskaia Amerika*, see pp. 35, 188, and 197.
70 V. Selivanov, "Latinskaia Amerika: Protiv diktata SShA," *Krasnaia Zvezda*, 3 June 1976, 3.
71 "Declaration of Havana," *Kommunist* 10 (1975): 97.
72 See round-table discussion, "Novye Tendentsii v Latinoamerikanskoi Politike SShA," *Latinskaia Amerika* 3 (1978): 150–68.
73 M. Vasiliev, "Sovremennyi 'Panamerikanizm,' Retorika i Politika," *Mezhdunarodnaia Zhizn'* 1 (1980): 33.
74 Genrikh A. Trofimenko, "Sredestva i Metody Vneshnei Politiki SShA," *Voprosy Istorii* 5 (1979): 59–77.
75 "Novye Tendentsii v Latinoamerikanskoi Politike SShA," 150.
76 Perhaps out of deference to *détente,* or because of uncertainty about the results of the uprising, the Soviet press remained contradictory in its assessment of the revolution's prospect.
77 Jorge Shafik Handal, "Trudnyi Put' Bor'by Sal'vadorskikh Kommunistov," *Kommunist* 3 (1977): 105–15 (especially 105 and 113–15).
78 S. A. Sergeev, "Latinskaia Amerika: God 1978," *Latinskaia Amerika* 1 (1979): 23.
79 V. G. Bushuyev and Iu. Kozlov, "Latinskaia Amerika: Novaia Rol' V Mezhdunarodnykh Otnosheniakh," *Kommunist* 12 (1978): 108–19 (especially 119).
80 Vsevolod Ovchinnikov, "A Step Toward Victory," *Pravda*, 19 July 1979, 5.
81 Quoted in Morris Rothenberg, "Since Reagan: The Soviets and Latin America," *Washington Quarterly* (Spring 1982): 176.
82 Quoted in Richard Feinberg, "Central America, the View from Moscow," *Washington Quarterly* (Spring 1982): 173.
83 Ibid.
84 Paul Seabury and Walter McDougall, eds., *The Grenada Papers* (San Francisco, CA: ICS, 1984), 10.
85 Shafik Handal, "Tsentral'naia Amerika: Krizis Voennykh Diktatur," *Latinskaia Amerika* 6 (1979): 23–35.
86 Handal, "Na Puti K Svobode," *Kommunist* 17 (1980): 103.
87 Howard J. Wiarda and Mark Falcoff, *The Communist Challenge in the Caribbean and Central America* (Washington: American Enterprise Institute for Public Policy Research, 1987), 88.
88 V. Skliar, *Latinskaia Amerika: Bor'ba Za Nezavisimost' i Sotsyal'nyi Progres* (Moscow: Znanie, 1980), 60.
89 See N. V. Dmitriev, "Politicheskie Manevry SShA v Nikarague," *Latinskaia Amerika* 7 (1980): 57–66.

90 Boris Ponomarev, "Neodolimost' Osvoboditel'nogo Dvizheniia," *Kommunist* 1 (1980): 25.
91 Ibid., 15.
92 Vasiliev, "Sovremennyi 'Panamerikanizm,' Ritorika i Politika," 30–40.
93 Ibid., 36.
94 E. V. Mitiaeva, "Vmeshatel'stvo SShA v Sal'vadore," *SShA* 7 (1980): 60.
95 For example, see N. N. Glagolev, "Ronald Reagan – Kandidat Respublikanskoi Partii," *SShA* 9 (1980): 105–8. See also O. N. Anichkin, "Sto dnei Prezidentstva Reigana," *SShA* 5 (1981): 42–46.
96 *The New York Times*, 25 February 1982.
97 See Morris Rothenberg, "Latin America in Soviet Eyes," *Problems of Communism* (Fall 1983): 4.
98 See Jiri Valenta, "Soviet Strategy in the Caribbean Basin," *U.S. Naval Institute Proceedings* (May 1982): 173–81.
99 Seabury and McDougall, eds., *The Grenada Papers*, 23.
100 E. V. Mitiaeva, "Povorot v Latinoamerikanskoi Politike," *SShA* 6 (1981): 81–84.
101 A. N. Glinkin, B. Martynov, and P. Iakovlev, *Evoliutsiia Latinoamerikanskoii Politiki SShA* (Moscow: Nauka, 1982), 141.
102 Ibid., 169.
103 Ibid., 180.
104 M. A. Oborotova, "Vneshnepoliticheskii Usloviia Razvitiia Revoliutsionnogo Protsessa (Tsentral'naia Amerika)," *Latinskaia Amerika* 7 (1982): 86–105.
105 A. Glinkin and P. Iakovlev, "Latinskaia Amerika v Global'noi Strategii Imperializma," *MEMO* 10 (1982): 65–83.
106 See Rothenberg, "Since Reagan," 177.

2 Latin America's role in the capitalist division of labor

1   Z. I. Romanova, "Latinskaia Amerika na Vneshnem Rynke: Problema Sootnosheniia Tsen," *Latinskaia Amerika* 6 (1971): 38–57.
2   A. Glinkin, and P. Iakovlev, "Latinskaia Amerika: Sovremennyi Etap Protivoborstva S Imperializmom," *MEMO* 7 (1976): 17.
3   Ibid., 17, 20.
4   Ibid., 20. For a similar analysis of the decline of Latin America within the world capitalist system, see N. N. Kholodov, *Latinskaia Amerika: Problemy Vneshnei Zadolzhennosti* (Moscow: Nauka, 1979).
5   L. Klochkovskii, and I. Shermet'ev, "Latinskaia Amerika Krizis Zavisimogo Kapitalizma," *MEMO* 4 (1978): 53–56.
6   A. N. Glinkin, "Latinskaia Amerika v Mezhdunarodnykh Otnosheniakh na Poroge 80kh Godov," *Latinskaia Amerika* 5 (1979): 21–36.
7   Viktor Vol'skii, "Latinskaia Amerika v Sisteme Sovremennogo Kapitalizma," *Latinskaia Amerika* 3 (1979): 14.
8   Ibid., 20.
9   Ibid., 22.
10 Ibid.

11 A. N. Glinkin, and A. I. Sizonenko, eds., *Vneshnaia Politika Stran Latinskoi Ameriki* (Moscow: Mezhdunarodnye Otnosheniia, 1982), 236–38.
12 Ibid., 239.
13 Ibid., 249–54.
14 Ibid., 259.
15 Iu. N. Paniev, "Nekotorye Aspekty Ekonomicheskikh Otnoshenii Latino-amerikanskikh Stran S EES," *Latinskaia Amerika* 3 (1982): 29.
16 Ibid., 30.
17 Ibid., 34.
18 Ibid., 31.
19 For a discussion of the Japanese penetration of Latin America, see Iu. Barsukov, "Iaponiia v Latinskoi Amerike," *MEMO* 7 (1975): 116–19.
20 See L. L. Klochkovskii, *Latinskaia Amerika v Sisteme Mirovykh Khoziaist-vennykh Sviazei* (Moscow: Mezhdunarodnye Otnosheniia, 1984), 29, 44.
21 V. O. Kistanov, "Platsdarm Iaponskikh Monopolii v Latinskoi Amerike," *Latinskaia Amerika* 4 (1976): 80–97.
22 Evgenii Primakov, "Zakon Neravnomernosti Razvitiia i Istoricheskie Sud'by Osvobodivshikhsia Stran," *MEMO* 12 (1980): 34–36.
23 Klochkovskii, *Latinskaia Amerika v Sisteme Mirovykh Khoziaistvennykh Sviazei*, 30–32.
24 Ibid., 33.
25 Quoted in Jerry F. Hough, *The Struggle for the Third World: Soviet Debates and American Options* (Washington, DC: The Brookings Institution, 1986), 237.

3 Latin America's role in the Third World

1 See David Kimchi, *The Afro-Asia Movement. Ideology and Foreign Policy of the Third World* (Jerusalem: Israel Universities Press, 1973), 160.
2 For a discussion of the emerging ties between Latin America and the Third World during the early 1970s, see James D. Theberge, *Latin America in the World System: The Limits of Internationalism* (Beverly Hills, CA and London: Sage Publications, 1975), 33–36.
3 Aaron Segal, "Perspektivy Dvukh Kontinentov," *Za Rubezhom* 6 (1966): 8–9.
4 For example, see A. P. Baryshev "Latinskaia Amerika v OON," *Latinskaia Amerika* 5 (1971): 15–25.
5 R. A. Tuzmukhamedov, "Neprisoedinenie 'Latino-Amerikanskii Etap'?" *Latinskaia Amerika* 1 (1972): 46.
6 Ibid., 49.
7 Ibid., 46–47.
8 Ibid., 60.
9 Ibid., 63.
10 Lev L. Klochkovskii, "Novyi Mezhdunarodnyi Ekonomicheskii Poriadok i Latinskaia Amerika," *Latinskaia Amerika* 2 (1976): 56.
11 Ibid., 58–59.
12 G. Z. Tanin, "Osobennosti Vneshnei Politiki Voennykh v 70e Gody," *Latinskaia Amerika* 1 (1979): 139.

13 Ibid.
14 Ibid., 140, 145.
15 M. L. Chumakova, "Evoliutsiia Vneshnei Politiki (Brazilia)," *Latinskaia Amerika* 4 (1980): 66.
16 Ibid., 67.
17 Glinkin, "Latinskaia Amerika v Mezhdunarodnykh Otnosheniakh na Poroge 80kh Godov," 32–33.
18 Anna Matlina, "Vneshnaia Politika: Samostoiatel'nost' v Usloviiakh Ekonomicheskoi Zavisimosti?" *Latinskaia Amerika* 6 (1980): 79–80.
19 Ibid., 88–89.
20 Ibid., 90.
21 V. N. Nikolaev, "Ot Belgrada k Gavane," *Latinskaia Amerika* 4 (1979): 8.
22 Ibid., 19.
23 Ibid.
24 Juan Cobo, "Idei Bandunga i Latinskaia Amerika," *Latinskaia Amerika* 5 (1980): 133–42.
25 Glinkin and Sizonenko, eds., *Vneshnaia Politika Stran Latinskoi Ameriki*, 275.
26 Ibid., 277.
27 For a detailed analysis of the USSR's changing attitude toward a new economic world order, see Elizabeth K. Valkenier, *The Soviet Union and the Third World: An Economic Bind* (New York: Praeger Publishers, 1985), 117–22.

4 Soviet views on Latin America's regional integration

1 See G. Pope Atkins, *Latin America in the International Political System* (New York: Free Press, 1977), 276.
2 Zoia I. Romanova, "Ekonomicheskaia Integratsiia v Latinskoi Amerike: Novyi Etap Protivorechii" (*Novaia i Noveishaia Istoriia* 3 1966): 79–81.
3 Ibid., 82.
4 Ibid., 83.
5 N. Iudanov, "Integratsiia Ograblennykh," *Mezhdunarodnaia Zhizn'* 3 (1965): 117–19.
6 A. Shul'govskii, "Latin America in the Modern World," *International Affairs* 9 (1966): 59.
7 Ibid., 63.
8 Ibid., 66.
9 Iu. Gvozdev, "Latin America: Integration Problems," *International Affairs* 10 (1968): 39–41.
10 Ibid., 44.
11 N. G. Zaitsev, "LAST Cherez Trudnosti i Protivorechiia," *Latinskaia Amerika* 3 (1975): 85.
12 Ibid., 92.
13 N. G. Zaitsev, "Latin America: Some Development Trends," *International Affairs* 11 (1976): 55.
14 Ibid., 58.
15 Glinkin and Sizonenko, eds., *Vneshnaia Politika Stran Latinskoi Ameriki*, 104.

16 Lev L. Klochkovskii, *The Economies of the Countries of Latin America* (Moscow: Progress Publishers, 1984), 355–66.
17 A. Kartsev, "Tsentral'naia Amerika: Integratsiia Pode Egidoi SShA," *Mezhdunarodnaia Zhizn'* 6 (1965): 108–9.
18 A. N. Glinkin, V. Vol'skii, and B. Gvozderov, eds., *Strany Latinskoi Ameriki v Sovremennykh Mezhdunarodnykh Otnosheniakh* (Moscow: Nauka, 1967), 239, 279.
19 Klochkovskii, *The Economies of the Countries of Latin America*, 372.
20 Oleg Konstantinov, "The New Andean Group," *New Times* 19 (1971): 29.
21 G. S. Efimova, and A. A. Lavut, "Andskaia Gruppa," *Latinskaia Amerika* 6 (1971): 70.
22 Ibid., 72.
23 S. Mishin, "Latin America: Two Trends of Development," *International Affairs* 6 (1976): 56.
24 Ibid., 57.
25 Ibid., 58.
26 Ibid.
27 A. Lavut, "Andskaia Gruppa," *MEMO* 11 (1975): 122.
28 *TASS*, 4 January 1977.
29 Vadim Listov, *Pravda*, 19 September 1977.
30 V. Iakubovski, *Pravda*, 21 May 1979.
31 V. Sudarev, "Andskaia Gruppa na Poroge 80kh Gedov," *MEMO* 12 (1980): 136–42.
32 Ibid., 141.
33 Ibid., 140–42.
34 E. V. Lyvkin, "Opyt Andskoi Gruppy Po Regulirovaniiu Deiatel'nosti Inostrannogo Kapitala," *Latinskaia Amerika* 4 (1982): 33.
35 Ibid., 36.
36 Glinkin and Sizonenko, eds., *Vneshnaia Politika Stran Latinskoi Ameriki*, 110.
37 Ibid., 111.
38 Ibid., 112.
39 For example, see V. B. Tarasov, "Novoe Ob'edinenie Amazonskii Pakt," *Latinskaia Amerika* 2 (1979): 71–81.
40 *Pravda*, 6 August 1975.
41 *Izvestiia*, 21 October 1975.
42 I. K. Shermet'ev, "Chto Lezhit v Osnove Segodniashnikh Problem?" *Latinskaia Amerika* 4 (1982): 5–9.
43 N. G. Zaitsev, "Vozmozhnosti i Protivorechiia Regional'nogo Ekonomicheskogo Sotrudnichestva," *Latinskaia Amerika* 4 (1982): 9–21.
44 Ibid., 15.
45 See N. Zinov'ev, *Latinskaia Amerika: Regional'noe Sotrudnichestvo i Problemy Razvitiia* (Moscow: Progress Publishers, 1983).

5 Soviet conclusions regarding Latin America's ability to conduct an independent foreign policy

1 Quoted in Hough, *The Struggle for the Third World*, 236.
2 Matlina, "Vneshniaia Politika: Samostoiatel'nosti v Usloviiakh Ekonomicheskoi Zavisimosti?" *Latinskaia Amerika* 6 (1981): 80.

3 Ibid., 89.

4 See "Latinskaia Amerika: Vneshniaia Politika i Ekonomicheskaia Zavisimost'," *Latinskaia Amerika* 9 (1981), 10 (1981), and 10 (1982).

5 Anatolii Glinkin's presentation in the conference titled, "Latinskaia Amerika: Vneshniaia Politika i Ekonomicheskaia Zavisimost'," *Latinskaia Amerika* 8 (1981): 43.

6 Ibid., 45.

7 Ibid.

8 Ibid., 49.

9 Shul'govskii, "Latinskaia Amerika: Vneshniaia Politika," 63.

10 Vitalii Fadin, "Latinskaia Amerika: Vneshniaia Politika i Ekonomicheskaia Zavisimost'," Part 2, *Latinskaia Amerika* 9 (1981): 55.

11 P. P. Iakovlev, "Latinskaia Amerika: Vneshniaia Politika i Ekonomicheskaia Zavisimost'," Part 2, *Latinskaia Amerika* 9 (1981): 57.

12 Ibid., 57.

13 V. N. Dmitriev, "Latinskaia Amerika: Vneshniaia Politika i Ekonomicheskaia Zavisimost'," Part 3, *Latinskaia Amerika* 10 (1982): 57.

14 Ibid.

15 Ibid., 59.

16 Matlina, "Vneshniaia Politika," 69–70.

17 Ibid., 71.

18 Ibid., 68.

19 V. P. Totskii, "Khristianskaiia Demokratiia v Politicheskoi Sisteme Stran Latinskoi Ameriki," *Latinskaia Amerika* 8 (1981): 58.

20 Ibid., 53.

21 Ibid., 55–56.

22 Maidonik, "Latinskaia Amerika: Vneshniaia Politika," *Latinskaia Amerika* 10 (1981): 73.

23 Quoted in Hough, *The Struggle for the Third World*, 236.

24 Lev L. Klochkovskii, "Latinskaia Amerika: Vneshniaia Politika i Ekonomicheskaia Zavisimost'," Part 2, *Latinskaia Amerika* 9 (1981): 50.

25 Ibid., 51.

26 E. S. Dabagyan, "Latinskaia Amerika Vneshniaia Politika i Ekonomicheskaia Zavisimost'," Part 3, *Latinskaia Amerika* 10 (1982): 53.

27 V. P. Sudarev, "Vneshnepoliticheskie Aspekty Andskoi Intergratsii," *Latinskaia Amerika* 6 (1981): 29.

28 Ibid., 30.

PART II

6 The Latin American church

1 For example, see A. F. Shul'govskii, "O Katolicheskom 'Tret' em Puti' v Latinskoi Amerike," *MEMO* 6 (1958): 101.

2 Iu. Gvozdev, "V Strane Zolotoi Legendy," *Nauka i Religia* 10 (1964): 83–87.

3 I. R. Grigulevich, "U Vlasti Levye Katoliki," *Nauka i Religia* 12 (1964): 82–83.

4 Orlando Millas, "Christian Democratic Reformism: The Chilean Exper-

iment," *World Marxist Review* 11 (1965): 69. For a more detailed discussion of the involvement of the Alliance for Progress, see Orlando Millas' article in the May 1966 issue of the *World Marxist Review*.

5 Ibid.

6 *Pravda*, 3 April 1966.

7 R. Ramírez, and N. Tsicgir', "Novoe Veianie v Kolumbiskoii Tserkvi," *MEMO* 11 (1965): 126–28.

8 Roque Dalton, "Catholics and Communists in Latin America: Some Aspects of the Present Situation," *World Marxist Review* 1 (1968): 86.

9 Ibid., 87.

10 I. R. Grigulevich, "Chili Pobeda Narodnykh Sil i Pozitsiia Tserkvi," *Nauka i Religia* 5 (1971): 69.

11 Dalton, "Catholics and Communists in Latin America," 84.

12 Ibid., 85.

13 Ibid., 85.

14 Ibid., 86.

15 Ibid., 85, 88.

16 M. Andreev, "Katolitsizm v Politicheskoi Zhizni Latino Amerikanskikh Stran," *MEMO* 6 (1968): 118.

17 Ibid., 116.

18 Ibid., 121.

19 I. R. Grigulevich, "Novoe i Staroe v Latino-Amerikanskom Katolitsizme," *Voprosy Nauchnogo Ateizma* 6 (1968): 359.

20 Ibid., 357.

21 Ibid., 362–67.

22 V. P. Andronova, *Kolumbia Tserkov' i Obshchestvo* (Moscow: Nauka, 1970), 72–211.

23 Ibid., 218–23.

24 I. R. Grigulevich, "Pobeda Narodnykh Sil i Pozitsiia Tserkvi," 65–69.

25 I. R. Grigulevich, *"Miatezhnaia" Tserkov v Latinskoyoi Amerike* (Moscow: Nauka, 1972), 139.

26 Ibid., 118.

27 Ibid., 133.

28 Ibid., 141–43.

29 Ibid., 143–47.

30 Ibid., 170–79.

31 Ibid., 181–84.

32 Ibid., 199–205.

33 Ibid., 217–59.

34 Ibid., 260.

35 Ibid., 255.

36 I. R. Grigulevich, "Katoliki, Marksisty, i Revoliutsionnye Protsessy v Latinskoi Amerike (a book review of Rosales' book by the same title), *Voprosy Nauchnogo Ateizma* 16 (1974): 313–16.

37 B. I. Koval', S. I. Semenov, and A. F. Shul'govskii, *Revoliutsionnye Protsessy v Latinskoi Amerike* (Moscow: Nauka, 1974), 306.

38 Ibid., 315.

39 Ibid., 316.
40 Ibid., 318.
41 A. N. Glinkin and A. F. Shul'govskii, eds., *Latinskaia Amerika: Problemy Edinstva Anti-Imperialisticheskikh Sil*, vol. 1 (Moscow: ILA, 1974), 214–17.
42 Ibid., 228.
43 I. R. Grigulevich, "Katoliki i Fashistskii Perevorot v Chili," *Voprosy Nauchnogo Ateizma* 18 (1975): 184–206.
44 For the text, see "Declaration of Havana," *Kommunist* 10 (1975): 88–109.
45 S. González, "Decisive Prerequisites for the Overthrow of Fascist Dictatorship," *World Marxist Review* 3 (1976): 110.
46 Ibid., 113.
47 Luis Corvolán, "Chiliiskaia Katolicheskaia Tserkov'," *Latinskaia Amerika* 6 (1977): 36.
48 Ibid., 37–38.
49 Ibid., 39.
50 A. F. Shul'govskii, ed., *Natsionalizm v Latinskoi Amerike: Politicheskie i Ideologicheskie Techeniia* (Moscow: Nauka, 1976), 160.
51 Ibid., 162–63.
52 Ibid., 164.
53 Ibid., 169.
54 Karen Khachaturov, "Imperializm i 'Miatezhnaia' Tserkov," *Mezhdunarodnaia Zhizn'* 8 (1977): 86–91.
55 V. P. Andronova, "Bor'ba za 'Teologiiu Osvobozhdeniia'," *Latinskaia Amerika* 9 (1980): 58.
56 Ibid., 61.
57 Ibid., 51–56.
58 I. R. Grigulevich, "Latinoamerikanskaia Tserkov' Na Poroge 80kh Godov," *Latinskaia Amerika* 9 (1980): 31–34.
59 Ibid., 35–37.
60 Ibid., 39.
61 V. Vol'skii *et al.*, eds., *Braziliia: Tendentsii Ekonomicheskogo i Sotsial'no-Politicheskogo Razvitiia* (Moscow: Nauka, 1983). See N. S. Konstantinova, "Polozhenie i Sovremennye Tendentsii v Katolicheskoi Tserkvi," 217–23.
62 A. F. Shul'govskii, ed., *Sovremennye Ideologicheskie Techeniia v Latinskoi Amerike* (Moscow: Nauka, 1983), 244–55.
63 Ibid., 243.
64 Ibid., 237.
65 Ibid.
66 Ibid., 239–40.

7 The Latin American armed forces

1 The term "army" will be used generically to include all the services of the armed forces.
2 Mangus Morner, *Race Mixture in the History of Latin America* (Boston: Little, Brown and Company, 1967), 88–89.
3 Anatolii Shul'govskii, "V Poiskakh Ideologicheskogo Kompasa," *Mezhdunarodnaia Zhizn'* 8 (1963): 112.

4 Alfredo Castro, "Tactics of the Struggle Against the Dictatorship in Brazil," *World Marxist Review* 9 (8) 1966: 45.
5 For examples of Soviet analysis of the armies of Asia and Africa, see A. Iskederov, "Armiia, Politika, Narod," *Izvestiia*, 17 January 1967, 2. See also G. Mirskii, "O Kharaktere Sotsial'nykh Sil Azii i Afriki," *Kommunist* 17 (1968).
6 Alfred Stepan, *The Military in Politics: Changing Patterns in Brazil* (Princeton, NJ: Princeton University Press, 1974), 3–56. (Although the study is limited to Brazil, its findings are applicable to most of Latin America.)
7 S. Kondrashov, "U.S.A. and Revolt in Brazil," *Izvestiia*, 4 May 1964, 2.
8 Iu. A. Antonov, *Braziliia: Armiia i Politika* (Moscow: Nauka, 1973), 194.
9 L. Kamynin, "The Revolt Against the Triumvirate," *Izvestiia*, 27 April 1965, 2.
10 For example, see "The American Gendarme with the Big Stick," *Pravda*, 19 April 1965, 5.
11 Charles McClane, *Soviet–Middle East Relations* (London: Central Asia Research Center, 1973), 35.
12 G. I. Mirskii, *Armiia i Politika v Stranakh Azii i Afriki* (Moscow: Nauka, 1970), 4.
13 L. Kamynin, "Fars bez pereodevaniia," *Izvestiia*, 29 October 1968, 5.
14 Quoted in Goure and Rothenberg, *Soviet Penetration of Latin America*, 82.
15 Oleg Ignat'ev, "Monopolii Diktuiut," *Pravda*, 8 December 1968, 5.
16 V. Levin, "Rashchioty i proschioty Pentagona," *Pravda*, 13 November 1969.
17 Conference of Communist and Workers' Parties (Moscow: Novosti Press, 1969).
18 Juan Cobo, *Literaturnaia Gazeta*, 11 December 1968, quoted in Goure and Rothenberg, *Soviet Penetration of Latin America*.
19 Juan Cobo, "The Peruvian Phenomenon," *New Times* 11 (1970): 21–24.
20 Iu. Antonov and V. Komarov, "Pentagon v Latinskoi Amerike," *Mezhdunarodnaia Zhizn'* 12 (1970): 81.
21 *Pravda*, 27 September 1970.
22 Cobo, "The Peruvian Phenomenon," 21.
23 Souza, "Revoliutsiia i Kontra Revoliutsiia v Latinskoi Amerike," 84. For a similar analysis, see J. Cobo and G. Mirskii, "O Nekotorykh Osobennostiakh Evoliutsii Armii Latinoamerikanskogo Kontinenta," *Latinskaia Amerika* 4 (1971): 42–51.
24 Boris Ponomarev, "Topical Problems of the Theory of Revolutionary Process," *Kommunist* 15 (1971): 62.
25 Ibid., 75.
26 Anatolii F. Shul'govskii, "Latinskaia Amerika: Armiia i Politika," *Latinskaia Amerika* 4 (1972): 9–10.
27 Ibid., 23.
28 N. S. Leonov, "Peru: Novaia Rol' Voennykh," *Latinskaia Amerika* 4 (1971): 86.
29 Iu. A. Antonov, "Armiia v Sotsial'no-Politicheskom Razvitii Brazilii 1961–1964," *Latinskaia Amerika* 4 (1971): 98–106.
30 Cobo and Mirskii, "O Nekotorykh Osobennostiakh Evoliutsii Armii: Latinoamerikanskogo Kontinenta," 50.

31 Silvio J. Mendiandua, "K Istorii Politicheskogo Militarizma v Latinskoi Amerike," *Latinskaia Amerika* 4 (1971): 55.
32 Anna A. Matlina, *Kritika Kontseptsii "Mirnoi Reguliruemoi Revolutsii" Dlia Latinskoi Ameriki* (Moscow: Nauka, 1971), 256.
33 Col. Iu. Sumbatian, "Vooruzhionnye Sily Latinskoi Ameriki," *Krasnaia Zvezda*, 20 August 1971.
34 A. Shul'govskii, ed., *Peru 150 let Nezauisimosti* (Moscow: ILA, 1971), 81.
35 Goure and Rothenberg, *Soviet Penetration of Latin America*, 84.
36 G. Mirskii, *Problems of the National Liberation Movement* (Moscow: Novosti Press, 1971), 66.
37 Jorge del Prado, "Is There a Revolution in Peru?" *World Marxist Review* 1 (1971): 20.
38 N. V. Rusinov and A. F. Feodorov, "Vooruzhionnye Sily Peru (do 10/1968)," *Latinskaia Amerika* 3 (1970): 179, 185.
39 Shul'govskii, *Latinskaia Amerika: Armiia i Osvoboditel'noe Dvizhenie*, 45.
40 Ibid., 36.
41 Ibid., 51.
42 Jorge del Prado, "The Revolution Continues," *World Marxist Review* 1 (1973): 65.
43 Ibid., 70.
44 Jorge del Prado, "Revoliutsionnyi Protsess v Peru i Pozitsiia Kommunisticheskoi Partii," *Kommunist* 13 (1973): 104.
45 Ibid., 111–12.
46 Anatolii Shul'govskii, "Kritika Nekotorykh Melkoburzhaznykh Kontseptsii o Roli Armii," *Latinskaia Amerika* 5 (1973): 66.
47 Ibid., 65–69.
48 For an example of standard Soviet praise of the Chilean army, see the text of the Spanish language broadcast of Radio Peace and Progress, 8 July 1973.
49 *Pravda*, 7 November 1970.
50 *New Times*, 2 April 1975.
51 Iurii Eliutin, "Latinskaia Amerika: Pentagon i Gonka Vooruzhenii," *Mezhdunarodnaia Zhizn'* 12 (1968): 63–70.
52 Konstantin Tarasov, *SShA i Latinskaia Amerika: Voenno-Politicheskie i Voenno–Ekonomicheskie Otnosheniia* (Moscow: Politizdat, 1972), 143.
53 Ibid., 168.
54 Konstantin Tarasov, "SShA-Latinskaia Amerika: Sistema Voenno-Ekonomicheskikh Otnoshenii," *Latinskaia Amerika* 2 (1976): 36.
55 Ibid., 51.
56 V. N. Selivanov, *Voennaiia Politika SShA v Stranakh Latinskoi Ameriki* (Moscow: ILA, 1970), 94.
57 Ibid., 101.
58 A. Aleksin, "'Tikhaia' Interventsiia SShA v Latinskoi Amerike," *Kommunist* 10 (1970): 97.
59 L. Padilla, J. Laborde, and E. Sousa, "Latin America: Anti-imperialist Fight and the Armed Forces," *World Marxist Review* 3 (1971): 91.
60 Ibid.
61 Cobo and Mirskii, "O Nekotorykh Osobennostiakh Evoliutsii Armii Latinoamerikanskogo Kontinenta," 49.

62 V. Tikhmenev, "Leninism i Revoliutsionnyi Protsess v Latinskoi Amerike," *Kommunist* 3 (1971): 114–19.
63 L. Padilla, "Some Lessons of Events in Bolivia," *World Marxist Review* 11 (1971): 24.
64 Ibid.
65 Stephen T. Hosmer and Thomas W. Wolfe, *Soviet Policy and Practice Toward Third World Conflicts* (Lexington, MA: Lexington Books, 1983), 43.
66 *Krasnaia Zvezda,* 3 June 1972.
67 TASS, 23 September 1972.
68 *Krasnaia Zvezda,* 13 March 1972.
69 *The Guardian,* 18 December 1973, and *The Daily Telegraph,* 26 February 1974.
70 TASS, 18 June 1971.
71 *Novoe Vremia,* 19 March 1971.
72 *The Guardian,* 14 July 1971.
73 Robert S. Leiken, "East Winds in Latin America," *Foreign Policy* 42 (1981): 96.
74 Hosmer and Wolfe, *Soviet Policy and Practice Toward Third World Conflicts,* 45.
75 Radio Moscow, 13 April 1972.
76 *Krasnaia Zvezda,* 26 May 1972.
77 TASS, 31 May 1972.
78 TASS, 17 September 1972.
79 *The Daily Telegraph,* 29 September 1972.
80 *Prensa Latina,* 23 May 1973.
81 Radio Peace and Progress, 8 July 1973.
82 *Krasnaia Zvezda,* 6 September 1973.
83 For a more complete discussion, see Aldo César Vacs, *Discreet Partners: Argentina and the USSR Since 1917* (University of Pittsburgh Press, 1985), 24–28.
84 *Pravda,* 30 July 1972.
85 *Krasnaia Zvezda,* 19 December 1972.
86 *Izvestiia,* 5 December 1973.
87 Anatolii Shul'govskii, "Vooruzhionnye Sily Chili: Ot 'apolitichnosti' k Konterrevoliutsii," *Latinskaia Amerika* 6 (1974): 32.
88 Ibid., 48.
89 Ibid., 43.
90 A. Shul'govskii, "Revolution and the Army in Latin America," *Soviet Military Review* 9 (1975): 46.
91 K. I. Zarodov, ed., *1,000 Dnei Revoliutsii* (Prague: MIR i Sotsializm, 1978).
92 Quoted in Cole Blasier, *The Giant's Rival,* K. R. Zarodv, ed., 86.
93 See M. Kudachkin and A. Kutsenkov, *Uroki Chili* (Moscow: Nauka, 1977).
94 Boris Ponomarev, "The World Situation and the Revolutionary Process," *World Marxist Review* 6 (1974): 11.
95 Goure and Rothenberg, *Soviet Penetration of Latin America,* 113.
96 *Uroki Chili,* 45.
97 Alvaro Delgado, "Against the Danger of Militarism," *World Marxist Review* 2 (1974): 103.
98 Anatolii Shul'govskii, "Ideologicheskie i Teoreticheskie Aspekty Revoliutsionnogo Protsessa v Peru," *Latinskaia Amerika* 4 (1975): 12–14.

99 S. A. Kazakov, "Vooruzhionnye Sily i Politicheskaia Vlast' v Argentine," *Latinskaia Amerika* 1 (1977), 59.

100 Ibid., 62–63.

101 Ibid., 63.

102 Ibid., 72.

103 Piotr Shiblin, "The Pentagon and Latin America," *New Times* 2 (1977): 25–26.

104 Ibid., 26.

105 A. F. Shul'govskii, Symposium on the Armies of Latin America, *Latinskaia Amerika* 3 (1977): 52.

106 Ibid., 55.

107 A. N. Glinkin, Symposium on the Armies of Latin America, 60.

108 G. I. Mirskii, Symposium on the Armies of Latin America, 67.

109 Ibid., 70.

110 J. Cobo, Symposium on the Armies of Latin America, 76.

111 Ibid., 78.

112 C. M. Khenkin, Symposium on the Armies of Latin America, 82–83.

113 Sergo Mikoian, Symposium on the Armies of Latin America, 143–44.

114 A. F. Shul'govskii, Symposium on the Armies of Latin America, 146–48.

115 Alain Joxe, "Latinoamerikanskie Voennye i Denatsionalizatsiia Gosudarstva," *Latinskaia Amerika* 6 (1977): 93–94.

116 Anna A. Matlina, "Imperializm i 'Revoliutsiia Voennykh,'" *Latinskaia Amerika* 5 (1978): 152.

117 Ibid., 152, 158.

118 For a discussion of Guevara's rehabilitation, see Robert S. Leiken, *Soviet Strategy in Latin America* (New York: Praeger Publishers, 1982), 36–38.

119 A. A. Sosnovskii, "Braziliia: Evoliutsiia Rezhima i Armiia," *Latinskaia Amerika* 11 (1981): 36–37. (For a similar analysis, see I. Shokina's chapter in Vol'skii *et al.*, *Braziliia*, 36–37.)

120 A. A. Sukhostat, "Politicheskaia Bor'ba v Usloviiakh Krizisa Voennogo Rezhima," *Latinskaia Amerika* 4 (1980): 44–48.

121 S. A. Sergeev, "Latinskaia Amerika: God 1978," *Latinskaia Amerika* 1 (1979): 23.

122 *Krasnaia Zvezda*, 8 July 1983.

8 Latin American labor unions

1 Gary K. Busch, *The Political Role of International Trade Unions* (New York: St. Martin Press, 1983), 136.

2 See Clissold, *Soviet Relations with Latin America 1918–1968*, 12–13.

3 Victor Alba, *Politics and the Labor Movement in Latin America* (Stanford, CA: Stanford University Press, 1968), 321.

4 Ibid., 325.

5 Ibid., p. 280.

6 Ibid., 328.

7 For an excellent analysis of the activities of the rural proletariat in Brazil prior to 1964, see Joseph H. Page, *The Revolution That Never Was: Northeast Brazil 1955–1964* (New York: Grossman Publishers, 1972).

8 Busch, *The Political Role of International Trade Unions*, 168.
9 For the text of the communiqué, see William E. Ratliff, *Castroism and Communism in Latin America 1959–1976* (Stanford, CA: AEI-Hoover Policy Studies, 1976), 195–98.
10 A. A. Kutsenkov, ed., *Rabochii Klass i Antiimperialisticheskaia Revoliutsiia v Azii, Afrike i Latinskoii Amerike* (Moscow: Nauka, 1969), 201–10.
11 M. Danilevich and A. Kondrat'eva, "Nekotorye Voprosy Rabochego Dvizheniia v Latinskoi Amerike," *Politicheskoe Samo Obrozovavie* 5 (1968): 76.
12 Ibid., 77.
13 R. Zinov'eva and L. Fel'dman, "Samodeiatel'noe Naselenie Latinskoi Ameriki," *MEMO* 4 (1969): 51–63.
14 B. I. Koval' and B. M. Merin, "Rabochee Dvizhenie Na Sovermennom Etape," *Latinskaia Amerika* 3 (1969): 43.
15 L. Pegusheva, "Profsoiuzy Latinskoi Ameriki," *Mezhdunarodnaia Zhizn'* 8 (1969): 155–57.
16 L. Pegusheva, "AFM–KPP v Latinskoi Amerike," *Novaia i Noveishaia Istoriia* 4 (1970): 56–66.
17 V. I. Ermolaev and A. F. Shul'govskii, *Rabochee i Kommuniticheskoe Dvizhenie v Latinskoi Amerike* (Moscow: Nauka, 1970), 43–44.
18 E. N. Pashentsev, "Zadachi Edinstva Profsoiuznogo Dvizhenia Peru (1968–1981gg.)," *Latinskaia Amerika* 12 (1981): 34, 35.
19 Busch, *The Political Role of International Trade Unions*, 173.
20 E. V. Makukhin, "Profsoiuzy i Narodnoe Edinstvo v Chili," *Rabochii Klass i Sovremennyi Mir* 1 (1973): 126–28.
21 *Uroki Chili*, 106.
22 Ibid., 112.
23 A. V. Kondrat'eva, "Khristianskii Sindikalizm v Latinskoi Amerike," *Rabochii Klass i Sovremennyi Mir* 1 (1973): 107–18.
24 See J. Gregory Oswald, *Soviet Image of Contemporary Latin America: A Documentary History 1960–1968* (Austin: University of Texas Press, 1970), 161.
25 A. V. Kondrat'eva, *Latinskaia Amerika: Problemy Bor'by Za Edinstvo Profsoiuznogo Dvizheniia* (Moscow: Nauka, 1976), 15.
26 Ibid., 61.
27 Ibid., 62–70.
28 Ibid., 84.
29 Ratliff, *Castroism and Communism in Latin America 1959–1976*, 223.
30 A. F. Shul'govskii, "Rabochii Klass Latinskoi Ameriki: Politicheskie i Ideologicheskie Problemy Bor'by," *Latinskaia Amerika* 6 (1976): 6–23.
31 Iu. I. Vizgunova, "Novye Aspekty v Bor'be Rabochego Klassa Latinskoi Ameriki (Meksika)," *Latinskaia Amerika* 2 (1977): 62–72.
32 B. Merin, ed., *Rabochii Klass i Revoliutsionnyi Protsess v Latinskoi Amerike* (Moscow: ILA, 1978).
33 Ibid., 23.
34 Ibid., 32.
35 Ibid., 162–68.
36 S. M. Khenkin, "Nekotorye Problemy Politiki Soiuzov Rabochego Klassa v Stranakh Latinskoi Amerike," *Rabochii Klass i Sovremennyi Mir* 6 (1978): 82.

37 A. F. Shul'govskii, ed., *Gospodstvuiuschie Klassy Latinskoi Ameriki* (Moscow: Nauka, 1978), 347–48.

38 Ibid.

39 L. V. Pegusheva, *Latinskaia Amerika: 'Panamerikanizm' v Rabochem Dvizhenii* (Moscow: Nauka, 1974), 222–25.

40 L. V. Pegusheva, "Sovremenye Tendentsie v Profsoiuznom Dvizhenii Latinskoi Ameriki (70e gody)," *Latinskaia Amerika* 10 (1981): 35–43.

41 Ibid., 41.

42 P. P. Iakovlev, "Rabochii Klass i Vneshnaia Politika Latinskoi Ameriki," *Latinskaia Amerika* 2 (1982): 5–19.

43 Ibid.

44 E. D. Stroganov, "Rol' Solidarnykh Vystupl'enii v Bor'be Revoliutsionnyky Sil Latinskoi Ameriki," *Rabochii Klass i Sovremennyi Mir* 5 (1982): 107–14.

45 B. I. Merin, *Proletariat i Revoliutsionnyi Protsess v Latinskoi Amerike* (Moscow: Nauka, 1985), 162.

46 For articulation of such views, see Busch, *The Political Role of International Trade Unions*, 178. See also, Robert S. Leiken, *Soviet Strategy in Latin America*, 34–35.

9 Bourgeois political parties

1 See Herbert S. Dinerstein, *Soviet Policy in Latin America* (Santa Monica, CA: Rand Corporation, 1966), 23.

2 For example, Alvaro Delgado stated that "Betancourt committed more atrocities than dictator Pérez Jiménez." In "Latin American Reformism Today," *World Marxist Review*, 7 (1967): 70.

3 See Nina Egorova, "Peru: The Belaúnde Compromises," *New Times* 2 (1965): 15–17.

4 Quoted in Oswald, *Soviet Image of Contemporary Latin America: A Documentary History 1960–1968* (Austin, TX: University of Texas Press, 1970), 119.

5 Ibid., 124.

6 Ibid., 120.

7 V. P. Beliaev *et al.*, *Politicheskie Partii Stran Latinskoi Ameriki: Ideologiia i Politika* (Moscow: Nauka, 1965), 16–19.

8 Ibid., 19–21.

9 Oswald, *Soviet Image of Contemporary Latin America*, 129.

10 Delgado, "Latin American Reformism Today," 66.

11 Ibid., 67.

12 E. V. Kovalev, "Khristianskie Demokraty i Problema Agrarnoi Reformy v Chili," *Voprosy Istorii* 6 (1969): 80–95.

13 I. Zorina, "Chili: Komy Prinadlezhit Vremia," *MEMO* 6 (1969): 123.

14 I. Zorina, *Revoliutsiia Ili Reforma v Latinskoi Amerike* (Moscow: Nauka, 1971), 203–51.

15 See S. S. Mikhailov, ed., *Osvoboditel'noe Dvizhenie v Latinskoi Amerike* (Moscow: Nauka, 1964).

16 Herbert Dinerstein, *Soviet Policy in Latin America*, 24.

17 S. Semionov, *Khristianskaia Demokratiia i Revoliutsionnyi Protsess v Latinskoi Amerike* (Moscow: Nauka, 1971), 300.

18 Ibid., 299.

19 Delgado, "Latin American Reformism Today," 72.

20 Kiva Maidonik, "Sumerki Liberal'nogo Reformizma," *Latinskaia Amerika* 5 (1970): 63.

21 Ibid., 59–60.

22 V. I. Ermolaev, "Eshchio Raz o Burzhuaznom Reformizme," *Latinskaia Amerika* 2 (1971): 102.

23 Ibid., 103, 106.

24 Ibid., 104.

25 M. F. Kudachkin, "Revoliutsionnye Preobrazovaniia i Burzhuaznyi Reformizm," *Latinskaia Amerika* 6 (1971): 5.

26 Ibid., 6–7.

27 Goure and Rothenberg, *Soviet Penetration of Latin America*, 134, and Blasier, *The Giant's Rival*, 34.

28 Jackson, *Castro, Kremlin, and Communism in Latin America*, 84–89.

29 For example, see Waldo Attias, "Chile: The Real Face of Reformism," *World Marxist Review* 2 (1968): 45–47.

30 For a more detailed discussion, see part I of this book.

31 A. Veber, "Sotsial-Demokratiia v Meniaiushchemsia Mire," *MEMO* 11 (1972): 32–33.

32 Ibid., 34.

33 K. M. Obyden, "Partii Sotsial-Demokraticheskoi Orientatsii v Latinskoi Amerike i Sotsintern," *Rabochii Klass i Sovremennyi Mir* 5 (1974): 49.

34 Ibid., 50–60.

35 Kudachkin and Kutsenkov, eds., *Uroki Chili*; see I. Zorina, "Revoliutsiia i Khristiano-Demokraticheskaia Partiia," 193, 197–202, 203, 204.

36 A. F. Shul'govskii, ed., *Natsionalizm v Latinskoi Amerike: Politicheskie i Ideologicheskie Techeniia* (Moscow, Nauka, 1976); see E. S. Dabagyan, "Natsional-nye-Reformistskie Partii i Ideologiia Natsionalizma," 45.

37 Ibid., 46.

38 Ibid., 54.

39 Ibid., 68.

40 E. S. Dabagyan, "Venetsuela: Evoliutsiia Ideologii i Politiki Partii Demokraticheskogo Deistve," *Latinskaia Amerika* 5 (1978): 37–50.

41 N. G. Sibilev, "Sotsial-Demokratiia: Novye Tendentsii v Vneshnei Politike," *Rabochii Klass i Sovremennyi Mir* 6 (1977): 124–26.

42 Ibid., 128.

43 B. I. Koval' and S. I. Semenov, "Latinskaia Amerika i Mezhdunarodnaia Sots-Demokratiia," *Rabochii Klass i Sovremennyi Mir* 4 (1978): 115.

44 Ibid., 118.

45 Ibid., 126.

46 Ibid., 125–28.

47 I. V. Danilevich, "Mezhdunarodnaia Sotsial-Democratiia i Latinskaia Amerika," *Latinskaia America* 2 (1978): 80.

48 Ibid., 90–91.

49 "Mezhdunarodnaia Sots-Demokratiia i Latinskaia Amerika," *Latinskaia Amerika* 4 (1978): 91–94.
50 Ibid., 95–97.
51 Ibid., 99–101.
52 Ibid., 103–5.
53 Ibid., 107–11.
54 Ibid., 115.
55 Ibid., 127–29.
56 Jorge Shafik Handal et al., "Mezhdunarodnaiia Sots-Demokratiia i Latinskaia Amerika," *Latinskaia Amerika* 5 (1979): 106–8.
57 Ibid., 115–18.
58 Yuri Gvozdev, "Christian Democracy at the Crossroads," *New Times* 36 (1980): 14.
59 Ibid.
60 Ibid.
61 Ibid.
62 Ibid., 15.
63 Ibid.
64 M. M. Gurvits, "Put' k Vlasti Partii COPEI," *Latinskaia Amerika* 12 (1980): 39–48.
65 Quoted in Hough, *The Struggle for the Third World*, 173.
66 M. F. Gornov and V. G. Tkatchenko, *Latinskaia Amerika: Opyt Narodnykh Koalitsii i Klassovaia Bor'ba* (Moscow: Politizdat, 1981), 246–48.
67 Ibid., 252.
68 Ibid., 110.
69 "Khristianskaia Demokratiia v Politicheskoi Sisteme Stran Latinskoi Ameriki," *Latinskaia Amerika* 1 (1982): 45–51.
70 Ibid., 52–58.
71 Ibid., 61–63.
72 Kiva Maidonik, "Khristianskaia Demokratiia v Politicheskoi Sisteme Stran Latinskoi Ameriki," *Latinskaia Amerika* 2 (1982): 35–43.
73 For a discussion of the debate, see Hough, *The Struggle for the Third World*, 172.
74 E. A. Kosarev, "Khristianskaia Demokratiia v Politicheskoi Sisteme Stran Latinskoi Ameriki," *Latinskaia Amerika* 2 (1982): 49–51.
75 V. P. Totskii, "Khristianskaia Demokratiia v Politicheskoi Sisteme Stran Latinskoi Ameriki," *Latinskaia Amerika* 2 (1981): 53–56.
76 *Latinskaia Amerika* 3 (1982): 68–69.
77 Shul'govskii, ed., *Sovremennye Ideologicheskie Techeniia v Latinskoi Amerike*. E. S. Dabagyan, "Sotsial-Demokraticheskie Kontseptsii," 198.
78 Ibid., 202.
79 Ibid., 206.
80 Ibid., 202, 206.
81 Ibid., 210.
82 Ibid., 224.
83 Ibid., 220.

10 Wars of national liberation or peaceful transformation?

1 For an excellent discussion of the changes in the sophistication of Soviet analysis of the dynamic within the Third World, see Hough, *The Struggle for the Third World*, esp. chs. 3 and 5.

2 B. I. Koval', "Problemy Natsional-Osvoboditel'nogo Dvizheniia v Programnykh Dokumentakh Kompartii Stran Latinskoi Ameriki," *Novaia i Noveishaia Istoriia* 2 (1964): 96.

3 Ibid., 99–102.

4 Ibid., 102.

5 Rodney Arismendi, "Some Aspects of the Revolutionary Process in Latin America Today," *World Marxist Review* 10 (1964): 19.

6 M. Kudachkin and N. Mostovets, "The Liberation Movement in Latin America," *Kommunist* 11 (1964): 121–30; here quoted from Oswald, *Soviet Image of Contemporary Latin America*, 26.

7 Oswald, *Soviet Image of Contemporary Latin America*, 27.

8 Ibid., 26.

9 Ibid., 31.

10 A. M. Sivolobov, "The Peasant Movement in Latin America," *Kommunist* 12 (1964): 100–7. From the translation by Oswald, *Soviet Image of Contemporary Latin America*, 170.

11 Ibid., 174.

12 Ibid.

13 "Natsional'no-Osvoboditel'noe Dvizhenie i Sotsial'nyi Progress," *Kommunist* 3 (1965): 23.

14 Ibid., 23.

15 Ibid., 24.

16 See Jacques Levesque, *The USSR and the Cuban Revolution: Soviet Ideological and Strategic Perspectives 1959–77* (New York: Praeger Publishers, 1978), 110.

17 Pedro Mota Lima, "The Revolutionary Process and Democracy in Latin America," *World Marxist Review* 8 (1965): 45–52.

18 José Manuel Fortuny, "Has the Revolution Become More Difficult in Latin America?" *World Marxist Review* 8 (1965): 45.

19 Ibid., 39.

20 Ibid., 42.

21 Ibid., 45.

22 L. Corvolán, "Alliance of Anti-Imperialist Forces in Latin America," *World Marxist Review* 7 (1967): 45.

23 Ibid.

24 C. Levano, "Lessons of the Guerrilla Struggle in Peru," *World Marxist Review* 9 (1967): 47–48.

25 Ibid., 48.

26 Ibid., 49.

27 Ramón López, "New Stage in Guerrilla Struggle in Colombia," *World Marxist Review* 2 (1967): 55.

28 "An Interview with Rodney Arismendi," *Za Rubezhom* 52 (1967): 9.

29 Ibid.

30 See Jackson, *Castro, Kremlin, and Communism in Latin America*.

31 For the notes on the Baku conference, see *Latinskaia Amerika* 3 (1972): 199–203.

32 "Latinskaia Amerika v Mirovom Revoliutsionnom Protsesse," *Latinskaia Amerika* 2 (1971): 5–15.

33 "Latin America: New Stage in Its Struggle," *New Times* 43 (1971): 21.
34 V. Tkatchenko, "Latinskaia Amerika: Problemy Osvoboditel'noi Bor'by," *Mezhdunarodnaia Zhizn'* 4 (1972): 13–21.
35 Ponomarev, "The World Situation and the Revolutionary Process," 10.
36 Brezhnev, *On Relations Between Socialist and Developing Countries*, 92.
37 "Sovremennyi Etap Osvoboditel'noi Revoliutsionnoi Bor'by v Latinskoi Amerike," *Latinskaia Amerika* 5 (1976): 21.
38 D. Lozinov, "The Liberation Struggle in Latin America," *International Affairs* 7 (1977): 40.
39 Kiva Maidonik, "Vokrug Urokov Chili," *Latinskaia Amerika* 5 (1974): 116.
40 Ibid., 117.
41 Ibid., 129.
42 Ibid., 130.
43 M. F. Kudachkin, "Nekotorye Uroki Revoliutsii," *Latinskaia Amerika* 2 (1975): 59–66.
44 "Sovremennyi Etap Osvoboditel'noi Revoliutsionni Bor'by," 12.
45 L. Corvolán, "Chile: The Unarmed Revolution," *World Marxist Review* 1 (1978): 37.
46 Ibid., 41.
47 Richard Feinberg, ed., *Central America the International Dimension of the Crisis* (New York: Holmes & Meier, 1982), 150.
48 Handal, "Trudnyi Put' Bor'by Sal'vadorskikh Kommunistov," 105–15.
49 Sergeev, "Latinskaia Amerika: God 1978.
50 Iosif Grigulevich, ed, *Nicaragua: Long Road to Victory* (Moscow: USSR Academy of Sciences, 1981), 170.
51 Ibid., 171.
52 Ibid., 176.
53 Ibid., 179–81.
54 Ibid., 194.
55 Ibid.
56 Ibid., 201.
57 B. I. Koval', "Leninskaya Kontseptsiia Mirovigo Revoliutsionnogo Protsessa i Sovremennost'," *Rabochii Klass i Sovremennyi Mir* 3 (1980): 8.
58 Ibid., 9.
59 Iu. Korolev, "Aktual'nost' Chiliiskogo Opyta," *Latinskaia Amerika* 9 (1980): 8, 13.
60 "Revolution: Ways to It," *World Marxist Review* 10 (1979): 57–58.
61 Ibid., 65.
62 Shafik Handal, "Na Puti K Svobode," *Kommunist* 17 (1980): 99.
63 T. E. Vorozheikina, "Revoliutsionnye Organizatsii Sal'vadora i Narodnoe Dvizhenie," *Latinskaia Amerika* 7 (1982): 23.
64 M. F. Gornov, "Latinskaia Amerika: Usilenie Bor'by Protiv Imperializma i Oligarkhii i Za Demokratiiu i Sotsial'nyi Progress," *Latinskaia Amerika* 7 (1982): 11.
65 Ibid., 12.
66 See Edme Domínguez Reyes, "Soviet Relations with Central America, the Caribbean, and Members of the Contadora Group," *The Annals of the*

American Academy of Political and Social Studies (Beverly Hills, CA: Sage Publications, 1985), 154.

67 Robert Wesson, *Year Book of International Communist Affairs* (Stanford, CA: The Hoover Institute Press, 1983), 70.

PART III

Introduction

1 See Elizabeth K. Valkenier, *The Soviet Union and the Third World: An Economic Bind* (New York: Praeger Publishers, 1985), 6.

2 Vacs, *Discreet Partners*, 15–17.

3 For a good chronology of Soviet activities in Latin America during the 1960s, see Viktor Vol'skii, *SSSR i Latinskaia America 1917–1967* (Moscow: Mezhdunarodnye Otnosheniia, 1967), 210–13.

4 For an excellent analysis of the Soviet approach toward Latin America during the 1960s, see Dinerstein, "Soviet Policy in Latin America," 80–90.

5 Levesque, *The USSR and the Cuban Revolution*, 138.

6 For a chart dating Soviet diplomatic ties with Latin America, see Blasier, *The Giant's Rival*, 17.

7 Quoted in Kurt London, ed., *The Soviet Union in World Politics* (Boulder, CO: Westview Press, 1980), 237.

8 Leiken, *Soviet Strategy in Latin America*, 19.

11 Case study: Mexico

1 For an excellent history of Soviet–Mexican relations during the 1920s, see Clissold, *Soviet Relations With Latin America 1918–1968*.

2 Donald L. Herman, ed., *The Communist Tide in Latin America: A Selected Treatment* (Austin, TX: University of Texas Press, 1973), 79.

3 Ibid., 80.

4 Ibid., 79.

5 See A. Sizonenko, ed., *SSSR-Meksika 50 Let* (Moscow: ILA, 1975), 66–70.

6 Yoram Shapira, *Mexico's Foreign Policy Under Echeverría* (Beverly Hills, CA and London: Sage Publications, 1978), 42.

7 Blasier, *The Giant's Rival*, 27.

8 Herman, *The Communist Tide in Latin America*, 81.

9 See Shapira, *Mexico's Foreign Policy Under Echeverría*.

10 For a documentation of Soviet–Mexican relations, see *Sovetsko–Meksikanskie Otnosheniia 1968–1980* (Moscow: Izdatel'stvo Politicheskoi Literatury, 1981).

11 Iu. Zakharov, "SSSR–Meksika: V Traditsiiakh Doveriia i Vzaimoponimania," *Mezhdunarodnaia Zhizn'* 7 (1978): 103.

12 Blasier, *The Giant's Rival*, 56–57.

13 Susan Kaufman Purcell, ed., *Mexico–United States Relations* (New York: Proceedings of the Academy of Political Sciences, 1981), 146.

14 Quoted in Zakharov, "SSSR–Meksika," 104.

15 Radio Moscow (in Spanish), 25 February 1982.
16 For example, see E. G. Lapshev, "Ideologicheskie Osnovy Vneshnei Politiki," *Latinskaia Amerika* 11 (1982): 102.
17 Zakharov, "SSSR–Meksika," 106.
18 Purcell, ed., *Mexico–United States Relations*, 152.
19 See Vol'skii, "Latinskaia Amerika v Sisteme Sovremennogo Kapitalizma," 6–31.
20 Lapshev, "Ideologicheskie Osnovy Vneshnei Politiki."

12 Case study: Chile

1 See Blasier, *The Giant's Rival*, 37.
2 See Vol'skii, *SSSR i Latinskaia Amerika 1917–1967*, 213.
3 For example, see Kovalev, "Khristianskie Demokraty i Problema Agrarnoi Reformy v Chili," 80–95, and Zorina, *Revoliutsiia Ili Reforma v Latinskoi Amerike*, 203–51.
4 For a more detailed discussion of Moscow's attitude toward Allende, see Leon Goure and Jaime Suchlicki, "The Allende Regime: Actions and Reactions," *Problems of Communism* (Spring 1971): 55–58.
5 Dinerstein, "Soviet Policy in Latin America," 88.
6 See Paul Sigmund, *The Overthrow of Allende* (University of Pittsburgh Press, 1977), 162.
7 *Pravda*, 7 November 1970.
8 Boris Ponomarev, "Topical Problems of the Theory of Revolutionary Process," as quoted in Hosmer and Wolfe, *Soviet Policy and Practice Toward Third World Conflicts*, 42.
9 Goure and Rothenberg, *Soviet Penetration of Latin America*, 99.
10 Jorge Texier, "General and Distinctive Features of the Liberation Process," *World Marxist Review*, 4 (1972): 106.
11 *Krasnaia Zvezda*, 29 August 1971, 3.
12 *Prensa Latina*, 23 May 1973, 87.
13 Paul Sigmund, "The Invisible Blockade and the Overthrow of Allende," *Foreign Affairs* 52 (1974): 336.
14 See Paul Sigmund, "The USSR, Cuba and the Revolution in Chile" in Robert H. Donaldson, ed., *The Soviet Union in the Third World* (Boulder, CO: Westview Press, 1981), 39.
15 See Joseph Nogee and John Sloan, "Allende's Chile and the Soviet Union," *Journal of Interamerican Studies and International Affairs* 3 (1979): 353.
16 Ibid., 353–54.
17 Goure and Rothenberg, *Soviet Penetration of Latin America*, 135.
18 Ibid., 142.
19 See Joan Urban, "Socialist Pluralism in the Soviet and Italian Perspective: The Chilean Catalyst," *Orbis* 18 (1974): 482–510.
20 See Konstantin Tarasov and Vyacheslav Zubenko, *The CIA in Latin America* (Moscow: Progress Publishers, 1984), 106–51.
21 Jonathan Steele, *Soviet Power: The Kremlin's Foreign Policy – Brezhnev to Chernenko* (New York: Touchstone Books, 1984), 219.

22 Ponomarev, "The World Situation and the Revolutionary Process," 10.
23 Ibid., 11.
24 Blasier, *The Giant's Rival*, 86.
25 See *1,000 Dnei Revoliutsii: Rukovoditeli KPCh ob Urokakh Sobytii v Chili* (Prague, 1978).
26 Cheddi Jaggan, "From Guyana to Chile," *World Marxist Review* (6/1974): 101–4.
27 Nina Tadeo, "Formulas for Counter Revolution Coups," *World Marxist Review* (6/1974): 108.
28 Karen Khachaturov, ed., *Ideologicheskaia Ekspantsiia SShA v Latinskoi Amerike* (Moscow: Mezhdunarodnye Otnosheniia, 1978), 12, 22.
29 Juan Cobo, "Latin America: Optimistic Perspective," *New Times* 29 (1975): 4–16.
30 See Kudachkin and Kutsenkov, eds., *Uroki Chili*.
31 Ibid., 25.
32 Ibid., 5–20.
33 Ibid., 45.
34 Ibid., 80.
35 Iosif Grigulevich, "Amerikanskii Imperializm Protiv Chiliiskogo Naroda," *Voprosy Istorii* 11 (1978): 52, 66.

13 Case study: Brazil and Argentina

1 Viktor Vol'skii, *SSSR i Latinskaia Amerika 1917–1967* (Moscow: Mezhdunarodnye Otnosheniia, 1967), 109.
2 Dinerstein, "Soviet Policy in Latin America," 85.
3 *Izvestiia*, 4 April 1964.
4 V. Kobysh, "Uspekhov tebe Braziliia," *Izvestiia*, 7 September 1964.
5 Vol'skii *et al.*, eds., *Braziliia*, 312.
6 J. Gregory Oswald and Anthony J. Strover, eds., *The Soviet Union and Latin America* (New York: Praeger Publishers, 1970), 84.
7 Dinerstein, "Soviet Policy in Latin America," 85.
8 Vol'skii, *SSSR i Latinskaia Amerika 1917–1967*, 213.
9 Goure and Rothenberg, *Soviet Penetration of Latin America*, 154.
10 Vol'skii *et al.*, eds., *Braziliia*, 311.
11 Oswald and Strover, eds., *The Soviet Union and Latin America*, 89.
12 Blasier, *The Giant's Rival*, 62.
13 Robert S. Leiken, "East Winds in Latin America," *Foreign Policy* 42 (1981): 96.
14 Vol'skii *et al.*, eds., *Braziliia*, 317.
15 Blasier, *The Giant's Rival*, 51–52.
16 *Pravda*, 5 July 1980.
17 See Vacs, *Discreet Partners*, 16.
18 Ibid.
19 Ibid., 18.
20 Ibid.
21 Blasier, *The Giant's Rival*, 30.

22 Vacs, *Discreet Partners*, 16.
23 Ibid., 22.
24 Ibid., 69.
25 Ibid., 40.
26 See section dealing with Soviet perceptions of Latin American military.
27 See "The Communists and the New Situation in Argentina," *World Marxist Review Information Bulletin* 7 (1976): 36–40.
28 *The Washington Post*, 7 November 1977.
29 Vacs, *Discreet Partners*, 45.
30 Ibid., 50.
31 Ibid., 55.
32 Ibid., 57.
33 Ibid., 83.
34 William H. Luers, "The Soviets and Latin America: A Three Decade U.S. Policy Tangle," *Washington Quarterly* (Winter 1984): 13.
35 Vojtech Mastny, "The Soviet Union and the Falklands War," *Naval War College Review* 36 (1983): 47.
36 *The New York Times*, 18 April 1982, 18.
37 Joseph G. Whelan, *The Soviet Union in the Third World: An Imperial Burden or Political Asset*, Congressional Research Service Report no. 85–40 S, 182.
38 Mastny, "The Soviet Union and the Falklands War," 47.
39 *Izvestiia*, 7 October 1977.

PART IV

Conclusions

1 Robert Cassen, ed., *Soviet Interests in the Third World* (London: RIIS, 1985), 114.
2 Ibid., 127.
3 Augusto Varas, "Latin American–Soviet Relations in the Eighties" (unpublished manuscript).

Epilogue

1 Karen Brutents, "Osvobodivshiesiia Strany v Nachale 80kh Godov," *Kommunist*, no. 3 (1984): 109.
2 Quoted in Hough, *The Struggle for the Third World*, 139.
3 *Notimex* 7 November 1987.
4 *Telam*, 6 November 1987.
5 *FIBIS–Latin America*, 6 November 1987.
6 Richard C. Schroeder, "Soviet's Latin American Influence," *Congressional Research Reports*, 6 March 1987.
7 *Noticias Argentinas*, 2 November 1987.
8 *O Estado de São Paulo*, 29 September 1987.
9 *Pravda*, 25 March 1988.
10 *TASS*, 1 March 1988.

11 *Radio Moscow*, 4 April 1988.
12 *FIBIS–Latin America*, 13 April 1987.
13 *O Estado de São Paulo*, 20 September 1987.
14 *Veja*, 7 November 1987.
15 *The News* (Mexico City), 2 January 1987.
16 V. Malevich in *La Republica* (Panama City), 4 January 1987.
17 *Gazeta Mercantil*, 25 March and 28 April 1987.
18 *Folha de São Paulo*, 3 May 1987.
19 *Excelsior* (Mexico), 3 April 1987.
20 Schroeder, "Soviet's Latin American Influence," 108.
21 TASS, 14 March 1988.
22 *Pravda*, 3 April 1988.
23 AFP, 10 April 1988.

Bibliography

"The American Gendarme with the Big Stick." *Pravda*, 19 April 1965.
"An Interview with Rodney Arismendi." *Za Rubezhom* 52 (1967): 9.
"The Communists and the New Situation in Argentina." *World Marxist Review Information Bulletin* 7 (1976): 36–40.
"Declaration of Havana." *Kommunist* 10 (1975): 88–109.
"Ekonomicheskaia Zavisimost'." Part 3. *Latinskaia Amerika* 10 (1982): 53.
"Khristianskaia Demokratiia v Politicheskoi Sisteme Stran Latinskoi Ameriki." *Latinskaia Amerika* 1 (1982): 45–51, 52–58, 61–63.
"Latin America: New Stage in Its Struggle." *New Times* 43 (1971): 21.
"Latinskaia Amerika v Morovom Revoliutsionnom Protsesse." *Latinskaia Amerika* 2 (1971): 5–16.
"Latinskaia Amerika: Vneshniaia Politika: Ekonomicheskaia Zavisimost'." *Latinskaia Amerika* 9 (1981), 10 (1981), and 10 (1982).
"Mezhdunarodnaia Sots-Demokratiia i Latinskaia Amerika." *Latinskaia Amerika* 4 (1978): 89–129.
"Natsional'no-Osvoboditel'noe Dvizhenie i Sotsial'nyi Progress." *Kommunist* 3 (1965): 23–24.
"Notes of the Baku Conference." *Latinskaia Amerika* 3 (1972): 199–203.
"Novye Tendentsii v Latinoamericanskoi Politike SShA." *Latinskaia Amerika* 3 (1978): 150–68.
"Pamiatnaia Zapiska Palmiro Tol'iatti." *Pravda*, 10 September 1964.
"Revolution: Ways to It." *World Marxist Review* 10 (1979): 57–58, 65.
"Sovremennyi Etap Osvoboditel'noi Revoliutsionnoi Bor'by Latinskaia Amerike." *Latinskaia Amerika* 2 (1976): 12, 26.
Uroki Chili. Prague, 1978.

Abramov, A. G. "Rol' Pentagona v Formirovanii Vneshnei Politiki SShA Poslednevgo Dvadsatiletiia." *Voprosy Istorii* 7 (1974): 97–112.
"Administratsiia Kartera i Latinskaia Amerika." *Latinskaia Amerika* 4 (1979): 100–160.
Alba, Víctor. *Politics and the Labor Movement in Latin America.* Stanford University Press, 1968.
Aleksin, A. "'Tikhaia' Interventsiia SShA v Latinskoi Amerike." *Kommunist* 10 (1970): 97.

229

Andreev, M. "Katolitsizm v Politicheskoi Zhizni Latinoamerikanskikh Stran."
    MEMO 6 (1968): 116, 118, 121.
Andronova, V. P. "Bor'ba za 'Teologiiu Osvobozhdeniia'." *Latinskaia Amerika* 9
    (1980): 51–56, 58, 61.
Kolumbia Tserkov' i Obshchestvo. Moscow: Nauka, 1970.
Anichkin, O. N. "Sto dnei Prezidentstva Reagana." *SShA* 5 (1981): 42–46.
Antonov, B. "Latinskaia Amerika Protiv Zasiliia SShA." *Mezhdunarodnaia
    Zhizn'* 7 (1971): 66–73.
Antonov, Iu. A. *Braziliia: Armiia i Politika.* Moscow: Nauka, 1973.
    Armiia v Sotsial'no-Politicheskom Razvitii Brazilii 1961–1964. Latinskaia Amerika
    4 (1971): 98–111.
Antonov, Iu. A., and V. Komarov. "Pentagon v Latinskoi Amerike." *Mezh-
    dunarodnaia Zhizn'* 12 (1970): 81–86.
Arismendi, Rodney. "Some Aspects of the Revolutionary Process in Latin
    America Today." *World Marxist Review* 10 (1964): 19.
Atkins, G. Pope. *Latin America in the International Political System.* New York:
    Free Press, 1977.
Attias, Waldo. "Chile: The Real Face of Reformism." *World Marxist Review* 2
    (1968): 45–47.
Barsukov, Iu. "Iaponiia v Latinskoi Ameriki." *MEMO* 7 (1975): 116–19.
Baryshev, A. P. "Latinskaia Amerika v OON." *Latinskaia Amerika* 5 (1971):
    15–25.
"Of Dominos and Pendulums." *New Times* 27 (1980): 13.
Beliaev, V. P. *et al. Politicheskie Partii Stran Latinskoi Ameriki: Ideologiia i Politika.*
    Moscow: Nauka, 1965.
Blasier, Cole. *The Giant's Rival.* University of Pittsburgh Press, 1983.
Bobovskii, Viktor. "V Tupike." *Pravda,* 27 May 1966.
Boiko, P. N., ed. *Braziliia: Ten'dentsie Ekonomicheskogo i Sots-Politicheskogo Raz-
    vitiia.* Moscow: Nauka, 1983.
Brener, Wolfgang W. "The Place of Cuba in Soviet Latin American Strategy."
    Studies on the Soviet Union 2 (1968): 91, 94.
Brezhnev, Leonid. *On Relations Between Socialist and Developing Countries.*
    Moscow: Progress Publishers, 1984, 591–605, 609.
Brutents, Karen. "Osvobodivshiesiia Strany v Nachale 80kh Godov." *Kommu-
    nist,* no. 3 (1984), 109.
Busch, Gary K. *The Political Role of International Trade Unions.* New York: St.
    Martin Press, 1983.
Bushuyev, V. G. "Latinskaia Amerika Na Novyekh Rubezhakh." *Mezhduna-
    rodnaia Zhizn'* 4 (1973): 47–59.
Latinskaia Amerika: Neobratimye Protsessy. Moscow: Znanie, 1973.
"Latinskaia Amerika v peredi Eshchio Trudnaia Bor'ba." *Kommunist Vooruz-
    hionnykh Sil* 21 (1973): 80.
"Latinskaia Amerika v Pervyi God Novogo desitiletiia." *Mezhdunarodnaia
    Zhizn'* 2 (1972): 64–72.
Veter' Perem'em nad Andami. Moscow: Politizdat, 1972.
Bushuyev, V. G. and Iu. Kozlov. "Latinskaia Amerika: Novaia Rol' V Mezh-
    dunarodnykh Otnosheniakh." *Kommunist* 12 (1978): 108–19.

Cassen, Robert, ed. *Soviet Interests in the Third World*. London: RIIS, 1985.
Castro, Alfredo. "Tactics of Struggle Against Dictatorship in Brazil." *World Marxist Review* 9 (8) 1966: 45.
Chumakova, M. L. "Evoliutsiia Vneshnei Politiki (Brazilia)." *Latinskaia Amerika* 4 (1980): 66–67.
Clissold, Stephen. *Soviet Relations with Latin America 1918–1968: A Documentary Survey*. New York: Oxford University Press, 1970.
Cobo, Juan. "Idei Bandunga i Latinskaia Amerika." *Latinskaia Amerika* 5 (1980): 133–42.
    "Latin America: Optimistic Perspective." *New Times* 29 (1975): 4–16.
Literaturnaia Gazeta, 11 December 1968. Quoted in Goure and Rothenberg. *Soviet Penetration of Latin America*. Coral Gables, FL: Miami University Press, 1975.
Cobo, Juan, and G. Mirski. "O Nekotorykh Osobennostiakh Evoliutsii Armii Latinoamerikanskogo Kontinenta." *Latinskaia Amerika* 4 (1971): 42–67.
Conference of Communist and Workers' Parties. Moscow: Novosti Press, 1969.
Corvolán, L. "Chile: The Unarmed Revolution." *World Marxist Review* 1 (1978): 37–41.
    "Chiliiskaia Katolicheskaia Tserkov'." *Latinskaia Amerika* 6 (1977): 36–39.
    "Alliance of Anti-Imperialist Forces in Latin America." *World Marxist Review* 7 (1967): 45.
Costo e Silva, Golbery do. *Geopolítica do Brasil*. Rio de Janeiro, 1967.
Dabagyan, E. S. "Sotsial-Demokraticheskie Kontseptsii" in A. F. Shul'govskii, ed., *Sovremennye Ideologtcheskie Techniia*. Moscow: Nauka, 1983.
    "Latinskaia Amerika Vneshniaia Politika i Ekonomicheskaia Zavisimost'." Part 3. *Latinskaia Amerika* 10 (1982): 53
    "Venetsuela: Evoliutsiia Ideologii i Politiki Partii Demokraticheskogo Deistva." *Latinskaia Amerika* 5 (1978): 37–50.
Daily Telegraph, 29 September 1972; 26 February 1974.
Dalton, Roque. "Catholics and Communists in Latin America: Some Aspects of the Present Situation." *World Marxist Review* 1 (1968): 85–88.
Danilevich, I. V. "Mezhdunarodnaia Sotsial-Demokratiia i Latinskaia Amerika." *Latinskaia Amerika* 2 (1978): 80, 90–91.
Danilevich, M., and A. Kondrat'eva. "Nekotorye Voprosy Rabochego Dvizheniia v Latinskoi Amerike." *Politicheskoe Samo Obrozovavie* 5 (1968): 76–77.
Delgado, Alvaro. "Against the Danger of Militarism." *World Marxist Review* 2 (1974): 103.
    "Latin American Reformism Today." *World Marxist Review* 7 (1967): 66, 67, 70, 72.
Dinerstein, Herbert S. *The Making of a Missile Crisis: October 1962*. Baltimore, MD: Johns Hopkins University Press, 1976.
    "Soviet Policy in Latin America." *The American Political Science Review* 1 (1967): 80–90.
Soviet Policy in Latin America. Santa Monica, CA: Rand Corporation, 1966.
Dmitriev, V. N. "Latinskaia Amerika: Vneshniaia Politika i Ekonomicheskaia Zavisimost'." Part 3. *Latinskaia Amerika* 10 (1982): 57–58.
    "Politicheskie Manevry SShA v Nikarague." *Latinskaia Amerika* 7 (1980): 57–66.

"Latinoamerikanskaia Politika Kartera: Itogi Pervogo Goda." *Latinskaia Amerika* 1 (1978): 150–63, 219–24.

Dolgov, Vladimir. "The Political Temperature Rises." *New Times* 34 (1979): 12–13.

Domínguez Reyes, Edme. "Soviet Relations with Central America, the Caribbean, and Members of the Contadora Group." *The Annals of the American Academy of Political and Social Studies*. Beverly Hills, CA: Sage Publications, 1985.

Efimova, G. S., and A. A. Lavut. "Andskaia Gruppa." *Latinskaia Amerika* 6 (1971): 70–72.

Egorova, Nina. "Peru: The Belaúnde Compromises." *New Times* 2 (1965): 15–17.

Eliutin, Iurii. "Latinskaia Amerika: Pentagon i Gonka Vooruzhenii." *Mezhdunarodnaia Zhizn'* 12 (1968): 63–71.

Ermolaev, V. I. "Eshchio Raz o Burzhuaznom Reformizme." *Latinskaia Amerika* 2 (1971): 102–6.

Ermolaev, V. I., and A. F. Shul'govskii. *Rabochee i Kommuniticheskoe Dvizhenie v Latinskoi Amerike*. Moscow: Nauka, 1970.

Fadin, Vitalii. "Latinskaia Amerika: Vneshniaia Politika i Ekonomicheskaia Zavisimost'." Part 2. *Latinskaia Amerika* 9 (1981): 51–55.

Fedoseev, P. N., and I. R. Grigulevich, eds. *Pan-Americanism: Its Essence and Evolution*. Moscow: Academy of Sciences Press, 1982.

Feinberg, Richard. "Central America, the View from Moscow." *Washington Quarterly* (Spring 1982): 173.

    ed. *Central America the International Dimension of the Crisis*. New York: Holmes & Meier, 1982.

Fortuny, José Manuel. "Has the Revolution Become More Difficult in Latin America?" *World Marxist Review* 8 (1965): 39, 42, 45.

Furtak, Robert K. "The Cuban Impact on Soviet Ideology and Strategy *vis-à-vis* the Third World." *Studies on the Soviet Union* 2 (1968): 112.

Galkin, V., ed. *Vneshniaia Politika Latinskoi Ameriki*. Moscow: ILA, 1982.

Garthoff, Raymond. *Detente and Confrontation: American Soviet Relations from Nixon to Reagan*. Washington, DC: The Brookings Institution, 1985.

Gelman, Harry. *The Brezhnev Politburo and the Decline of Detente*. Ithaca, NY: Cornell University Press, 1984.

Gerechev, M. "Porochnyi Krug Politiki SShA v Latinskoi Amerike." *MEMO* 4 (1967): 54–65.

Glagolev, N. N. "Ronald Reagan – Kandidat Respublikanskoi Partii." *SShA* 9 (1980): 105–8.

Glinkin, A. N. "Latinskaia Amerika: Vneshniaia Politika i Ekonomicheskaia Zavisimost'." *Latinskaia Amerika* 8 (1981): 43, 45, 49.

    "Latinskaia Amerika v Mezhdunarodnykh Otnosheniakh na Poroge 80kh Godov." *Latinskaia Amerika* 5 (1979): 21–36.

    "Aiakucho Traditsiia i Sovremennost'." *Latinskaia Amerika* 1 (1975): 5–16, 184.

Glinkin, A., and P. Iakovlev. "Latinskaia Amerika v Global'noi Strategii Imperializma." *MEMO* 10 (1982): 65–83.

"Latinskaia Amerika: Sovremennyi Etap Protivoborstva S Imperializmom." *MEMO* 7 (1976): 17–33.

Glinkin, A. N., B. Martynov, and P. P. Iakovlev. *Evoliutsiia Latinoamerikanskoii Politiki SShA*. Moscow: Nauka, 1982.

"Novye Tendentsii v Latinoamerikanskoi Politike SShA." *Latinskaia Amerika* 3 (1978): 150–68.

Glinkin, A. N., and A. A. Matlina, eds. *Vneshnepoliticheskie Doktriny i Kontseptsii Stran Latinskoi Ameriki*. Moscow: ILA, 1980.

Glinkin, A. N., and A. F. Shul'govskii, eds. *Latinskaia Amerika: Problemy Edinstva Anti-Imperialisticheskikh Sil*, vol. 1. Moscow: ILA, 1974.

Glinkin, A. N., and A. I. Sizonenko, eds. *Vneshniaia Politika Stran Latinskoi Ameriki*. Moscow: Mezhdunarodnye Otnosheniia, 1982.

Glinkin, A. N., V. Vol'skii, and B. Gvozderov, eds. *Strany Latinskoi Ameriki v Sovremmenykh Mezhdunarodnykh Otnosheniakh*. Moscow: Nauka, 1967.

Godson, Roy. *Labor in Soviet Global Strategy*. New York: Crane Russak, 1984.

Golubiov, V. "Eksport kontra-revolutsyi v politike amerikanskogo neokolonializma." *Kommunist Vooruzhionnykh Sil* 21 (1966): 28.

Gonionskii, S. "Krizis v OAG." *Mezhdunarodnaia Zhizn'* 12 (1970): 39.

González, S. "Decisive Prerequisites for the Overthrow of Fascist Dictatorship." *World Marxist Review* 3 (1976): 110, 113.

Gornov, M. F. "Latinskaia Amerika: Usilenie Bor'by Protiv Imperializma i Oligarkhii i Za Demokratiiu i Sotsial'nyi Progress." *Latinskaia Amerika* 7 (1982): 11, 12.

Gornov, M. F., and V. G. Tkatchenko. *Latinskaia Amerika: Opyt Narodnykh Koalitsii i Klassovaia Bor'ba*. Moscow: Politizdat, 1981.

Goure, Leon, and Morris Rothenberg. *Soviet Penetration of Latin America*. Coral Gables, FL: Miami University Press, 1975.

Goure, Leon, and Jaime Suchlicki. "The Allende Regime: Actions and Reactions." *Problems of Communism* (Spring 1971): 55–58.

Grigulevich, I. R. "Latinoamerikanskaia Tserkov' Na Poroge 80kh Godov." *Latinskaia Amerika* 9 (1980): 31–34, 35–37, 39.

"Amerikanskii Imperializm Protiv Chiliiskogo Naroda." *Voprosy Istorii* 11 (1978): 52–66.

"Katoliki i Fashistskii Perevorot v Chili." *Voprosy Nauchnogo Ateizma* 18 (1975): 184–206.

"Miatezhnaia" Tserkov v Latinskoyoi Amerike. Moscow: Nauka, 1972.

"Katoliki, Marksisty, i Revoliutsionnye Protsessy v Latinskoi Amerike." *Voprosy Nauchnogo Ateizma* 16 (1974): 313–16.

"Chili Pobeda Narodnykh Sil i Pozitsiia Tserkvi." *Nauka i Religia* 5 (1971): 69.

"Novoe i Staroe v Latino-Amerikanskom Katolitsizme." *Voprosy Nauchnogo Ateizma* 6 (1968): 357, 362–67.

"U Vlasti Levye Katoliki." *Nauka i Religia* 12 (1964): 82–83.

Grigulevich, I. R., ed. *Nicaragua: Long Road To Victory*. Moscow: USSR Academy of Sciences, 1981.

Guardian, 14 July 1971; 18 December 1973.

Gurvits, M. M. "Put' k Vlasti Partii COPEI." *Latinskaia Amerika* 12 (1980): 39–48.

Gvozderov, Boris. "Latinskaya Amerika: V poiskakh Novekh Reshenii." *Pravda*, 29 January 1975.

Neokolonializm SShA v Latinskoi Amerike. Moscow: Nauka, 1970.

Neokolonializm SShA v Latinskoi Amerike. Moscow: Nauka, 1968.

"Latin America: Wall Street's New Tactics." *New Times* 36 (1967): 19–21.

Gvozdev, Iu. "Christian Democracy at the Crossroads." *New Times* 36 (1980): 14, 15.

"The Lessons of Nicaragua." *New Times* 47 (1978): 22–24.

"Latin America: Integration Problems." *International Affairs* 10 (1968): 39–41, 44.

"V Strane Zolotoi Legendy." *Nauka i Religia* 10 (1964): 83–87.

Halperin, Maurice. *The Rise and Decline of Fidel Castro.* Berkeley, CA: University of California Press, 1972.

Handal, Jorge Shafik. "Na Puti K Svobode." *Kommunist* 17 (1980): 93, 103.

"Mezhdunarodnaiia Sots-Demokratiia i Latinskaia Amerika." *Latinskaia Amerika* 5 (1979): 106–8, 115–18.

"Tsentral'naia Amerika Krizis Voennykh Diktatur." *Latinskaia Amerika* 6 (1979): 23–35.

"Trudnyi Put' Bor'by Sal'vadorskikh Kommunistov." *Kommunist* 3 (1977): 105–15.

Herman, Donald L, ed. *The Communist Tide in Latin America: A Selected Treatment.* University of Texas Press, 1973.

Hoffmann, Erik, and Frederik Ferlon. *The Soviet Conduct of Foreign Policy.* New York: Aledine Publishing Co., 1980.

Hosmer, Stephen T., and Thomas W. Wolfe. *Soviet Policy and Practice Toward Third World Conflicts.* Lexington, MA: Lexington Books, 1983.

Hough, Jerry F. *The Struggle for the Third World: Soviet Debates and American Options.* Washington, DC: The Brookings Institution, 1986.

Iakhnatov, Iulii. "After Lengthy Negotiations." *Pravda,* 14 August 1977.

Iakovlev, P. P. "Rabochii Klass i Vneshniaia Politika Latinskoi Ameriki." *Latinskaia Amerika* 2 (1982): 5–20.

"Latinskaia Amerika: Vneshniaia Politika i Ekonomicheskaia Zavisimost'." Part 2. *Latinskaia Amerika* 9 (1981): 57–58.

Iakubovski, V. *Pravda,* 21 May 1979.

Ignat'ev, Oleg. "Monopolii Diktuiut." *Pravda,* 8 December 1968.

"Dlinnye Ruki Monopolii." *Pravda,* 9 January 1967.

Iskederov, A. "Armiia, Politika, Narod." *Izvestiia,* 17 January 1967.

Iudanov, N. "Integratsiia Ograblennykh." *Mezhdunarodnaia Zhizn'* 3 (1965): 117–19.

Izvestiia, 4 April 1964; 5 December 1973; 21 October 1975; 7 October 1977.

Jabber, Paul, and Roman Kolkwitcz. "The Arab–Israeli Wars of 1967 and 1973." In Stephen Kaplan, ed. *Diplomacy of Power: Soviet Armed Forces as Political Instrument.* Washington, DC: The Brookings Institution, 1981.

Jackson, Bruce D. *Castro, Kremlin, and Communism in Latin America.* Baltimore, MD: Johns Hopkins University Press, 1969.

Jaggan, Cheddi. "From Guyana to Chile." *World Marxist Review* (June 1974): 101–4.

Johnson, Cecil. *Communist China and Latin America 1959–1967.* New York: Columbia University Press, 1970.

Joxe, Alain. "Latinoamerikanskie Voennye i Denatsionalizatsiia Gosudarstva." *Latinskaia Amerika* 6 (1977): 93–94.

Kalinin, Ia. "Imperializm i Razvivaiushchiesia Strany." *Latinskaia Amerika* 2
(1973): 210–11.

Kamynin, L. "Premier of an Old Play" (in English). *Izvestiia*, 15 April 1970.

"Fars bez pereodevaniia." *Izvestiia*, 29 October 1968.

"Inter-American Force a Weapon of Neo-Colonialism." *International Affairs* 3
(1967): 28.

"The Revolt Against the Triumvirate" (in English). *Izvestiia*, 27 April 1965.

Karnow, Stanley. *Vietnam: A History*. New York: Viking Press, 1983.

Karol, K. S. *Guerrillas in Power: The Course of the Cuban Revolution*. New York:
Hill & Wang, 1970.

Kartsev, A. "Tsentral'naia Amerika: Integratsiia Pode Egidoi SShA." *Mezhdunarodnaia Zhizn'* 6 (1965): 108–9.

Kazakov, S. A. "Vooruzhionnye Sily i Politicheskaia Vlast' v Argentine."
Latinskaia Amerika 1 (1977): 59, 62–63, 72.

Khachaturov, Karen, ed. *Ideologicheskaia Ekspantsiia SShA v Latinskoi Amerike*.
Moscow: Mezhdunarodnye Otnosheniia, 1978, 12, 22.

"Imperializm i 'Miatezhnaia' Tserkov." *Mezhdunarodnaia Zhizn'* 8 (1977):
86–92.

Khenkin, S. M. "Nekotorye Problemy Politiki Soiuzov Rabochego Klassa v
Stranakh Latinskoi Amerike." *Rabochii Klass i Sovremennyi Mir* 6 (1978): 82.

Kholodkov, N. N. *Latinskaia Amerika: Problemy Vneshnei Zadolzhennosti*.
Moscow: Nauka, 1979.

Kimchi, David. *The Afro-Asia Movement. Ideology and Foreign Policy of the Third
World*. Jerusalem: Israel Universities Press, 1973.

Kissinger, Henry A. *The Years of Upheaval*. Boston, MA: Little, Brown & Company, 1982.

Kistanov, V. O. "Platsdarm Iaponskikh Monopolii v Latinskoi Amerike."
Latinskaia Amerika 4 (1976): 80–97.

Klochkovskii, L. L. *Latinskaia Amerika v Sisteme Mirovykh Khoziaistvennykh Sviazei*. Moscow: Mezhdunarodnye Otnosheniia, 1984.

"Latinskaia Amerika: Vneshniaia Politika i Ekonomicheskaia Zavisimost'."
Part 2. *Latinskaia Amerika* 9 (1981): 50, 51.

"Ekonomicheskaia Strategiia Monopolii SShA v Latinoamerikanskom
Raione." *Latinskaia Amerika* 1 (1979): 57–59.

"Novyi Mezhdunarodnyi Ekonomicheskii Poriadok i Latinskaia Amerika."
Latinskaia Amerika 2 (1976): 55–70.

ed. *The Economies of the Countries of Latin America*. Moscow: Progress Publishers, 1984.

Klochkovskii, L., and I. Shermet'ev. "Latinskaia Amerika Krizis Zavisimogo
Kapitalizma." *MEMO* 4 (1978): 53–66.

Kobysh, V. "Uspekhov tebe Braziliia." *Izvestiia*, 7 September 1964.

Kokoshin, A. A. *SShA: Za Fasadom Global'noi Politiki*. Moscow: Politizdat, 1982.

Kondrashov, S. *Izvestiia*, 4 April 1964.

"USA and Revolt in Brazil." *Izvestiia*, 4 May 1964.

Kondrat'eva, A. V. *Latinskaia Amerika: Problemy Bor'by Za Edinstvo Profsoiuznogo
Dvizheniia*. Moscow: Nauka, 1976.

"Khristianskii Sindikalizm v Latinskoi Amerike." *Rabochii Klass i Sovremennyi Mir* 1 (1973): 107–19.

Konstantinov, Oleg. "The New Andean Group." *New Times* 19 (1971): 29.

Konstantinova, N. S. "Polozhenie i Sovremennye Tendentsii v Katolicheskoi Tserkvi," 217–23. In Viktor Vol'skii, ed. *Braziliia*. Moscow: Nauka, 1983.

Korionov, V. "The Mask Is Torn Off" (in English). *Pravda*, 29 September 1965.

"Mechtaniia Obrechionykh." *Kommunist* 15 (1965): 109.

Korolev, Iu. "Aktual'nost' Chiliiskogo Opyta." *Latinskaia Amerika* 9 (1980): 8, 13.

Kosarev, E. A. "Khristianskaia Demokratiia v Politicheskoi Sisteme Stran Latinskoi Ameriki." *Latinskaia Amerika* 2 (1982): 49–51.

"Ekonomika i Mirnyi Put' Revoliutsii." *Latinskaia Amerika* 4 (1977): 92–95.

Koval', B. I. "Leninskaya Kontseptsiia Mirovogo Revoliutsionnogo Protsessa i Sovremennosti." *Rabochii Klass i Sovremennyi Mir* 3 (1980): 8.

"Vliianie Mirovogo Sotsializma Na Rost Politicheskogo Soznania Proletariata Latinskoi Ameriki." *Latinskaia Amerika* 2 (1974): 33.

"Problemy Natsional-Osvoboditel'nogo Dvizheniia v Programnykh Dokumentakh Kompartii Stran Latinskoi Ameriki." *Novaia i Noveishaia Istoriia* 2 (1964): 96, 99–102.

Koval', B. I., and B. M. Merin. "Rabochee Dvizhenie Na Sovermennom Etape." *Latinskaia Amerika* 3 (1969): 43.

Koval', B. I., and S. I. Semenov. "Latinskaia Amerika i Mezhdunarodnaia Sots-Demokratiia." *Rabochii Klass i Sovremennyi Mir* 4 (1978): 115, 118, 125–26.

Koval', B. I., S. E. Semenov, and A. F. Shul'govskii. *Revoliutsionnye Protsessy v Latinskoi Amerike*. Moscow: Nauka, 1974.

Kovalev, E. V. "Khristianskie Demokraty i Problema Agrarnoi Reformy v Chili." *Voprosy Istorii* 6 (1969): 80–95.

Krasnaia Zvezda, 29 August 1971; 13 March 1972; 16 May 1972; 3 June 1972; 19 December 1972; 6 September 1973; 8 July 1983.

Kudachkin, M. F. "Nekotorye Uroki Revoliutsii." *Latinskaia Amerika* 2 (1975): 57–66.

"Realities of Present-day Latin America." *New Times* 27 (1973): 18–20.

"Revoliutsionnye Preobrazovaniia i Burzhuaznyi Reformizm." *Latinskaia Amerika* 6 (1971): 5–7.

Kudachkin, M. F., and A. A. Kutsenkov, eds. *Uroki Chili*. Moscow: Nauka, 1977.

Kudachkin, M., and N. Mostovets. "The Liberation Movement in Latin America" (in English). *Kommunist* 11 (1964): 121–30.

Kutsenkov, A. A., ed. *Rabochii Klass i Antiimperialisticheskaia Revoliutsiia v Azii, Afrike i Latinskoii Amerike*. Moscow: Nauka, 1969.

Kuzentsov, Vasilii. "Obostrenie Ekonomicheskikh Protiovrechnii." *Latinskaia Amerika* 2 (1976): 86.

Lapshev, E. G. "Ideologicheskie Osnovy Vneshnei Politiki." *Latinskaia Amerika* 11 (1982): 102.

Lapskii, V. "Common Sense Prevails" (in English). *Izvestiia*, 17 February 1977.

Lavut, A. "Andskaia Gruppa." *MEMO* 11 (1975): 122.

Leibzon, B. "The Leninist Criteria for Revolutionaries: The Forms of Armed Struggle" (in English). *Kommunist* 8 (1968): 38–51.

Leiken, Robert S. *Soviet Strategy in Latin America*. New York: Praeger Publishers, 1982.

"East Winds in Latin America." *Foreign Policy* 42 (1981): 96.

Leonidov, R. "Aggressive US Policy in Latin America." *International Affairs* 2 (1967): 54–59.

Leonov, N. S. "Peru: Novaia Rol' Voennykh." *Latinskaia Amerika* 4 (1971): 86.

Levano, C. "Lessons of the Guerrilla Struggle in Peru." *World Marxist Review* 9 (1966): 47–49.

Levesque, Jacques. *The USSR and the Cuban Revolution: Soviet Ideological and Strategic Perspectives 1959–77*. New York: Praeger Publishers, 1978.

Levin, V. "Class Struggle in Latin America." *New Times* 24 (1970): 17–18.

"Rashchioty i proschioty Pentagona." *Pravda*, 13 November 1969.

"The Big Stick's Modern Version." *New Times* 39 (1967): 13.

"Novye Konkistadory." *Pravda*, 19 September 1967.

"OAG Orudie Imperializma SShA." *Kommunist Vooruzhionnykh Sil* 2 (1965): 83.

Levinson, Jerome, and Juan de Onís. *The Alliance That Lost Its Way*. Chicago, IL: Quadrangle Books, 1970.

Listov, Vadim. *Pravda*, 19 September 1977.

"Otpor Narastaet." *Pravda*, 3 July 1970.

Litvarin, P., and L. Iakovlev. "Novyi Etap v Amerikano-Brazil'skikh Otnosheniiakh." *SShA* 4 (1980): 55–63.

London, Kurt, ed. *The Soviet Union in World Politics*. Boulder, CO: Westview Press, 1980.

López, Ramón. "New Stage in the Guerrilla Struggle in Latin America." *World Marxist Review* 2 (1967): 65.

Lovienko, A. "The Vicious Circle of the Alliance for Progress." *International Affairs* 3 (1967): 33.

Lozinov, D. "The Liberation Struggle in Latin America." *International Affairs* 7 (1977): 40.

Luers, William H. "The Soviets and Latin America: A Three Decade U.S. Policy Tangle." *Washington Quarterly* (Winter 1984): 13.

Lukin, Viktor. "Kontseptsiia Tsentrov sily' i Latinskaia Amerika." *Latinskaia Amerika* 8 (1980): 5–20.

Evoliutsiia Amerikanskikh Kontseptsii. Moscow: Nauka, 1966.

Lunin, V., and P. Iakovlev. "Latinskaia Amerika: Kurs Vashingtona." *Mezhdunarodnaia Zhizn'* 2 (1980): 24–33.

Lyvkin, E. V. "Opyt Andskoi Gruppy Po Regulirovaniiu Deiatel'nosti Inostrannogo Kapitala." *Latinskaia Amerika* 4 (1982): 33–39.

McClane, Charles. *Soviet–Middle East Relations*. London: Central Asia Research Center, 1973.

Maidonik, Kiva. "Khristianskaia Demokratiia v Politicheskoi Sisteme Stran Latinskoi Ameriki." *Latinskaia Amerika* 2 (1982): 35–43.

"Vokrug Urokov Chili." *Latinskaia Amerika* 5 (1974): 116, 117, 129, 130.

"Imperializm i razvivaiushchiesia Strany." *Latinskaia Amerika* 2 (1973): 211.

"Sumerki Liberal'nogo Reformizma." *Latinskaia Amerika* 5 (1970): 59–60, 63.

Maksimov, V. T. "Amerikanskie Programmy Obshchestvennoi Bezopasnosti." *Latinskaia Amerika* 3 (1975): 113–23.

Mashbitz, Ia. "Latinskaia Amerika v Mezhdunarodnom Kapitalisticheskom Razdele Truda." *MEMO* 11 (1964): 29–39.

Mastny, Vojtech. "The Soviet Union and the Falklands War." *Naval War College Review* 36 (1983): 47.

Matlina, Anna. "Vneshniaia Politika: Samostoiatel'nosti v Usloviiakh Ekonomicheskoi Zavisimosti." *Latinskaia Amerika* 8 (1981): 68–72.

"Vneshniaia Politika: Samostoiatel'nost' v Usloviiakh Ekonomicheskoi Zavisimosti?" *Latinskaia Amerika* 6 (1980): 76–92.

"Imperializm i 'Revoliutsiia Voennykh.'" *Latinskaia Amerika* 5 (1978): 152, 158.

Kritika Kontseptsii "Mirnoi Reguliruemoi Revoliutsii" Dlia Latinskoi Ameriki. Moscow: Nauka, 1971.

Kritika Kontseptsii Mirnoi Reguliruemoi "Revoliutsii." Moscow: ILA, 1968.

Matveev, V. "Agressivnye deistviia amerikanskogo imperializma." *Kommunist* 9 (1965): 98–99.

Makukhin, E. V. "Profsoiuzy i Narodnoe Edinstvo v Chili." *Rabochii Klass i Sovremennyi Mir* 1 (1973): 126–27.

May, Ernest R. *The Making of the Monroe Doctrine.* Cambridge, MA: Harvard University Press, 1975.

Mendiandua, Silvio J. "K Istorii Politicheskogo Militarizma v Latinskoi Amerike." *Latinskaia Amerika* 4 (1971): 55.

Merin, B. I. *Proletariat i Revoliutsionnyi Protsess v Latinskoi Amerike.* Moscow: Nauka, 1985.

Tsentral'naiia Amerika i SShA. Moscow: Znanie, 1971.

ed. *Rabochii Klass i Revoliutsionnyi Protsess v Latinskoi Amerike.* Moscow: ILA, 1978.

Mikhailov, S. S., ed. *Osvoboditel'noe Dvizhenie v Latinskoi Amerike.* Moscow: Nauka, 1964.

Mikoian, Sergo. "America at the Moment of Truth." In Viktor Vol'skii, ed. *Pan-Americanism: Its Essence and Evolution.* Moscow: USSR Academy of Sciences Press, 1982.

Symposium on the Armies of Latin America, Part 2, *Latinskaia Amerika* 4 (1977): 143–44.

Millas, Orlando. "Christian Democratic Reformism: The Chilean Experiment." *World Marxist Review* 11 (1965): 69.

Mirskii, G. *Problems of the National Liberation Movement.* Moscow: Novosti Press, 1971.

Armiia i Politika v Stranakh Azii i Afriki. Moscow: Nauka, 1970.

"O Kharaktere Sotsial'nykh Sil Azii i Afriki." *Kommunist* 17 (1968).

Mishin, S. "Latin America: Two Trends of Development." *International Affairs* 6 (1976): 56, 57, 58.

Mitiaeva, E. V. "Povorot v Latinoamerikanskoi Politike." *SShA* 6 (1981): 81–84.

"Vmeshatel'stvo SShA v Sal'vadore." *SShA* 7 (1980): 60.

Morner, Magnus. *Race Mixture in the History of Latin America.* Boston, MA: Little, Brown and Co., 1967.

Mostovets, N. V., ed. *SShA i Latinskaia Amerika*. Moscow: Nauka, 1978.

Mota Lima, Pedro. "The Revolutionary Process and Democracy in Latin America." *World Marxist Review* 8 (1965): 45–52.

New Times, 2 April 1975.

New York Times, 25 February 1982; 18 April 1982.

Nikolaev, V. N. "Ot Belgrada k Gavane." *Latinskaia Amerika* 4 (1979): 8, 19, 23.

Nixon, Richard M. *The Memoirs of Richard Nixon*. New York: Grosset & Dunlap, 1978.

Nogee, Joseph, and John Sloan. "Allende's Chile and the Soviet Union." *Journal of Interamerican Studies and International Affairs* 3 (1979): 353.

Novoe Vremia, 14 March 1971.

Oborotova, M. A: "Vneshnepoliticheskii Usloviia Razvitiia Revoliutsionnogo Protsessa (Tsentral'naia Amerika)." *Latinskaia Amerika* 7 (1982): 86–106.

Obyden, K. M. "Partii Sotsial-Demokraticheskoi Orientatsii v Latinskoi Amerike i Sotsintern." *Rabochii Klass i Sovremennyi Mir* 5 (1974): 49, 56, 60.

Onskii, S. "SShA–Latinskaia Amerika: Trudnyi Dialog." *Mezhdunarodnaia Zhizn'* 6 (1974): 75–85.

Oswald, J. G. *Soviet Image of Contemporary Latin America: A Documentary History 1960–1968*. University of Texas Press, 1970.

Oswald, J. G., and Anthony J. Strover, eds. *The Soviet Union and Latin America*. New York: Praeger Publishers, 1970.

Ovchinnikov, Vsevolod. "A Step Toward Victory" (in English). *Pravda*, 19 July 1979.

Padilla, L. "Some Lessons of Events in Bolivia." *World Marxist Review* 11 (1971): 24.

Padilla, L., J. Laborde, and E. Souza. "Latin America: Anti-imperialist Fight and the Armed Forces." *World Marxist Review* 3 (1971): 91.

Page, Joseph H. *The Revolution That Never Was: Northeast Brazil 1955–1964*. New York: Grossman Publishers, 1972.

Paniev, Iu. N. "Nekotorye Aspekty Ekonomicheskikh Otnoshenii Latinoamerikanskikh Stran S EES." *Latinskaia Amerika* 3 (1982): 29–34.

Pashentsev, E. N. "Zadachi Edinstva Profsoiuznogo Dvizhenia Peru (1968–1981gg.)." *Latinskaia Amerika* 12 (1981): 34, 35.

Pavlovskii, V. "Karibskie Narody Zhazhduiut Svobody." *Kommunist* 8 (1982): 100–109.

Pegusheva, L. V. "Sovremenye Tendentsie v Profsoiuznom Dvizhenii Latinskoi Ameriki (70e gody)." *Latinskaia Amerika* 10 (1981): 35–43.

Latinskaia Amerika: 'Panamerikanizm' v Rabochem Dvizhenii. Moscow: Nauka, 1974.

"AFM-KPP v Latinskoi Amerike." *Novaia i Noveishaia Istoriia* 4 (1970): 56–66.

"Profsoiuzy Latinskoi Ameriki." *Mezhdunarodnaia Zhizn'* 8 (1969): 155–57.

Ponomarev, Boris. "Neodolimost' Osvoboditel'nogo Dvizheniia." *Kommunist* 1 (1980): 15, 25.

"The World Situation and the Revolutionary Process." *World Marxist Review* 6 (1974): 10.

"Topical Problems of the Theory of Revolutionary Process" (in English). *Kommunist* 15 (1971): 62.

Prado, Jorge del. "Is there a Revolution in Peru?" *World Marxist Review* 1 (1971): 20.

"Revoliutsionnyi Protsess v Peru i Pozitsiia Kommunisticheskoi Partii." *Kommunist* 13 (1973): 104, 111–12.

"The Revolution Continues." *World Marxist Review* 1 (1973): 65–70.

Pravda, 3 April 1966; 27 September 1970; 7 November 1970; 30 July 1972; 30 January 1977; 5 July 1980; 6 August 1987.

Prensa Latina, 23 May 1973.

Primakov, Evgenii. "Zakon Neravnomernosti Razvitiia i Istoricheskie Sud'by Osvobodivshikhsia Stran." *MEMO* 12 (1980): 34–36.

Purcell, Susan Kaufman, ed. *Mexico–United States Relations*. New York: Proceedings of the Academy of Political Sciences, 1981.

Radio Moscow, 13 April 1972.

Radio Moscow (in Spanish), 25 February 1982.

Radio Peace and Progress (in Spanish), 8 July 1973.

Ramírez, R., and N. Tsigir'. "Novoe Veianie v Kolumbiskoii Tserkvi." *MEMO* 11 (1965): 126–28.

Ratiani, G. "Punta del Este: Gur'kie uroki." *Pravda*, 18 May 1967.

Ratliff, William E. *Castroism and Communism in Latin America 1959–1976*. Stanford CA: AEI-Hoover Policy Studies, 1976.

Romanova, Zoia I. "Latinskaia Amerika na Vneshnem Rynke: Problema Sootnosheniia Tsen." *Latinskaia Amerika* 6 (1971): 38–56.

"Ekonomicheskoe Osnovanie Gospodtsva SShA v Latinskoi Amerike." *Latinskaia Amerika* 2 (1970): 108–24.

"Neokolonializm SShA v Latinskoi Amerike." *Novaia i Noveishaia Istoriia* 4 (1968): 22–38.

Problemy Ekonomicheskoi Integratsii v Latinskoi Amerike. Moscow: Nauka, 1965.

"Ekonomicheskaia Integratsiia v Latinskoi Amerike: Novyi Etap Protivorechii." *Novaia i Noveishaia Istoriia* 3 (1966): 79–81, 82, 83.

Romantsev, Iurii V. "SShA–OAG–Kuba: Proval Blokady." *SShA* 10 (1975): 61–65.

Rosales, Juan. *World Marxist Review* 3 (1976): 46–53.

Rothenberg, M. "Since Reagan: The Soviets and Latin America." *Washington Quarterly* (Spring 1982): 176, 177.

"Latin America in Soviet Eyes." *Problems of Communism* (Fall 1983).

Rusakov, E. "Protivorechiia Ostaiutsia." *Pravda*, 21 April 1975.

Rusinov, N. V., and A. F. Feodorov. "Vooruzhionnye Sily Peru (do 10/1968)." *Latinskaia Amerika* 3 (1970): 179, 185.

Schlesinger, Arthur M., Jr. *A Thousand Days*. Boston, MA: Houghton Mifflin Co., 1965.

Schroeder, Richard C. "Soviets' Latin American Influence." *Congressional Research Reports*, 6 March 1987.

Seabury, Paul, and Walter McDougall, eds., *The Grenada Papers*. San Francisco, CA: ICS, 1984.

Segal, Aaron. "Perspektivy Dvukh Kontinentov." *Za Rubezhom* 6 (1966): 8–9.

Selivanov, V. "Latinskaia Amerika v Planakh Imperializma SShA." *Kommunist Vooruzhionnykh Sil* 21 (1978): 80–85.

"Latinskaia Amerika: Protiv diktata SShA." *Krasnaia Zvezda*, 3 June 1976.

Ekspansiia SShA v Latinskoi Amerike. Moscow: Voinizdat, 1975.

Voennaiia Politika SShA v Stranakh Latinskoi Ameriki. Moscow: ILA, 1970.

Semionov, S. *Khristianskaia Demokratiia i Revoliutsionnyi Protsess v Latinskoi Amerike*. Moscow: Nauka, 1971.

Sergeev, S. A. "Latinskaia Amerika: God 1978." *Latinskaia Amerika* 1 (1979): 20–25.

Sergeev, K. S., and V. G. Tkatchenko. *Latinskaia Amerika: Bor'ba Za Nezavisimost'*. Moscow: IMO, 1975.

Shapira, Yoram. *Mexico's Foreign Policy Under Echeverría*. Beverly Hills, CA., and London: Sage Publications, 1978.

Shermet'ev, I. K. "Chto Lezhit v Osnove Segodniashnikh Problem?" *Latinskaia Amerika* 4 (1982): 5–9.

Shevchenko, Arkady. *Breaking With Moscow*. New York: Knopf, 1985.

Shiblin, Piotr. "The Pentagon and Latin America." *New Times* 2 (1977): 25–26.

Shul'govskii, A. "Latinskaia Amerika: Vneshniaia Politika i Ekonomicheskaia Zavisimost'." *Latinskaia Amerika* 8 (1981): 60–63.

Symposium on the Armies of Latin America. *Latinskaia Amerika* 3 (1977): 52–83.

"Venetsuely i Kolumbii." *Latinskaia Amerika* 4 (1977): 161–66.

"Rabochii Klass Latinskoi Ameriki: Politicheskie i Ideologicheskie Problemy Bor'by." *Latinskaia Amerika* 6 (1976): 6–23.

"Ideologicheskie i Teoreticheskie Aspekty Revoliutsionnogo Protsessa v Peru." *Latinskaia Amerika* 4 (1975): 12–14.

"Vooruzhionnye Sily Chili: Ot 'apolitichnosti' k Konterrevoliutsii." *Latinskaia Amerika* 6 (1974): 32, 43–48.

"Revolution and the Army in Latin America" (in English). *Soviet Military Review* 9 (1975): 46.

"Kritika Nekotorykh Melkoburzhaznykh Kontseptsii o Roli Armii." *Latinskaia Amerika* 5 (1973): 65–69.

Latinskaia Amerika: Armiia i Osvoboditel'noe Dvizhenie. Moscow: Znanie, 1972.

"Latinskaia Amerika: Armiia i Politika." *Latinskaia Amerika* 4 (1971): 23.

"Latin America in the Modern World." *International Affairs* 9 (1966): 59, 63–66.

"V Poiskakh Ideologicheskogo Kompasa." *Mezhdunarodnaia Zhizn'* 8 (1963): 112.

"O Katolicheskom 'Tret'om Puti' v Latinskoy Amerike." *MEMO* 6 (1958): 101.

ed. *Sovremennye Ideologicheskie Techeniia v Latinskoi Amerike*. Moscow: Nauka, 1983.

ed. *Gospodstvuiuschie Klassy Latinskoi Ameriki*. Moscow: Nauka, 1978.

ed. *Natsionalizm v Latinskoi Amerike: Politicheskie i Ideologicheskie Techeniia*. Moscow: Nauka, 1976.

ed. *Peru 150 let Nezauisimosti*. Moscow: ILA, 1971.

Sibilev, N. G. "Sotsial-Demokratiia: Novye Tendentsii v Vneshnei Politike." *Rabochii Klass i Sovremennyi Mir* 6 (1977): 124–28.

Sigmund, Paul E. "The USSR, Cuba and the Revolution in Chile." In Robert H.

Donaldson, ed. *The Soviet Union in the Third World*. Boulder, CO: Westview Press, 1981.

"The U.S. and Latin America." *Foreign Affairs* 60 (Winter 1981): 645.

The Overthrow of Allende. Pittsburgh University Press, 1977.

"The Invisible Blockade and the Overthrow of Allende." *Foreign Affairs* 52 (1974): 336.

Sivolobov, A. M. "The Peasant Movement in Latin America" (in English). *Kommunist* 12 (1964): 100–7.

Sizonenko, A., ed. *SSSR–Meksika 50 Let*. Moscow: ILA, 1975.

Skidmore, Thomas E. *Politics in Brazil 1930–1964: An Experiment in Democracy*. New York: Oxford University Press, 1973.

Skliar, V. *Latinskaia Amerika: Bor'ba Za Nezavisimost' i Sotsyal'nyi Progres*. Moscow: Znanie, 1980.

Sosnovskii, A. A. "Braziliia: Evoliutsiia Rezhima i Armiia." *Latinskaia Amerika* 11 (1981): 36–37.

Souza, Rubén. "Revoliutsiia i Kontra Revoliutsiia v Latinskoi Amerike." *Kommunist* 1 (1975): 84.

Sovetsko–Meksikanskie Otnosheniia 1968–1980. Moscow: Izdatel'stvo Politicheskoi Literatury, 1981.

Spirin, V. "Imperializm SShA i Latinoamerikanskaia Revoliutsiia." *SShA* 8 (1971): 27–42.

Steele, Jonathan. *Soviet Power: The Kremlin's Foreign Policy – Brezhnev to Chernenko*. New York: Touchstone Books, 1984.

Stepan, Alfred. *The Military in Politics: Changing Patterns in Brazil*. Princeton University Press, 1974.

Stroganov, E. D. "Rol' Solidarnykh Vystupl'enii v Bor'be Revoliutsionnykh Sil Latinskoi Ameriki." *Rabochii Klass i Sovremennyi Mir* 5 (1982): 107–14.

Sudarev, V. "Vneshnepoliticheskie Aspekty Andskoi Intergratsii." *Latinskaia Amerika* 6 (1981): 29–30.

"Andskaia Gruppa Na Poroge 80kh Godov." *MEMO* 12 (1980): 136.

Sukhostat, A. A. "Politicheskaia Bor'ba v Usloviiakh Krizisa Voennogo Rezhima." *Latinskaia Amerika* 4 (1980): 44–48.

Sumbatian, Iu. "Latinskaia Amerika na Novykh Rubezhakh." *Kommunist Vooruzhionnykh Sil* 3 (1975): 79–83.

"Vooruzhionnye Sily Latinskoi Ameriki." *Krasnaia Zvezda*, 20 August 1971.

Tadeo, Nina. "Formulas for Counter Revolution Coups." *World Marxist Review* (June 1974): 108.

Tanin, G. Z. "Osobennosti Vneshnei Politiki Voennykh v 70e Gody." *Latinskaia Amerika* 1 (1979): 139.

Tarasov, K. *Tainaia Voina Imperializma SShA v Latinskoi Amerike*. Moscow: Politizdat, 1978.

"SShA i Latinskaia Amerika: Voenno-Ekonomicheskikh Otnoshenii." *Latinskaia Amerika* 2 (1976): 36, 51.

SShA i Latinskaia Amerika: Voenno-Politicheskie i Voenno-Ekonomicheskie Otnosheniia. Moscow: Politizdat, 1972.

"Alliance for Monopolies." *International Affairs* 1 (1968): 33.

Tarasov, Konstantin, and Vyacheslav Zubenko. *The CIA in Latin America*. Moscow: Progress Publishers, 1984.

Tarasov, V. B. "Novoe Ob'edinenie Amazonskii Pakt." *Latinskaia Amerika* 2 (1979): 71–81.

TASS, 18 June 1971; 31 May 1972; 17 September 1972; 23 September 1972; 4 January 1977.

Texier, Jorge. "General and Distinctive Features of the Liberation Process." *World Marxist Review* 4 (1972): 106.

Theberge, James D. *Latin America in the World System: The Limits of Internationalism.* Beverly Hills, CA, and London: Sage Publications, 1975.

Tikhmenev, V. "Leninism i Revoliutsionnyi Protsess v Latinskoi Amerike." *Kommunist* 3 (1971): 117–19.

Tkatchenko, V. "Latinskaia Amerika: Problemy Osvoboditel'noi Bor'by." *Mezhdunarodnaia Zhizn'* 4 (1972): 13–21.

Totskii, V. P. "Khristianskaiia Demokratiia v Politicheskoi Sisteme Stran Latinskoi Ameriki." *Latinskaia Amerika* 8 (1981): 53–56.

Trofimenko, Genrikh A. "Strategiia i Metody Vneshnei Politiki SShA." *Voprosy Istorii* 5 (1979): 59–77.

Tsigir', N. "Latinskaia Amerika-SShA protivobrstvo obostriaetsia." *Mezhdunarodnaia Zhizn'* 3 (1970): 143–48.

Tuchin, R. "Washington Props the Junta" (in English). *Izvestiia*, 13 January 1981.

Turkatenko, N. D. "Korporatsii SShA i Politika Vashingtona v Latinskoi Amerike." *Latinskaia Amerika* 5 (1974): 25–41.

Tuzmukhamedov, R. A. "Neprisoedinenie 'Latino-Amerikanskii Etap'?" *Latinskaia Amerika* 1 (1972): 46–63.

Ulam, Adam B. *Dangerous Relations: The Soviet Union in World Politics, 1970–1982.* New York: Oxford University Press, 1983.

Urban, Joan. "Socialist Pluralism in the Soviet and Italian Perspective: The Chilean Catalyst." *Orbis* 18 (1974): 482–509.

Vacs, Aldo César. *Discreet Partners: Argentina and the USSR Since 1917.* University of Pittsburgh Press, 1985.

Valenta, Jiri. "Soviet Strategy in the Caribbean Basin." *US Naval Institute Proceedings* (May 1982): 173–81.

Valkenier, Elizabeth K. *The Soviet Union and the Third World: An Economic Bind.* New York: Praeger Publishers, 1985.

Varas, Augusto. "Latin American–Soviet Relations in the Eighties." Unpublished manuscript.

Vasiliev, M. "Sovremennyi 'Panamerikanizm,' Ritorika i Politika." *Mezhdunarodnaia Zhizn'* 1 (1980): 30–40.

"'Novyi Podkhod' SShA k Latinskoi Amerike." *Mezhdunarodnaia Zhizn'* 5 (1971): 58–68.

Veber, A. "Sotsial-Demokratiia v Meniaiushchemsia Mire." *MEMO* 11 (1972): 32–33, 34.

Veshnevskii, G. "Uzakonivatom Bezzakonie." *Pravda*, 22 September 1965.

Vishnia, G. F. *SShA–Latinskaia Amerika: Vneshnopolitichskie Otnosheniia v Sovremenykh Usloviakh.* Moscow: Nauka, 1978.

"SShA i Latinskaia Amerika Vzaimootnosheniia v Usloviiakh Razriadki." *MEMO* 8 (1975): 83–89.

Vizgunova, Iu. I. "Novye Aspekty v Bor'be Rabochego Klassa Latinskoi Ame-riki (Meksika)." *Latinskaia Amerika* 2 (1977): 62–72.

Vol'skii, Viktor. "Latinskaia Amerika v Sisteme Sovremennogo Kapitalizma." *Latinskaia Amerika* 3 (1979): 6–31.

"Put' Perekhoda K Sotsializmu." *Latinskaia Amerika* 2 (1975): 66–72.

"New Stage of the People's Struggle" (in English). *Pravda*, 10 March 1968.

SSSR : Latinskaia Amerika 1917–1967. Moscow: Mezhdunarodnye Otnoshe-niia, 1967.

Vol'skii, Viktor, P. N. Boiko, and A. N. Glinkin, eds. *Braziliia: Tendentsii Ekonomicheskogo i Sotsial'no-Politicheskogo Razvitiia*. Moscow: Nauka, 1983.

Vorozheikina, T. E. "Revoliutsionnye Organizatsii Sal'vadora i Narodnoe Dvizhenie." *Latinskaia Amerika* 7 (1982): 23.

Washington Post, 7 November 1977.

Wesson, Robert. *Year Book of International Communist Affairs*. Stanford, CA: The Hoover Institute Press, 1983.

Whelan, Joseph G. *The Soviet Union in the Third World: An Imperial Burden or Political Asset*. Congressional Research Service Report No. 85–40 S.

Wiarda, Howard J., and Mark Falcoff. *The Communist Challenge in the Caribbean and Central America*. Washington: American Enterprise Institute for Public Policy Research, 1987.

Yelutin, Y. "U.S.–Latin America Equal Partnership?" *International Affairs* 8 (1970): 65–72.

Zaitsev, N. G. "Vozmozhnosti i Protivorechiia Regional'nogo Ekonomiches-kogo Sotrudnichestva." *Latinskaia Amerika* 4 (1982): 9–14, 15.

"Latin America: Some Development Trends." *International Affairs* 11 (1976): 55–58.

"LAST Cherez Trudnosti i Protivorechiia." *Latinskaia Amerika* 3 (1975): 85.

Zakharov, Iu. "SSSR–Meksika: V Traditsiiakh Doveriia i Vzaimoponimaniia." *Mezhdunarodnaia Zhizn'* 7 (1978): 103–5.

Zarodov, K. I., ed. *1,000 Dnei Revoliutsii: Rukovoditeli KPCh ob Urokakh Sobytii v Chili* (Prague: Mir i Sotsializm, 1978).

Zinov'ev, N. *Latinskaia Amerika: Regional'noe Sotrudnichestvo i Problemy Razvitiia*. Moscow: Progress Publishers, 1983.

Zinov'eva, R., and L. Fel'dman. "Samodeiatel'noe Naselenie Latinskoi Ame-riki." *MEMO* 4 (1969): 51–63.

Zorina, I. "Revoliutsiia i Khristiano-Demokraticheskaia Partiia." In M. F. Kudachkin and A. A. Kutsenkov, eds. *Uroki Chili*. Moscow: Nauka, 1977.

Revoliutsiia Ili Reforma v Latinskoi Amerike. Moscow: Nauka, 1971.

"Chili: Komy Prinadlezhit Vremia." *MEMO* 8 (1969): 123.

Index

245

Soviet and East European Studies

The following series titles are now out of print: